Praise fo

"Breathless just reading it."
—Professor Noam Choms ... itute of Technology

"Guilt by Association is a magnificent, timely and persuasive study of how stealth, deceit and cunning helped create today's perilous situation in the Middle East and the high stakes for all of us in the presidential race."

—Paul Findley, Member of Congress 1961-1983
(first Congressman openly removed by the Israel lobby)

"Carefully researched, explosively revelatory, powerful, compelling and certain to be highly contentious, this book must be widely read for precisely those reasons. A broader knowledge of the how and why of our involvement in the Middle East is of critical importance to America, domestically as well as globally."

—Ambassador Edward L. Peck, Deputy Director,
Cabinet Task Force on Terrorism,
Reagan White House; former Chief of Mission, Baghdad

Guilt by Association

How Deception and Self-Deceit Took America to War

Guilt by Association

How Deception and Self-Deceit Took America to War

Jeff Gates

State Street Publications

Guilt by Association
How Deception and Self-Deceit Took America to War

Published by State Street Publications

For additional copies or bulk orders, see www.criminalstate.com
To correspond with author or publisher:
State Street Publications
3408 State Street, Suite A
Santa Barbara, CA 93105

Book design by:
Arbor Books, Inc.
19 Spear Road, Suite 301
Ramsey, NJ 07446
www.arborbooks.com

Printed in the United States of America

Guilt by Association
How Deception and Self-Deceit Took America to War
Jeff Gates

1. Title 2. Author 3. Politics/Political Science/Religion

Additional books by the author:
The Ownership Solution (1998)
Democracy at Risk (2000)

Library of Congress Control Number: 2008908446

ISBN 10: 0-9821315-0-X
ISBN 13: 978-0-9821315-0-3

Table of Contents

Preface

Control of the Oval Office is the goal of the criminality chronicled in this account. Those identified are bipartisan in their politics, systemic in the scope and scale of their corruption and ruthless in the execution of their geopolitical goals. Unlike criminal syndicates identified in the past, this operation has sustained itself over generations through an extremist ideology that organizes its activities across time and distance.

I claim no unique qualifications to write this book save one: In November 2002 I met a person who will be identified in future books in the *Criminal State* series. He was attending a conference in London at which I was a speaker. I had published two books endorsed by well-known people, one of whom is related to this person who, for the moment, I will call John Doe.

From 1980-1987, I served as counsel to the U.S. Senate Committee on Finance working with Russell Long of Louisiana. The

Senator's father, Huey Long, was Governor of Louisiana (1928-32) and U.S. Senator until 1935 when he was assassinated at age 42 while preparing to mount a presidential campaign. His son, then 16, was elected to the Senate in 1948 along with Lyndon Johnson from neighboring Texas.

In 1933, President Franklin Delano Roosevelt appointed James Farley as postmaster general and chairman of the Democratic National Committee. In April 1935, Farley commissioned the nation's first-ever "scientific" political poll. His "penny postcard" poll confirmed that if Huey Long campaigned for the presidency in 1936, Roosevelt would not be reelected. Long could not win, the results showed, but his candidacy would ensure FDR's loss to any Republican challenger and set the stage for a Long presidential bid in 1940.

Huey Long was assassinated five months after the poll results were released. Fifty years later, Russell Long remained confident that Roosevelt's people killed his father. Soon after I first met John Doe in London, he assured me that if I agreed to undertake the research and analysis for this series, the evidentiary trail would identify who killed Huey Long and why. The facts since assembled point not to Roosevelt's people but to the syndicate identified in this account.

The multi-volume *Criminal State* series will chronicle the operations of that syndicate as experienced by John Doe since his birth in 1952. Since 1982, he has profiled that criminality from the inside. Without exception, those identified share an ideological bias sympathetic to Israel. Based on research and analysis pivoting off that quarter-century experience, *Guilt by Association* identified Arizona Senator John McCain as an "asset" of this trans-generational syndicate. [The term "asset" is described in the introduction.]

The election of John McCain as president would embolden those skilled at displacing facts with deceit. He is not the only asset in the 2008 presidential field. Nor, if elected, would he be the first asset to serve in the White House. However, John McCain is the most problematic of the 2008 candidates, as the facts will demonstrate.

In April 2005, after Florida Governor Jeb Bush had contacted John Doe, an attempt was made to force Doe's car into a bridge abutment on the MacArthur Causeway in Miami. After that incident, Doe was induced by a syndicate operative to relocate to Gila County,

Arizona. While residing in John McCain's home state, Doe was subjected to serial criminal stalking with the complicity of officials at the local, state and federal levels. As of July 2008, the Supreme Court of Arizona had commenced proceedings to disbar one of several attorneys identified as complicit. Evidence of statewide racketeering and conspiracy is part of a public court record in a lawsuit filed in the Gila County courts.

For two years (July 2005 to July 2007), John Doe and I shared a house in Strawberry, Arizona, 90 miles north of Phoenix, where we completed the research and analysis for the *Criminal State* series. While we identified and profiled those stalking him in Arizona, law enforcement authorities ignored appeals for assistance. Since July 2007, Doe and I have shared a house in Tempe, Arizona.

Waging War by Way of Deception

Not until early February 2008 did it become clear that John McCain's presidential aspirations might be realized. A subsequent analysis of his political supporters revealed the same networks of syndicate operatives stalking John Doe. Doe's experience with organized crime in Arizona dates from 1973 when he relocated from Michigan to attend Arizona State University in Tempe where McCain opened his first district office after his election to Congress in 1982.

The facts confirm that the same criminal syndicate still stalking John Doe with impunity is still waging war on the U.S.—with impunity. Just as Doe's experience revealed complicity within the U.S. government, many of the operatives identified in this account work inside governments. *Guilt by Association* explains *how* this criminality operates hidden in plain view and, thus far, with impunity.

Those identified specialize in waging war by way of deception. Oftentimes, for example, an incident will be staged to provoke a reaction by the "mark." While the *agent provocateur* fades into the background, the mark emerges in the foreground to be discredited by his response. The *modus operandi* is ancient; the means for taking it to global scale are unique to the Information Age and to those skilled at displacing facts with what people can be induced to *believe.*

This book was written with the immediate goal of alerting the public to the perils of John McCain becoming commander-in-chief of a nation already riddled with organized crime, extremism and treason. Another goal is to ensure that, if elected, Barack Obama does not continue his behavior of pandering to those complicit in the conduct described.

Guilt by Association offers a multi-layered analysis. Each of the chapters can be read separately or the entirety reviewed in the sequence provided. Supporting endnotes include supplemental evidentiary trails that will be developed in the *Criminal State* series. Additional analytical tools and topical analyses will be posted on the *Criminal State* website (www.criminalstate.org) which also offers a subscription newsletter, educational materials and a subscriber blog.

Accountability for this trans-generational criminality requires transparency and the good faith efforts of those with line responsibility for law enforcement and national security. Citizen involvement is essential. Those readers skeptical of conspiracy theories (as am I) are urged to engage the facts and note the lack of conjecture common to such theories.

Guilt by Association shows why the presence of organized crime and extremism inside government requires that Americans revisit our duty as citizens if we hope to remain free. As crafted by Founders who sought to liberate this nation from an earlier form of tyranny, the Declaration of Independence offers strategic advice that remains relevant:

> ...when a long train of abuses and usurpations, pursuing invariably the same Object evinces a design to reduce them under absolute Despotism, it is their right, it is their duty, to throw off such Government, and to provide new Guards for their future security.

With facts confirming a need for informed Americans "to provide new Guards for their future security," this book is dedicated to those who served our nation honorably in the Middle East.

—Jeff Gates, Tempe, Arizona (September 11, 2008)

Introduction

We do not govern Egypt, we govern the governors of Egypt.
—Lord Cromer (1841-1917)

America faces the greatest challenge of its 232-year history—its credibility in tatters, its security at risk, its finances awry, its future in jeopardy and its leadership adrift. A John McCain presidency is poised to make matters worse. Possibly far worse. However, that does not mean a Barack Obama presidency would be better, only less worse.

Six decades ago, an enclave of Jewish elites and extremists induced Harry Truman, a Christian Zionist president, to recognize Zionism as a sovereign entity in the Middle East. Rather than operate as a loyal ally, that enclave has proven itself an enemy. The consistency of Israel's behavior since its founding in 1948 confirms how organized crime expanded to global scale behind the façade of a sovereign state.

> Zionism is routinely described as a national movement for the return of Jewish people to their homeland and the resumption

> of Jewish sovereignty in the Land of Israel.[1] Christian Zionists believe that the Jews' return to Israel will hasten the second coming of Christ. The Zionism chronicled in this account describes a transnational organized crime agenda featuring financial and political domination by elites and extremists.

Blinded by sympathy for a faith whose members were subjected to atrocities during World War II, America's post-war leadership embraced an alliance with an elitist and fundamentalist subculture within Judaism's broader faith tradition. Sixty years of hard experience have since confirmed the illusion of a common interest between an inclusive secular democracy and an exclusivist theocratic state. Though many Americans have long sensed that something fundamental was amiss in this alliance, the facts have not been available to support that intuition—until now.

Though politically branded a war hero due to his prisoner of war status in Vietnam, John McCain aided the pro-Israeli agenda that took America to war in Iraq based on intelligence fixed around a prearranged goal that he promoted as a U.S. Senator. His campaign touts his skills as commander-in-chief for an unnecessary war that he helped initiate.

The known facts confirm that the war in Iraq is the product of a trans-generational syndicate skilled at displacing facts with (false) beliefs. Those masterful at manipulating thoughts and beliefs are also responsible for enabling organized crime to expand to a global scale. Those who "fixed" the intelligence to justify invading Iraq require a series of reliable and pliable allies in the White House in order to expand this conflict to include Iran.

Saddam Hussein played no role in the mass murder of 9/11 and Iraq posed no threat to the U.S. with weapons of mass destruction. Nor did the secular Iraqi dictator have ties to the religious fundamentalists of Al Qaeda, mobile biological laboratories or the alleged "yellowcake" uranium from Niger. Yet Senator McCain insisted that the U.S. commit its blood and treasure to a war he now proposes we expand to Iran. Senator Obama has proposed that the U.S. quickly withdraw, leaving dynamics in place that this conflict was certain to create.

The Real Threat to Jews

To restore trust in government requires proof of *how* our trust was betrayed to induce the U.S. invasion of Iraq for Greater Israel. To face that uncomfortable fact, this account describes how—through our entangled alliance with Jewish Zionists and our embrace of extremist Christian Zionists—the U.S. discredited itself in the court of public opinion. So long as the U.S. defends the indefensible behavior of such extremists, America will be seen as guilty of Israel's crimes.

Induced by an ally to wage wars without adequate justification and to shower upon it advantages denied to others, America continues to deceive itself at its own peril while this network of extremists endangers the broader Jewish community by associating them with this treasonous conduct. This account will be attacked as a conspiracy theory, dismissed as a diatribe, depicted as a rant and worse. The text will be nitpicked and the author scorned, discredited and described as delusional or cast as a bigot and an anti-Semite for presenting facts that show *how* the state of Israel induced America to fight its wars for territorial expansion.

The year 2007 saw publication of *The Israel Lobby and U.S. Foreign Policy* by scholars John J. Mearsheimer and Stephen M. Walt. Though both professors had distinguished records as academics and authors of well-received books on foreign policy, they were attacked as anti-Semites for suggesting that policies promoted by the lobby are damaging to America's national interests, to Israel's long-term security and to moderate Jews who do not share the lobby's extremist views.

This entangled alliance will remain perilous to U.S. national security until those complicit in this extremism are identified, indicted and prosecuted. To the detriment of the broader Jewish community, neither John McCain nor Barack Obama has shown any inclination to perform that essential task. To the detriment of U.S. national security, even the highly critical Mearsheimer-Walt book suggested that the Israel lobby is just another lobby that is simply more successful than other interest groups in Washington. That simplistic portrayal misleads Americans about the agenda pursued by foreign agents *posing* as a domestic lobby.

The threat to Jews is from neither Iran nor Islamo-fascists. The danger lies with the behavior of elites and extremists within the

Jewish community and the impact they wield on America through the Israel lobby and the broader criminal syndicate described in this account. Their impact is magnified by those in the Christian Zionist community who pursue their narrow interests to the detriment of U.S. national security.

Since the 1967 Six-Day War, charges of "Jew hater" and "Holocaust-denier" have been deployed to discredit those who criticize Israeli policies, and to misdirect and intimidate those who seek to identify the common source of the provocations that evoke extremism. With another pro-Israeli president in the White House, not only would Tel Aviv's agenda wield more influence over U.S. policy but also terrorism would become more prevalent as a means for manipulating lawmakers. While Barack Obama's repeated loyalty oaths to Israel were at the core of his spring 2008 presidential primary campaign, he at least distinguishes between Israelis and their series of extremist governments.[2]

Chapter 1 describes the sophisticated game theory that underlies today's unconventional warfare and clarifies who had the means, motive and opportunity to "fix" U.S. intelligence around the goal of invading Iraq. Only as this treason is made transparent and its operatives exposed can Americans, including Jewish-Americans, be confident they live in a nation governed by values consistent with a democracy.

By his unwavering support for Tel Aviv regardless of its behavior, John McCain has confirmed that his sympathies lie with those who deceived America to wage a war on behalf of fundamentalists who have long planned to expand the Land of Israel to include Greater Israel. By his repeated pledges of allegiance to Israel, Barack Obama signaled he may prove equally submissive to an agenda set by this syndicate.

McCain Family Secrets

No public record has yet documented what happened to John McCain while a prisoner of war in Vietnam. Only he and his captors know the abuses and indignities to which he was subjected. While no one dares make an issue of his psychological health, his quick temper is a well-documented fact as is the delight he takes in humiliating his staff and dismissing those colleagues who question his fitness to command.

Nor has any public record examined the geopolitical implications of the organized crime network that encouraged and financed his political ambitions, as described in Chapter 2. That lineage includes Canada's Bronfman clan, Prohibition-era bootleggers whose family fortune capitalized the World Jewish Congress. Barack Obama's political career shares that suspect network with roots in Chicago's organized crime.

Chapter 3 reviews the organized crime implications of John McCain's role in the "Keating Five" network of senators and their success in delaying reforms required to halt a $153 billion fraud in the thrift industry. That nationwide fraud bears striking similarities to the 2008 credit crisis, including a role played in both episodes by Alan Greenspan who helped Arizonan Charles Keating recruit the Keating Five.

The meltdown of the U.S. mortgage market reveals at its core the same syndicate network as the financial "pump-and-dump" that typified the savings and loan fraud two decades earlier. In both cases, overlapping groups of operatives profited both on the financial upside and on the lucrative downside as families lost their homes in distressed sales while financial sophisticates profited off their misery.

The multi-decade role of Cincinnati's Carl Lindner is also examined. McCain campaign supporter Charles Keating served as counsel to Lindner prior to leading a $3.4 billion fraud from the Phoenix office of Lincoln Savings & Loan. That fraud, financed and controlled by "junk bond king" Michael Milken,[3] traces its origins to the same network behind the political ascendancy of Ronald Reagan, the president to whom McCain compares himself as a "true conservative."[4]

A Christian Zionist, Lindner describes himself as "the largest non-Jewish contributor to Jewish causes in the U.S." John Hagee, the Christian Zionist leader of Christians United for Israel, endorsed McCain for president before leading hundreds of the Zionist faithful on a "solidarity trip" to Israel in March 2008 following McCain's visit there with Connecticut Senator Joe Lieberman, a Jewish Zionist and his closest political ally.

Chapter 4 chronicles how Navy Admiral John S. McCain Jr., the Senator's father, helped President Lyndon Johnson cover up the Israeli killing of 34 American servicemen aboard the *USS Liberty* during the 1967 Six-Day War. That omission from the candidate's war-hero biography may help explain his unwavering support for policies crafted in Tel Aviv, often to the detriment of U.S. national security. Like his father, Senator McCain also aided the *USS Liberty* cover-up.

Making the Case

John McCain's reform of campaign finance law was a "perfect fit" for the Diaspora-based fundraising used by the Israel lobby. "The McCain-Feingold" legislation—co-sponsored with Senator Russ Feingold of Wisconsin—illustrates a key means by which this criminality became politically systemic. Their reforms boosted the amount (from $1,000 to $2,300) that candidates can lawfully receive from individuals in primary and general elections. This change enables a couple to give a combined $9,200 (4 x $2,300) to political candidates.

Importantly, that reform also doubled the funds candidates can receive *without regard to where their supporters reside.* A candidate in Iowa, say, may have only a few pro-Israeli constituents. That candidate can now be induced to support Israeli policies as a nationwide network of pro-Zionists contribute to that campaign. That funding strategy has long been deployed with success by the Israel lobby to shape U.S. policy. Under the guise of reform, McCain-Feingold doubled its impact.

The process works like this. Candidates are summoned for in-depth interviews by the Israel lobby—the American Israel Public Affairs Committee (AIPAC).[5] Those found sufficiently committed to AIPAC's agenda are provided a list of donors who can be relied on to "max out" their campaign contributions. Below is the first of many examples to show *how* an extremist few can wield so much influence over so many:

> "Bundlers" raise funds for candidates.[6] After McCain-Feingold reforms became effective in 2003, any experienced AIPAC-identified bundler should be able to raise $1 million for a candidate by contacting 10 friends in the Diaspora.
>
> The bundler and spouse "max out" for $9,200 and call ten others, say, in Manhattan, Miami and Beverly Hills. Each of them max out (10 x $9,200) and call 10 others for a total of 11. [111 x $9,200 = $1,021,200.] Assuming AIPAC endorsed

the candidate, one call could fund a modest campaign in many Congressional districts. No one knows the full impact of this political operation over the past six decades.

From Tel Aviv's perspective, that political leverage is leveraged yet again because fewer than 10% of House races (typically 35 to 50 Congressional districts) are competitive in any election cycle.[7] That makes the long-term leverage even greater for those—such as AIPAC—motivated to sustain this financial focus over multiple cycles.

Are the resources available in this network to sustain a nationwide pro-Israeli electoral strategy behind the cover of McCain-Feingold reform? According to *Jewish Achievement*, 42% of the largest political donors to the 2000 election cycle were Jewish.[8] Of the *Forbes 400* richest Americans, 25% are Jewish.[9] The limitation was not donor money; donors were limited by how much money they could lawfully contribute to AIPAC-screened candidates. McCain removed a key constraint on that influence-wielding strategy.

May 2008 saw the emergence of "joint fundraising committees" that "funneled funds to the candidates' primary campaigns (that's the $2,300 part), to the national party (up to $28,500) and, in McCain's case, to state parties as well ($10,000 each)."[10] An individual can donate up to $65,500 to parties and political action committees. Substitute that figure for $2,300 to calculate the potential impact of wealthy pro-Israelis in today's post-reform environment.

This nontransparent influence by elites and extremists can be wielded in plain sight, with impunity and under cover of free speech, free elections, free press and even the freedom of religion. Here's where the self-deceit component becomes critical in order for Americans to *believe* that this misuse of freedom is genuinely consistent with freedom.

To buy time on the public's airwaves, money raised from AIPAC's nationwide network is paid to media outlets owned in substantial part by members of the same network. As McCain and Feingold knew, presidents, senators and congressmen come and go but those who collect the checks rack up the favors that amass real political influence. Over the span of six decades of focused funding and single-issue advocacy, the Israel lobby amassed formidable political clout.

Repeal of Representative Government

America's federal system of governance was meant to ensure that members of the House represent the concerns of Americans who reside in Congressional districts in this country, *not* a nationally dispersed network (a Diaspora) concerned about a foreign country (Israel). Similarly, federal elections were meant to hold Senators accountable to concerns of constituents who reside in the states they represent—not policies sought by those living in other states or by a foreign state.

John McCain "reformed" representative government by granting a nationwide network of pro-Israeli elites and Jewish fundamentalists greater influence over election results in every state and Congressional district. With that reform, this network gained more political power—wielding influence that is disproportionate to their numbers, indifferent to their place of residence and often contrary to America's interests.

AIPAC could organize donors in New York, Florida and California to elect a U.S. Senator, say, in sparsely populated Idaho. The hypothetical Congressional candidate in rural Iowa may find his or her campaign flush with funds not from concerned constituents but from members of an AIPAC bundler's network who may never set foot in the state.[11] By granting this Diaspora greater sway over elections in both houses of Congress, McCain-Feingold granted Tel Aviv even more power over U.S. policy-making.

McCain proposed his reforms only after the Senate Ethics Committee cited his poor judgment for assisting the Keating Five in a massive financial fraud. As we shall see, his judgment continues to deteriorate at an accelerating pace as evidenced by his marketing as "reform" this step toward the repeal of representative government.[12]

War Waged in the Mental Environment

> Success will be less a matter of imposing one's will and more a function of shaping behavior of friends, adversaries, and most importantly, *the people in between.*
>
> —Defense Secretary Robert M. Gates (October 10, 2007)

By positioning themselves as *the people in between*, an ideologically aligned few (within a broader faith community) can leverage their modest numbers to wield substantial influence—while making that broader community appear complicit by association. According to the Jewish Virtual Library, 1.7% of the U.S. population is Jewish while 80% of those worldwide who identify themselves as Jewish live either in Israel or the U.S., a nation of 300 million. Approximately 5 million Jews live in each nation.

Yet as *Adbusters* editor Kalle Lasn pointed out, 26 of the 50 most influential neoconservatives who induced America to wage war in Iraq are Jewish (52%). In appraising *how* the U.S. was deceived to wage this war, he noted: "The point is simply that the neocons seem to have a special affinity for Israel that influences their political thinking and consequently American foreign policy in the Middle East." Lasn was promptly attacked as "anti-Semitic" when he titled his article, "Why Won't Anyone Say They're Jewish?"[13]

> The term "neoconservative" is identified with an aggressive foreign policy pursued with disdain for seeking consensus through multilateral organizations such as the United Nations. "Neocons" embrace a globalist free-market agenda backed by military intervention and a domestic emphasis on defense capability. The neocon community is predominantly made up of people and organizations with a pro-Zionist perspective.[14]

Vancouver-based *Adbusters* is subtitled *The Journal of the Mental Environment*. The mental domain is where this disproportionate influence is wielded and where the real war is being waged. The national mental state is the *in between* battleground where *the people in between* displace facts with what people can be deceived to believe.

Thus the widely shared *false belief* that U.S. national security was threatened by Iraqi weapons of mass destruction and the consensus (a shared belief—regardless of the facts) that the Saddam Hussein had operative ties with Al Qaeda.[15] Such fact-displacing beliefs are induced by the combined effect of politics, media, academia, think tanks and popular culture.

While enabling an extremist subculture to leverage its political influence through campaign contributions, McCain-Feingold also authorized unlimited contributions to "527" organizations. That reform bears the number of the tax code provision granting tax-exempt status to issue-advocacy groups ("527s"). Citing free speech, that reform enables the well-to-do to contribute unlimited amounts to issue campaigns so long as their funding is not coordinated with a candidate campaign—where dollar limits apply.

In effect, the wealthy no longer face any limit on funds they can donate (indirectly) to support candidates known to support a particular issue. The impact of this 2002 reform was seen in the 2004 presidential campaign when Swift Boat Veterans for Truth, a "527" organization, mounted a well-funded campaign to discredit John Kerry, the Democratic presidential candidate, by challenging his military record as a Swift Boat commander in Vietnam.

Pivoting off the publication of *Unfit for Command* by John O'Neill, a Swift Boat commander, and Jerome Corsi, an Israeli asset, that effort invested more than $22 million in an issue campaign not directly coordinated with the Bush presidential campaign. The political result helped elect to the presidency a Born Again Christian with personal beliefs strongly sympathetic to Zionism. Cincinnati-based American Financial Group, Carl Lindner's firm (and family members), contributed $1,223,000 to the Swift Boat Vets campaign—532 times more than Lindner could have contributed in the general election to the Bush-Cheney presidential campaign.[16]

The success of that campaign is evidenced by the fact that "Swift Boating" entered the political vocabulary to describe a campaign designed to discredit a political candidate while avoiding limits on campaign contributions. In 2006, Vice President Dick Cheney opened baseball season by throwing the first pitch at a Lindner-owned Cincinnati Reds baseball game. A pitch by President Bush opened the 2007 season in Cincinnati's Great American Ball Park (Lindner's insurance firm operates as the Great American Insurance Company).[17]

Failed Foreign Policy

The McCain campaign touts his foreign policy credentials as his top qualification for office. Yet he remained silent while political and financial power concentrated in the same hands abroad, creating oligarchies worldwide with staggering concentrations of wealth. Though proclaimed a "true conservative" by President Bush, the silence of McCain and Obama on that global trend suggests a failure by both candidates to grasp *how* the fast-globalizing merger of political with financial power threatens democracies and markets.

> *Oligarchy*—a small group of people who together govern a nation or control an organization, often for their own purposes; a nation governed by an organization controlled by an oligarchy; government or control by a small group of people.

Globally, *Forbes* identified 1,125 billionaires in 2008 with a net worth of $4.4 trillion.[18] That's up from 946 billionaires with personal wealth of $3.5 trillion in 2007, an increase from 476 billionaires worth $1.4 trillion in 2003. By 2007, India's 40 billionaires possessed a combined wealth of $351 billion, up from $170 billion in just one year. In 2006, China had 15 billionaires. By 2007 the ranks of its billionaires had swollen to more than 100 according to the widely watched Hurun Report.[19] By January 2008 *China Daily* reported 146 billionaires residing in that "communist" nation.[20]

Chapter 6 describes *how* these trends were set in motion, *why* these oligarchies were 100% predictable, and *how* these developments threaten freedom worldwide. These trends trace their origins to a common source: the embrace of a shared mindset (a consensus belief) that we were induced to freely choose by *the people in between.*

Neither McCain nor Obama voiced concern that the "oligarchization" of Russia under President Boris Yeltsin led President Vladimir Putin to restore a strong central government and revive state ownership. Nor did either candidate question *how* Russia chose that course after escaping seven decades of state ownership under oppressive Soviet rule. Instead John McCain urged that Russia be expelled from the G-8 meetings of industrial nations. Rather than promote dialogue with Russian leaders, he championed mega-thief Mikhail Khodorkovsky, a notorious operative in Moscow's criminal elite. Chapter 5 describes *how* this greatest fraud in history was orchestrated by the same transnational syndicate that induced the U.S. to wage war in the Middle East.

Much as Russia's vast natural resources were systematically looted by a predominantly Ashkenazi elite, the U.S. economy is being systematically hollowed out by financial forces that trace their intellectual origins to the same transnational network, a history to which we will return in the next book in the *Criminal State* series.

> *Ashkenazim* are descended from the medieval Jewish communities of the Rhineland who migrated eastward to areas that became Poland, Hungary, Russia and Eastern Europe. Ashkenazi Jews make up approximately 80% of Jews worldwide and 85% of American Jews. Often applicable as a broad ethnicity, Ashkenazim became moneylenders in the 12th and 13th centuries for secular rulers.
>
> By the 1700s and 1800s, Poland was the center of Ashkenazi Jewry though many Polish Jews fled to Amsterdam and Germany. By the end of the 19th century, Jews immigrated to other areas of Europe, Australia, South Africa and the United States. After World War II, the U.S. became the primary home for Ashkenazi Jews.[21]

West versus East

If America continues on this "consensus" course, it will quickly become a two-class society and a second-rate nation owned largely by a financial elite and foreign interests.[22] The current version of free trade was certain to fund an emboldened China with purchasing power we freely sent abroad based on our shared *belief* in a "consensus" economic model. Yet even as Beijing reinvests our money in modernizing its military and buying commodities in this hemisphere, Senator McCain has only praise for unfettered free trade.

America's viability and credibility continue to slip due to our unwavering support for Israel regardless of its conduct or the prevalence of its operatives inside the U.S. government. Yet, like Obama, McCain continues to insist: "When it comes to the defense of Israel, we simply cannot compromise." Rather than promote dialogue with Iran, an ally until 1979, John McCain threatens an attack—not to protect national security but to show America's backing for Israel. While in Tel Aviv, Barack Obama even promised to coordinate U.S. policy on Iran with Israel.[23]

If Iran is attacked, soaring oil prices will damage not only the U.S. but also China whose needs for imported energy ensure upward pressure on energy prices. China's competitiveness will decline as Beijing, to offset rising fuel costs, is forced to raise wages or reduce energy subsidies. Its investment in commodities will grow to offset erosion in the value of its dollar reserves. Its demand for commodities will fuel inflation in the U.S. As the dollar falls and the interest paid on U.S. securities rises, Americans will experience self-reinforcing recessionary pressures of stagnation and inflation. As China shifts its reserve currency out of dollars, downward pressure on the dollar will grow.

The next global conflict may be between China and the U.S., leaving Russia a self-sufficient spectator able to draw on its vast resources of energy, commodities and labor, including oil and gas exports that generate foreign reserves. America is poised to emerge far weaker as globalization—*at our insistence*—follows the "Washington" consensus. China will remain a mass-production center while Russia emerges unscathed under the influence of a predominantly Ashkenazi oligarchy.

Lastly, to grasp the systemic nature of this phenomenon requires a brief review of fast-emerging financial trends and an overview of *how* treason can operate hidden in plain view. But first a few words about the financial component, an area where those identified have long excelled.

Pocketbook Issues

In a 2008 poll, 81% of Americans agreed that the U.S. is on the wrong track, up from 35% in early 2002. Just 4% agree the country is better off than it was five years ago.[24] Economic trends are systematically reducing many Americans to a state of virtual servitude, including those returning from military service in the Middle East. Yet our freedom was sure to be endangered when, by consensus, we embraced a worldview that equates free will with the freedom allowed financial markets to work *their* will worldwide, as shown in Chapter 6.

As market freedom displaced personal freedom as a national priority, incomes stagnated and the super-rich emerged. In 1982, $91 million was required for inclusion on the *Forbes 400* list of richest

Americans. Average wealth was then $200 million on a list that featured 13 billionaires. By 2007, $1.3 billion was required just for inclusion in that elite group as their combined wealth grew by $290 billion in 2006 alone.

Yet John McCain has pledged his support for "supply-side" policies certain to accelerate this divide. Meanwhile U.S. government debt is on track to top $10,000 billion in 2009 (up from $900 billion in 1980) while federal obligations surged to more than $53,000 billion. David Walker, comptroller general of the U.S., put our fiscal health in perspective by urging in August 2007 that we "learn from the fall of Rome."[25] By July 2008, the nation was in a fiscal freefall as the White House conceded a record $482 billon deficit for the 2009 fiscal year.[26]

With the 2008 war-spending bill, operations in Iraq and Afghanistan exceed $860 billion.[27] With overall costs running an estimated $12 billion per month, this war already surpasses the $670 billion (in 2007 dollars) for the 12-year war in Vietnam. Just as the U.S. could not then, without inflation, fund both "guns and butter" (military and social programs), a future bout of inflation is certain. Stagflation (slow growth plus inflation) will sow unemployment while eroding the perilous retirement prospects for 78 million Baby Boomers.

Yet pro-Israeli war-planner Paul Wolfowitz, then deputy secretary of defense, assured a trusting public that Iraqis would welcome U.S. troops with flowers and sweets and the anticipated $50 billion cost for the war would be paid from oil proceeds by a grateful and peaceful Iraq. Instead, we are covering the cost by borrowing, largely abroad, while ignoring the advice of George Washington who warned against "ungenerously throwing upon posterity the burden which we ourselves ought to bear."

Long-term economic and social costs may push the overall war expense closer to $3 trillion by 2017, 60 times what Wolfowitz predicted.[28] For the first time in American history, every cent of a war's cost has been borrowed. Yet even that figure omits reconstruction costs for Iraqi infrastructure destroyed or badly damaged by a war waged on the basis of fixed intelligence and biased analyses provided by pro-Israeli neocons and their collaborators inside government and the media.

How could we have gotten it so completely wrong? Who—*precisely who*—would have the motivation to ensure that America mis-stepped so badly in this volatile, oil-rich region?

Here are a few of the uncomfortable questions that readers must answer for themselves: Who has the stable nation-state intelligence required to sustain such an operation *inside* the U.S. government? Who has the means, motive and opportunity at the local, state and federal level? The facts point to the same ideologically aligned network that fixed U.S. intelligence around the invasion of Iraq as a goal sought long before the attacks of September 11, 2001.

Treason Hidden in Plain Sight

To grasp the nontransparent nature of this syndicate's operation requires a grasp of how it can function in plain sight yet without detection. That requires a few clarifying words about the terminology of deception.

The 2008 presidential candidates are not agents but "assets" of extremist pro-Israelis, also known as Colonial Zionists.[29] The founders of Israel considered themselves from the outset entitled to operate above the law in order to expand the Land of Israel to its God-given borders, an extensive realm known as Greater Israel that includes much of the oil-rich Middle East. Few in numbers but skilled at leveraging their influence for geopolitical gain, these elites and extremists excel at waging unconventional warfare.

In waging such warfare, Defense Secretary Robert Gates aptly points to *the people in between* as the challenge. Those *in between* routinely emerge as the most ardent supporters of presidential candidates—of both parties—who, in turn, earn their commitment by their loyal support for Israel no matter how extreme its policies. And regardless how much damage those policies inflict on U.S. national security.

In waging what Director of Central Intelligence Michael Hayden calls today's "intelligence wars," the accessibility and reliability of intelligence are key factors that separate the victor from the vanquished. There too lie the perils of an entangling alliance with a nation of religious fundamentalists skilled at manipulating intelligence and preying on people's beliefs.

To prevail at modern-day warfare, these enemies of moderation and informed consent deploy *agents*, *assets* and *sayanim* (volunteers), as explained below. This modern-day mix of non-transparency, sophisticated psychological operations (psy-ops) and lengthy pre-staging makes this form of warfare particularly perilous to an open society where freedom of speech, press, assembly and religion provide these operatives a dependable cover. For those complicit, freedom becomes a means to undermine freedom.

The motto of Israel's foreign intelligence service (the Mossad) has long been "by way of deception shalt thou wage war." Known for their global reach, Mossad operatives provide a skilled cadre of specialists in psy-ops, assassinations and undercover operations. To leverage the impact of their modest numbers, Israeli strategists rely on three key categories of operatives when waging unconventional warfare:

> ***Agents*** possess the conscious mental state that connects their mind to a crime. Intent distinguishes premeditated murder from lesser crimes that involve death, such as involuntary manslaughter. Intent determines the extent of culpability based on the actor's state of mind. Agents operate with premeditation and what the law calls "extreme malice" or an "evil mind."
>
> From 1981-1985, U.S. Navy intelligence analyst Jonathan Pollard stole 360 cubic feet of classified U.S. intelligence documents (more than one million pages) on Soviet arms shipments, Pakistani nuclear weapons, Libyan air defense systems and other data sought by Tel Aviv. Convicted as an Israeli agent, Pollard is serving a life sentence in a federal prison in North Carolina. Even while imprisoned, the Pollard case may have continued to play a role in aiding how Tel Aviv communicates with its operatives. For example, 10 days before the mass murder of 9/11, Israel announced a $1 million grant to this Israeli super-spy.[30] With oversight by a few case officers (*katsas*) and well-trained agents, sophisticated operations can be accomplished with pre-staged assets and a network of cooperative *sayanim*.

Assets are people profiled such that, within an acceptable range of probabilities, they can be relied upon to behave consistent with their personality profile. Assets lack the state of mind required for criminal culpability because they lack the *conscious intent* to commit a crime. Nevertheless, they can contribute to a criminal operation simply by pursuing their subconscious personal needs, typically for recognition, influence, money, sex, drugs or ideology.

Put a profiled asset in a pre-staged time, place and circumstance (such as a presidency) and psy-ops specialists can be confident that—*within an acceptable range of probabilities*—an asset will behave consistent with their profile, much as Bill Clinton behaved with White House intern Monica Lewinsky. Just as Christian Zionist presidents from Harry Truman to G.W. Bush were reliable and pliable advocates for pro-Israeli policies, the consistency of a candidate's conduct confirms his or her qualifications as a pro-Israeli *asset*.

Sayanim (singular *sayan*) play an essential support role. Hebrew for *volunteers* or *helpers, sayanim* are shielded from culpability by being told only enough to perform their narrow role. Though they may play an essential task in the commission of a far broader crime, these volunteers could pass a polygraph test because Mossad recruiters ensure they are kept ignorant of the intended result.

Akin to military reservists, *sayanim* are activated when their skills are required to support Israeli operations. They agree to remain "on call" for missions they *believe* are in the best interest of Israel. In effect, *sayanim* operate as a cost-effective undercover corps. When not engaged in an operation, they gather and report intelligence useful to Israel. The assistance of *sayanim* may be logistics, medical care or intelligence gathering. *Sayanim* also operate as *the people in between* in legislative bodies worldwide. Morris Amitay, a former executive director of the Israel lobby (AIPAC), explains:

> There are a lot of guys at the working level up here [on Capitol Hill]…who happen to be Jewish, who are willing…to look at certain issues in terms of their Jewishness…These are all guys who are in a position to make the decision in these areas for those senators…You can get an awful lot done just at the staff level.[31]

As federal grand juries are impaneled to identify and indict *the people in between* who are involved in this trans-generational operation, how many *sayanim* should the Federal Bureau of Investigation expect to identify? No one knows. Former Mossad case officer Victor Ostrovsky wrote in 1990 that the Mossad had 7,000 *sayanim* on which it could rely in London alone.[32] If that volunteer population is divided by London's 1990 population of 6.8 million, *sayanim* then represented one-tenth of one percent of the population of that capital city.

If the capital of the United States is, say, four times more important to Israel's geopolitical goals than the capital of the United Kingdom, does that mean the FBI should expect four times more *sayanim* per capita in Washington, D.C.? What about *sayanim* in New York, Los Angeles, Miami, Atlanta, Boston, Cleveland, Denver, Phoenix, Minneapolis, Chicago, Philadelphia, Houston, St. Louis, San Diego, Seattle, Tampa? No one knows. And Tel Aviv is unlikely to volunteer the information.

Chapter 7 describes how, by our own self-deceit, America blinded itself to the possibility of trans-generational treason as the toxic charge of anti-Semitism was hurled at anyone seeking to identify the common source of this criminality. Chapter 8 examines the Obama candidacy and shows why a Democratic presidency may offer no real alternative to the Republican McCain, particularly on key issues affecting national security.

Chapter 9 suggests how to identify these on-call pro-Israeli operatives while America is waging war in the Middle East for Greater Israel. What *sayanim* are not told by their *katsas* (case officers) is that a Mossad operation may endanger not only Israel but also the broader Jewish community when operations are linked to extremism, terrorism, organized crime, espionage and treason. Though *sayanim* "must be 100 percent Jewish,"[33] Ostrovsky reports in *By Way of Deception* (1990):

> ...the Mossad does not seem to care how devastating it could be to the status of the Jewish people in the Diaspora if it was known. The answer you get if you ask is: "So what's the worst that could happen to those Jews? They'd all come to Israel. Great![34]

True Friendship

In combination, agents, assets and *sayanim* offer a powerful force multiplier for waging unconventional warfare as Israeli operations proceed in plain view yet non-transparently and with legal impunity. It is just such *people in between* who make such warfare so perilous to U.S. national security—so long as Israel is considered an ally.

On April 22, 2008, federal authorities arrested Ben-Ami Kadish who, like Jonathan Pollard, took classified documents home for Israeli agents to photograph in his basement.[35] The contact for Kadish was Josef Yagur, the same Israeli embassy "scientific attaché" that handled Pollard. Though the documents were stolen between 1979 and 1985, contacts between Kadish and Yagur were still ongoing in 2008. Kadish says he acted out of his *belief* that he was helping Israel.[36]

The Pollard affair revealed an Israel Defense Ministry unit that fulfilled intelligence and equipment-gathering missions for Israel's nuclear reactor at Dimona. That operation also served as a "theft contractor" for the Israeli security industry.[37] Kadish reportedly confessed to giving Israel 50-100 documents about nuclear weapons, fighter jets and air defense missiles from the Picatinny Arsenal in New Jersey ("Home of American Firepower").[38] He was first employed there in October 1963.

Kadish's handler at the Israeli embassy was in touch by phone and email as recently as April 20, 2008 when he reportedly instructed Kadish to lie to U.S. investigators. Kadish claims he never took anything in payment except small gifts and an occasional meal—suggesting he was a typical *sayan*. The Pollard-Kadish espionage case covers 45 years of treason (1963-2008). This case illustrates the challenge facing national security when confronted with how to identify and indict those complicit in a multi-decade operation involving agents, assets and *sayanim* as well as those operating under cover of diplomatic immunity granted an ally.

An Israeli Foreign Ministry spokesman explained that the government had "guidelines" that "prohibit this type of activity in the U.S." The spokesman added, "The relations between Israel and the United States have always been based on true friendship and similarity of values and interests."[39] Commentators wondered if reopening the Pollard spy case would renew 2003 concerns about Israeli defense ties with China. It took Tel Aviv until 1998 to admit that Pollard had been an agent acting on its behalf and awarded him Israeli citizenship.[40]

Americans were led to *believe* that Israel is a trustworthy ally. They have also been led to believe that either party's presidential nominee would be a trustworthy leader. Those marketing such portrayals are the same *people in between* who led Americans to *believe* that Iraq posed a present danger to national security. Should another pro-Israeli asset become president, those skilled at waging unconventional warfare will enjoy as commander-in-chief a powerful ally willing to wage perpetual global war on the pretense of defending America from "Islamo" fascism.

To make the case against John McCain, *Guilt by Association* documents the perils a McCain presidency would pose to the prospects for peace and prosperity both here and abroad. Though Barack Obama has a less extensive record, the candidate's enthusiastic embrace of pro-Zionist policies suggests an Obama administration would likewise pay little attention to the nation's most pressing problem: ridding America of the systemic criminality and treason chronicled in this account.

Chapter 1

Game Theory and the Mass Murder of 9/11

I want to tell you something very clear, don't worry about American pressure on Israel, we, the Jewish people control America, and the Americans know it.

—Israeli Prime Minister Ariel Sharon, October 3, 2001[1]

Unconventional warfare relies on game theory and the application of mathematical models to anticipate the response to staged provocations. Reactions become "perfectly predictable" in the sense that they are foreseeable *within an acceptable range of probabilities.* Israeli mathematician and game theory economist Robert J. Aumann received the 2005 Nobel Prize in economic science. Co-founder of the Center for Rationality at Hebrew University, this Jerusalem resident conceded that "the entire school of thought that we have developed here in Israel" has turned "Israel into the leading authority in this field."[2]

The target of a staged provocation can be a person, a company, an economy, a legislature, a nation or even an entire culture such as Islam or Christianity. With a well-executed provocation, the anticipated response of the "mark" can even become a weapon in the arsenal of the *agent provocateur*. Thus, for instance, America's anticipated response to 9/11 would enable an *agent provocateur* to foresee that the mark (the U.S.) would deploy its military to avenge that attack. With fixed intelligence, that attack could be redirected to wage a long-planned war in Iraq—not for U.S. interests but on behalf of Greater Israel.

Orchestrating a war with Iraq required the displacement of an inconvenient truth (that Iraq played no role in 9/11) with what people could be induced to *believe*. The emotionally wrenching nature of that event played a key fact-displacing role. With the nationally televised mass murder of nearly 3,000 people, a widely shared sense of grief, shock and outrage made it easier for the mark to *believe* that a known Evil Doer in Iraq was responsible, regardless of the facts.

That displacement of facts with beliefs also required a period of "preparing the minds" so that Americans would readily ignore the facts and put their faith in a pre-staged fiction. Those responsible for inducing the March 2003 invasion began "laying the mental threads" (mental associations) more than a decade earlier. Notable among those mental threads was the 1993 publication of an article in *Foreign Affairs* by Harvard professor Samuel Huntington. By the time his article appeared in book-length form in 1996 as *The Clash of Civilizations*, more than 100 academies and think tanks were prepared to promote it, pre-staging a "clash consensus" five years before 9/11.

Also published in 1996 under the guidance of Richard Perle was *A Clean Break* (subtitled *A New Strategy for Securing the Realm*). A member since 1987 of the U.S. Defense Policy Advisory Board, Perle became its chairman in 2001. As an adviser to Israeli Prime Minister Benjamin Netanyahu, Perle's Pentagon post helped lay more mental threads for removing Saddam Hussein, a key theme of *A Clean Break*—published five years before 9/11.

Articles, books and even Pentagon insiders were not enough. People in policy circles were also required to lend the authority of their office to Israel's cause. That role was ably filled by Senators John McCain, Joe Lieberman, a Jewish Zionist from Connecticut, and Jon Kyl, a Christian Zionist from Arizona, when they co-sponsored the Iraq Liberation Act of 1998. Echoing Perle's neoconservative themes in *A Clean Break*, their bill laid another mental thread when it called for the removal of Saddam Hussein three years before 9/11 and appropriated $97 million for that purpose. Distracted by mid-term elections and an impeachment proceeding stemming from his liaisons with Monica Lewinsky, Bill Clinton signed the bill into law October 31, 1998.

After 9/11, McCain and Lieberman became inseparable travel companions and irrepressible advocates for the invasion of Iraq. Looking "presidential" aboard the aircraft carrier *USS Theodore Roosevelt* in January 2002, McCain waved an admiral's cap while proclaiming, alongside Lieberman, "On to Baghdad."

By Way of Deception

An understanding of *applied* game theory helps to grasp the sophistication with which pro-Israeli neoconservatives "prepared the minds" of the American public to invade Iraq in response to 9/11. The confidence with which that game theory strategy was advanced could be seen in the behavior of Deputy Defense Secretary Paul Wolfowitz. Four days after 9/11, in a principals' meeting with President Bush at Camp David, he proposed that the U.S. military invade Iraq. At that time, there was no intelligence suggesting Iraqi involvement and bin Laden was thought to be in Afghanistan.

Neocons were frustrated when, following the First Gulf War in 1991, President George H.W. Bush declined to remove Saddam Hussein. Wolfowitz then proposed a No-Fly Zone in northern Iraq. The Mossad already had agents working in the northern Iraqi city of Mosul for at least a decade prior to the March 2003 U.S. invasion.[3] Reports of Saddam's connections to Al Qaeda also involved Mosul—reports that proved to be false.[4] Mosul also emerged in November 2004 as a center of the post-invasion insurgency that destabilized Iraq.[5]

The potential use of game theory to provoke the U.S. invasion of Iraq dates from an earlier staged incident when Tel Aviv displayed its expertise in deceiving the U.S. to deploy its military in the region. As with the war in Iraq, that incident involved a provocation that induced the U.S. to rely on intelligence fixed around a predetermined goal.

> The pre-staging: in February 1986, the Mossad launched Operation Trojan, a broadcasting operation in Tripoli meant

> to make it appear that the Libyan leadership was transmitting terrorist instructions to their embassies worldwide.[6]
>
> The orchestration: though the Israeli transmissions failed to deceive Spanish or French intelligence, U.S. intelligence was reassured when a trusted ally (Israel) confirmed the messages were legitimate. With Mossad operatives tied into terrorist cells throughout Europe, it was only a matter of time before an American would become a victim.
>
> The provocation: an April 5 terrorist attack on Berlin's La Belle Discotheque killed an American serviceman.
>
> The game theory deployment: on April 14, 160 American, British and German aircraft dropped sixty tons of bombs on Libya, killing 40 civilians, including the adopted two-year-old daughter of Libyan leader Moamer al Qadhafi.

In terms of game theory math, the "terrorist" attack at La Belle Discotheque was not just probable but "perfectly predictable"—*within an acceptable range of probabilities.* With President Ronald Reagan on record promising to retaliate against any country found to support terrorism, the orchestration was complete, awaiting only the death of an American abroad as the provocation required to trigger Israel's planned deployment of the U.S. military.

The attack on Libya not only scuttled negotiations for the release of hostages in Lebanon, it also led to the retaliatory execution of American University of Beirut librarian Peter Kilburn who had been held hostage for 16 months. That deadly reaction to an Israeli-orchestrated provocation also served Tel Aviv's strategic goals as the Cold War drew to a close. Operation Trojan raised the global profile of "radical Islam" as a plausible new Evil Doer and the next threat to American security.

In combination, those events also laid the mental threads (and "prepared the minds") to enhance the plausibility of *The Clash of Civilizations*, the emergence of "Islamo-fascism" and, with 9/11, the reasonableness of a "global war on terrorism." With Israeli confidence boosted by its success in simultaneously deceiving, endangering and discrediting its ally, Iraq and Saddam Hussein became Tel Aviv's next target. According to the assessment of a senior Mossad operative five years before the first Gulf War and 15 years before 9/11:

> After the bombing of Libya, our friend Qadhafi is sure to stay out of the picture for some time. Iraq and Saddam Hussein are the next target. We're starting now to build him up as the big villain. It will take some time, but in the end, there's no doubt that it'll work.[7]

Laying the Mental Threads

Tel Aviv's Iraqi campaign took longer than its Libyan campaign because Iraq was secular, modern and moderate (arguably because of its despotic leader). Its neighbors, on the other hand, were often non-secular, anti-modern and growing steadily more radical—often in response to serial Israeli provocations. Iraq also was allied with Jordan, a friend of Israel and an enemy of both Syria and Iran. As a follow-up to Operation Trojan, pro-Israeli networks began to saturate the political mind space with tales of evildoing by Saddam and the risks that his regime posed to the U.S. and others.[8]

As an operation for "preparing the minds" to accept as plausible *The Clash of Civilizations*, Operation Trojan also confirmed again for the Arab world that America would favor Israel in any Arab-Israeli conflict no matter how outrageous Israel's behavior—including Tel Aviv routinely deceiving its key ally, advocate and arms supplier.

That opinion has since been routinely reconfirmed. For instance, during Israel's July 2006 invasion of Lebanon, the U.S. dispatched to Tel Aviv an emergency supply of laser-guided bombs. Israel Defense Forces departed Lebanon leaving more than 100,000 unexploded cluster bomblets, the bulk of them fired in the final hours of the invasion when Israel knew their withdrawal was imminent. That U.S.-discrediting strategy ensured that American-made munitions would continue to kill and maim Lebanese civilians, primarily children, long after Israel Defense Forces withdrew, leaving more than 1,000 Lebanese, mostly civilians, dead.[9] And ensuring the U.S. could be portrayed as guilty by association.

Rather than punish the Israelis for this war crime, however, the U.S. military replenished Tel Aviv's diminished stock of munitions and the U.S. Congress enacted legislation in 2007 pledging Tel Aviv an additional $30 billion in arms over the next decade at a time when Israel was already the world's fourth largest arms supplier. At every turn in this entangled alliance, Americans were made to appear guilty by association. We became an accessory to war crimes and an accomplice in oppression as self-deceit once again led us to *believe* Israel is an ally.

Jerome Corsi, co-author of the 2004 Swift Boat account *Unfit for Command*, again played a role in 2006 in advancing a prepare-the-minds agenda. Two weeks after the Israeli invasion of Lebanon, he and co-author Jim Gilchrist launched their new book *Minutemen* at Ground Zero, the Manhattan site of 9/11. The book's message: due to the president's failed immigration policies, Hezbollah terrorists were infiltrating the U.S. from Mexico. Had another terrorist attack occurred on U.S. soil, *Minutemen* would have added a thread of plausibility to the claim that the attack was traceable to Hezbollah-sponsor Iran.

In an earlier effort to prepare-the-minds to make such an attack on Iran appear reasonable, Corsi published *Atomic Iran* in March 2005. As with *Minutemen*, Corsi argued that Israel or the U.S. should preemptively bomb the "mad mullahs" of Iran. That too was a lay-the-mental-threads publication designed to help displace facts with what people could be induced to *believe* was true. Plausibility was enhanced when anti-immigrant newscaster Lou Dobbs featured Gilchrist and Corsi on Time Warner's Cable News Network (CNN).

Fast-forward to April 2007 when candidate McCain described how President Bush and he agreed that America has a responsibility to protect Israel from Iran and an obligation to ensure that Iran does not develop nuclear weapons.[10] Consistent with the pro-Israeli position espoused throughout his political career, McCain continued to provide cover for Israeli game theorists even as more mental threads were being laid to make it appear rational for the U.S. to expand the war to Iran.

Corsi again emerged in August 2008 with his release of *The Obama Nation*, a caustic attack on the Democratic candidate published in an attempt to help elect John McCain (though Corsi has said he will not vote for McCain). As before, CNN promoted the author of *Atomic Iran* in a lengthy interview with talk-show host Larry King. With strong pre-release sales and a first edition print run of 475,000 copies, the book immediately topped *The New York Times* best-seller list in the lead-up to the presidential nominating conventions.

Entropy as a Game Theory Weapon

The Second Intifada (Palestinian uprising or, literally, a "shaking off") dates from September 2000 when Ariel Sharon led an armed march to Jerusalem's Temple Mount. When, after a year of calm, suicide bombings recommenced, Sharon and Netanyahu observed that only when Americans "feel our pain" would they understand the plight of Israelis. Both men mentioned a weighted body count of 4,500 to 5,000 Americans lost to terrorism—the initial estimate of those who died a year later in the twin towers of New York City's World Trade Center.[11]

When successful, game theory warfare leaves the mark both discredited and depleted by its reaction to a well-timed provocation. Thus the strategic success of 9/11 as the U.S. was portrayed as irrational when its reaction—the invasion of Iraq—triggered a deadly insurgency. That insurgency, in turn, was a reaction to the U.S. invasion of a nation that played no role in the provocation. As the cost in blood and treasure expanded, the U.S. became overextended militarily, financially and diplomatically.

As the mark (in this case, the U.S.) emerged in the foreground, the *agent provocateur* faded into the background—but only after leaving dynamics at work that steadily depleted the mark of its credibility, resources and resolve. The effect catalyzed *entropy* in the form of widespread cynicism, insecurity, distrust and disillusionment.

> Adapted from physics, *entropy* implies energy that is unavailable to do work. It also suggests disorder, deterioration, loss of information and systemic transformation. Throughout this account, entropy suggests the declining capacity of the U.S. to defend its interests due to the activities of an enemy within.[12]

Those masterful at game theory can wage wars on multiple fronts with minimal resources. One proven strategy: Pose as an ally of a well-armed nation likely to deploy its military in response to a mass murder. In this case, the result destabilized Iraq, creating crises that could subsequently be exploited to long-term strategic advantage. The resulting entropy undermined U.S. national security by weakening its military, discrediting its leadership, degrading its financial condition and disabling its political will. In game theory terms these results were *perfectly predictable*—within an acceptable range of probabilities.

In the asymmetry that typifies unconventional warfare, those who are few in numbers must devise means to leverage their impact.

The game theorists identified in this account lay mental threads and manipulate the mental environment by shaping perceptions that become consensus opinions. By steadily displacing facts with what people can be induced to believe, *the people in between* amplify the impact of deception, enabling the defeat of an opponent with vastly superior resources.

Intelligence wars can be waged in plain sight and under the cover of widely shared consensus beliefs. By manipulating beliefs, intelligence wars can be won *from the inside out* by inducing people to freely choose the very forces that imperil their freedom. Thus the role of self-deceit and, in the Information Age, the disproportionate power wielded by those with outsized influence in media, pop culture, politics, academia and think tanks.

Thus, for example, by putting our faith in the wisdom of financial markets, Americans freely chose a mindset certain to undermine democracies on a global scale. [See Chapter 6.] By branding America with the money-myopic "Washington" consensus, we simultaneously discredited ourselves and disavowed our espoused values while "our" economic model unleashed financial forces certain to create oligarchies worldwide. Those *perfectly predictable* results made America appear hypocritical, devious and even dangerous—i.e., not credible.

Therein lies the force-multiplier of induced beliefs as a means to wage intelligence wars from the shadows. At the operational core of such unconventional, mental-environment warfare is found *the people in between.* Skilled at game theory and imbedded in the intelligentsia, they anticipate the mark's response and incorporate that response in *their* arsenal. Pre-staging often spans generations as chronicled the chapters that follow.

Multi-Point Persuasion

In addition to Senators McCain, Lieberman and Kyl, others with authority also fueled the deceptions that led to war in Iraq. Former CIA Director James Woolsey focused on persuading the public that Mohammed Atta, a 9/11 hijacker, met with a senior Iraqi intelligence official in Prague. Woolsey had earlier joined other neoconservatives in signing a January 1998 letter to Bill Clinton from the Project for a New American Century urging the removal of Saddam Hussein.

Though the Prague account was unlikely and has since been

accepted as false, that report lent incremental plausibility to the "mental threads" then being laid to persuade America to view Iraq as a present danger. As pro-Israeli neoconservatives and the Israel lobby manipulated U.S. lawmakers to invade Iraq, Vice President Cheney delivered a series of saber rattling, prepare-the-mind speeches showcasing false, flawed and fixed intelligence. Moments of candor went largely unreported. For example, Philip Zelikow, executive director of the 9/11 Commission, informed a University of Virginia audience on September 10, 2002:

> Why would Iraq attack America or use nuclear weapons against us? I'll tell you what I think the real threat [is] and actually has been since 1990—it's the threat against Israel. And this is the real threat that dare not speak its name, because the Europeans don't care deeply about that threat, I will tell you frankly. And the American government doesn't want to lean too hard on it rhetorically, because it's not a popular sell.[13]

Zelikow omitted that candor in the 9/11 Commission report.[14]

Ernst Hollings, former Senator from South Carolina, offered a similarly candid post-invasion analysis for which he was labeled an anti-Semite. Like Zelikow, Hollings first noted that Iraq was not a direct threat to the U.S. When asked why we invaded Iraq, he responded: "The answer everyone knows…is because we want to secure our friend Israel."[15] Only an occasional journalist dared speak out—and often only once due to the vitriolic attacks that immediately ensued. Before the invasion, Robert Novak portrayed the conflict as "Sharon's war."[16] Journalist Michael Kinsley noted that "the lack of public discussion about the role of Israel…is the proverbial elephant in the room: Everybody sees it, no one mentions it."[17]

U.S. presidential candidates have learned not to challenge Tel Aviv's agenda for the Middle East. During the 2004 presidential campaign, presidential candidate Howard Dean called for the U.S. to take a more "even-handed role" in the Arab-Israeli conflict. Fellow Democrat Joe Lieberman lambasted him as "irresponsible" and accused him of selling Israel down the river. Senior Democrats in the House leadership jointly signed a letter criticizing Dean's comment as his candidacy faded.[18] After that, no other candidate dared suggest evenhandedness.

> ***Note:*** the long-running friction between Israelis and Palestinians is often described as a "conflict." The facts suggest it should more accurately be described as an "occupation," the description used in this analysis.

Emotion Management

A confluence of events in the aftermath of 9/11 affected the decision-making environment in response to those attacks, as did the timing of incidents in the lead-up to a U.S. Senate resolution in support of the invasion of Iraq.

- September 18, 2001—the first envelope was mailed to the office of a U.S. Senator containing weapons-grade anthrax (its origins remain a subject of contention).[19] The first of five anthrax victims was the photo editor of the *Sun*, a tabloid published in Florida near where cells of 9-11 terrorists trained.[20]
- October 3, 2001—Israeli Prime Minister Ariel Sharon announced: "I want to tell you something very clear, don't worry about American pressure on Israel, we, the Jewish people control America, and the Americans know it."[21]
- October 4, 2001—a White House leak, traced to Deputy Defense Secretary Wolfowitz, confirmed that the U.S. would invade Iraq.
- October 5, 2001—Israeli Prime Minister Ariel Sharon warned the U.S.: "Do not try to appease the Arabs at our expense. This is unacceptable to us. Israel will not be Czechoslovakia. Israel will fight terrorism."[22]
    - Sharon's comparison of the 9/11 terrorists to Hitler and of President George Bush to British Prime Minister Neville Chamberlain (who sought to appease Adolph Hitler) elicited a terse response from Secretary of State Colin Powell.[23]

  - Within hours of Powell's comment, Israel displayed its political invincibility when Sharon launched an invasion by Israel Defense Forces of Palestinian areas in Hebron.
  - Soon thereafter, a scandal involving Sharon threatened to destabilize his coalition government by threatening to remove the policy-maker essential for negotiations in the region.
  - The White House quickly silenced Sharon's critics in government, confirming that even the threat of entropy can be deployed as a strategic weapon by those skilled at game theory.
- October 6-8, 2001—in response to leaks, President Bush restricted intelligence-sharing to eight senior Congressional leaders. Congressman Tom Lantos rushed to the White House to protest.
  - The White House relented and the information flow re-commenced. When asked on *Meet the Press* in September 2002—six months before the invasion—about the prospects for war in Iraq, Lantos said: "The train has already left the station."
  - Speaking to the Israeli Knesset that same month, Lantos boasted: "You won't have any problem with Saddam. We'll be rid of the bastard soon enough. And in his place we'll install a pro-Western dictator, who will be good for us and for you."

The facts suggest that Lantos was referring to Ahmad Chalabi, head of the London-based Iraqi National Congress. Since the mid-1980s Chalabi had been groomed for a leadership role in post-invasion Iraq by neoconservatives Richard Perle and Paul Wolfowitz.[24] Chalabi is the serial liar whose "fixed" intelligence was routinely reported as news by *New York Times* reporter Judith Miller.[25]

Chalabi's bogus sources provided false intelligence on mobile biological weapons laboratories. Secretary of State Powell humiliated himself and discredited the U.S. when he relied on Chalabi's source (code name "Curveball") to justify an invasion of Iraq in February

2003 testimony before the U.N. Security Council. *The Man Who Pushed America to War,* a 2008 chronicle of Chalabi's exploits in deceit, confirmed that John McCain and Joe Lieberman were his earliest and most reliable Senate supporters commencing in 1991, a full decade before 9/11.[26]

Chalabi boasted to the Senate Committee on Appropriations in June 2002 that he placed 108 intelligence reports in major publications.[27] With appropriations from the McCain/Lieberman-sponsored Iraq Liberation Act of 1998, U.S. defense and intelligence agencies paid Chalabi's Iraqi National Congress $340,000 per month through May 2004.[28] Rather than deny he lied to the American public, Chalabi bragged about his manipulation: "We are heroes in error."

On October 2, 2002, random sniper attacks began around the Washington, D.C. area, killing ten people and wounding three over a three-week period. The effect created widespread insecurity and heightened anxiety as Washington became a city under siege the day before debate began on Senate Resolution 46, introduced by Senator Joe Lieberman, to authorize the use of U.S. armed forces against Iraq.[29]

Political Management

In late March 2002, in response to a Palestinian suicide bombing, Ariel Sharon dispatched Israel Defense Forces to take control of major Palestinian areas in the West Bank. President Bush demanded that Sharon halt the incursions and dispatched Secretary of State Powell to commence regional damage control meant to pressure all sides to start negotiations. Former Israeli Prime Minister Benjamin Netanyahu proved correct when he commented that Powell's trip "won't amount to anything."

While Powell was in the region, the Israel lobby and Christian Zionist evangelical leaders urged that Bush back off the pressure on Israel. Describing himself "an Israeli at heart,"[30] Texas Congressman Tom DeLay, House Majority Leader (2003-2005), was particularly outspoken. So was Congressman Richard Armey, Majority Leader from 1995-2003. Armey conceded in September 2002 that "my No. 1 priority in foreign policy is to protect Israel."[31]

Senate Minority Leader Trent Lott also lobbied Bush to ease up on Israel. Christian Zionist evangelicals, one of Bush's key political constituencies, urged that their members flood the White House with letters and emails. Christian Zionist leaders Jerry Falwell and Gary Bauer demanded an end to the pressure on Sharon to withdraw from the West Bank. The Conference of Presidents of Major American Jewish Organizations, the premier fundraising arm of the Israel lobby, sponsored a rally in Washington with the United Jewish Communities.

The House and Senate ignored Bush's objections and passed pro-Israeli resolutions by large margins (94 to 2 in the Senate and 352 to 21 in the House). Both resolutions cited America's "solidarity with Israel." The Armey-championed House resolution stated that the U.S. and Israel are "now engaged in a common struggle against terrorism." In early May 2002, a House appropriations subcommittee chaired by New York congresswoman Nita Lowey approved $200 million for Israel to fight terrorism, a proposal opposed by the Bush administration. They lost and President Bush reluctantly signed the legislation.

By the time Powell returned from the region and reappraised the political landscape, he knew who controlled U.S. foreign policy in the region, as did America's commander-in-chief. The systemic entropy injected into the U.S. political system ensured that America's senior leadership was precluded from doing the necessary work required to defend national security.

Fast-forward two years to April 2004, 13 months after the invasion of Iraq; Ariel Sharon was again in the Oval Office for a visit with the Christian Zionist president. On April 14, the two leaders announced in a White House photo opportunity that due to "realities on the ground" these two leaders—with no Palestinians present—agreed that Israel could retain land belonging to the Palestinians and that the Palestinians would not be able to return.

Prior to this announcement, all parties had agreed that these contentious issues would be negotiated with the Palestinians. As any game theorist could have foreseen, that joint statement set off a new round of violence in the Middle East—endangering U.S. troops, further destabilizing Iraq and discrediting America in the court of public opinion, particularly in the volatile Middle East, where the declaration galvanized insurgents loyal to radical Sheik Moqtada al Sadr.

As is common with Israeli-orchestrated provocations, the pre-staging ensured that the impact would include an emotional component certain to add outrage to the response. Just three weeks before the Bush-Sharon announcement, Israel had assassinated Hamas leader Sheik Ahmed Yassin. Because Israel used U.S.-made Hellfire missiles, many in the Arab world shared the belief that Washington approved Tel Aviv's murder of this paraplegic in his wheelchair. Three days after the Bush-Sharon announcement, Israel assassinated Sheikh Yassin's successor, Abdel Aziz Rantisi, ensuring that the proposed "roadmap for peace" lost traction and scuttling any prospect for peace (aka entropy).

Developed by the "Quartet" comprising the U.S., Russia, the European Union and the U.N., the roadmap had been presented to Israel and the Palestinian Authority on April 30, 2003. Yet months before its release, the proposal was criticized in detail in U.S. media outlets as neocon commentators ridiculed it as "a map without a destination," a "map to nowhere" and "road kill." After Bush's June 2003 trip to the Middle East to promote the proposal, Sharon ordered seven assassinations in five days. Those murders followed his promise to Colin Powell in May that Israel would cease targeted assassinations in order not to inflame the situation unless the killings involved a "ticking bomb."

In the interim, Israelis continued to provoke Palestinians at every turn with searches, arrests, house demolitions, the bulldozing of crops and orchards, collective punishments and generally ensuring that the Palestinians knew that they remained an imprisoned people and an immobilized population—as the peace process was held hostage to the mentality of domination, subjugation, intimidation and provocation.

Terror As a Tactic

The facts confirm that Israel and its collaborators in the U.S. are serial provocateurs and key architects of the terrorism against which Tel Aviv seeks America's military and diplomatic protection and the financial support of U.S. taxpayers. The timeline below points to a common source of terrorism orchestrated by extremists to exert geopolitical leverage while portraying themselves as victims. In each of the bombings in Israel, the victims were killed at venues frequented by recent Russian émigrés.

The consistency of the fact patterns, moreover, suggests that only a stable nation-state with world-class intelligence capabilities could orchestrate terrorist acts with such perfect timing. In each case, note the role of *time, place and circumstance* in manipulating the public mind space (the mental environment) to advance an agenda—a global war on terrorism—sought by pro-Israeli elites and extremists:

- On April 12, 2002, *at the same moment* Secretary of State Colin Powell was meeting with Ariel Sharon, a suicide bombing occurred in Israel, killing 8 and injuring 22.[32]
- On May 10, 2002, *at the same moment* President Bush was meeting with Ariel Sharon, a suicide bombing occurred in Israel.[33]
- On June 11, 2003, *on the same day* Ariel Sharon visited the White House, a suicide bombing killed 17 and wounded 100 on a bus in Jerusalem.
- On November 11, 2003, *while the president of Italy was visiting* the U.S., Italy suffered its greatest wartime casualties since WWII when 19 Italians were killed in Iraq.
- On November 20, 2003, *while President Bush was visiting Prime Minister Tony Blair* in London, the British envoy to Istanbul was among 27 killed by a blast.
- On November 30, 2003, *while the president of Spain was visiting the U.S.*, seven Spanish intelligence officers were killed in Iraq, along with two Japanese diplomats.
- *On that same day*, Senator Joe Lieberman warned in a widely reported speech that the war in Iraq could mark the beginning of a "global religious war" (aka *The Clash*) commencing with a civil war in the Middle East, with Arabs killing Arabs.
    - By January 2004, Iraqis were being killed and injured by other Iraqis, including Arab-on-Arab violence by suicide bombers.
    - By March 2004, 143 people were killed in one day in attacks on two sacred sites in Iraq.[34]
    - By August 2004, Joe Lieberman, senior Democrat on the Governmental Affairs Committee, was given

    responsibility for crafting the Senate's response to the 9/11 Commission report.[35]
  - By September 2004, Senators Lieberman and Carl Levin had emerged as key architects of the intelligence reform legislation crafted in response to the report.[36]
  - By January 2007, Senator Lieberman had assumed chairmanship of the Senate Committee on Homeland Security.

- On August 28, 2003, while pro-Israeli forces in the U.S. were lobbying U.S. lawmakers to expand the war by invading Iran, an Israeli ship (*Zim Antwerp I*) was impounded in Germany carrying Israeli arms and military equipment bound from Israel to Iran.[37]
- On October 13, 2004, *Maariv International* reported from Tel Aviv that George Ben Bachi, a 36-year-old Israeli citizen, was released from Iraq's Abu Ghraib prison. A Moroccan-born Jew, he was apprehended near the Iraqi-Jordanian border with Barazan Tikhriti, Saddam Hussein's half-brother and Iraqi chief of intelligence.
- At 3:55 a.m. on May 5, 2005 (8:55 a.m. in London), two IEDs (improvised explosive devices) exploded in front of a Manhattan office building that includes the office of the British consulate. In London, financial markets commenced a sharp decline an hour later just as voters were going to the polls. The political impact contributed to a sharp reduction in the Labor Party's majority in the 646-seat Parliament—from 160 to 66. Had Tory leader Michael Howard—running on a platform opposing Prime Minister Tony Blair on Iraq—been elected, he would have become Britain's first Jewish Prime Minister since Benjamin Disraeli.

Why would any media outlet suggest that these well-timed incidents were orchestrated by anyone other than a nation state with the stable intelligence, means, motive and opportunity to benefit from them?

Why would commentators suggest these events are traceable to anyone other than pro-Israeli operatives working inside governments in the U.S. and abroad? Who, other than those within that subculture, would suggest such an implausible possibility?

Chapter 2

Organized Crime in Arizona

Ten thousand Jews are selling booze without the law's permission.
To fill the needs of a million Swedes who voted Prohibition.
—Elliott Wadsworth

The trans-generational influence of organized crime on the U.S. presidency will be chronicled in the forthcoming *Criminal State* series. *Guilt by Association* focuses primarily on the organized crime lineage that positioned the 2008 candidates for the White House. This chapter chronicles the history of the state of Arizona as a key node in the node-and-network system of organized crime that nurtured John McCain's political career.

This chapter opens with a rhyme that comes from Assistant Treasury Secretary Elliott Wadsworth and refers to the fact that the law that made Prohibition a reality on January 16, 1920 was authored by Minnesota Congressman Andrew J. Volstead. Wadsworth understood that, in practical terms, the Volstead Act capitalized organized crime, established a continent-wide distribution network for criminal activities, and identified a network of corrupt politicians for future operations.

When the U.S. banned the manufacture and sale of alcohol, the stage was set for massive profits by those willing to operate outside the law and those willing to ship alcohol across the U.S.-Canadian border. After founding Distillers Corporation in Montreal in 1924, Sam Bronfman acquired Joseph E. Seagram & Sons in Waterloo, Ontario in 1928. That same year organized crime convened in Cleveland, Ohio.[1] By 1929, this criminal elite was ready to form the National Crime Syndicate at its first-ever conclave in Atlantic City, New Jersey. To escape prying ears, the mobsters rolled up their trousers and cut most of their deals while standing knee-deep in the waters of the Atlantic.

> Conceived by New York's Meyer Lansky and Frank Costello and by Chicago's Johnny Torrio, conclave attendees meeting at the posh Breakers Hotel included Al "Scarface" Capone, Benjamin "Bugsy" Siegel, Charlie "King" Solomon, Max Hoff, Waxey Gordon (né Irving Wexler), "Nig" Rosen, Sam Lazar, Charlie Schwartz, Moses "Moe" Dalitz, Dutch Schultz, Longy Zwillman, Hymie Weiss, Lou Rothkopf, Leo Berkowitz, Abe Bernstein and (reportedly) Chicago's Moses Annenberg who Torrio financially backed to buy *The Daily Racing Form.* [2]

Like the infamous Al Capone, Chicago mob boss Johnny Torrio moved to the Windy City from the orthodox Jewish neighborhood of Williamsburg in New York City's Brooklyn borough where he and Capone proved themselves sufficiently violent to oversee the Chicago Outfit. At the Atlantic City conclave, Meyer Lansky emerged as syndicate chairman and chief financial officer. While in their early teens on Manhattan's Lower East Side, he and Bugsy Siegel rose to prominence as killers-for-hire. The Polish Lansky (Mieir Suchowljanksy) and Italian Charles "Lucky" Luciano oversaw "Murder, Inc.," a syndicate assassination affiliate that ensured the smooth operations of this nationwide network.[3]

To reduce the violence that accompanied territorial disputes and attracted unwanted public scrutiny, the Atlantic City gathering divided the U.S. into 24 exclusive markets. A syndicate member was put in charge of each territory, with the New York City area home to five territories and Las Vegas designated an open city with syndicate oversight. At the conclave, Tom Lazia represented Kansas City's Pendergast political machine—a point to keep in mind when considering Harry Truman's political lineage and his recognition of Israel in 1948.[4]

Psychological Profile

In the course of researching the criminality chronicled in this account, it became essential to find a psychological profile that accurately described those identified as key operatives. The online *Compact Oxford English Dictionary* offered an appropriate clinical definition of those morally and ethically dissociated from the society in which they live. The descriptors in **bold** have proven reliable in accurately describing those chronicled in this account:

> *psychopathy* n. A mental disorder roughly equivalent to antisocial personality disorder, but with emphasis on affective and interpersonal traits such as **superficial charm, pathological lying, egocentricity, lack of remorse, and callousness** that have traditionally been regarded by clinicians as characteristic of psychopaths, rather than social deviance traits such as need for stimulation, parasitic lifestyle, poor behavioral controls, impulsivity, and irresponsibility that are prototypical of antisocial personality disorder.
>
> Whether psychopathy and antisocial personality disorder share a common referent is an open question. Compare sociopathy. psychopath n. A person with psychopathy. psychopathic adj. [From Greek psyche mind + pathos suffering]

The Real Syndicate

In November 1931 Meyer Lansky convened in Manhattan's Franconia Hotel a Jews-only sequel to the Atlantic City conclave. When Philadelphia bootleg king Waxey Gordon refused to work with the cover provided by Italians and Sicilians (aka "the Mickey Mouse Mafia"),[5] he was murdered. That risk to the Jewish-dominated syndicate was handled by replacing him with "Nig" Rosen and "Boo Boo" Hoff.[6]

Moe Dalitz attended each conclave—Cleveland (1928), Atlantic

City (1929) and Manhattan (1931). Operating out of the Great Lakes area, the Cleveland node in the syndicate network prospered when "the Jewish Navy" shuttled Bronfman booze across Lake Erie for nationwide distribution. Dalitz soon became the syndicate equivalent of a regional manager.

He oversaw much of the liquor bootlegged into the U.S. across the Detroit River, a narrow strip of water separating Michigan from Ontario and from the Bronfman-owned Seagram & Sons distilleries in nearby Waterloo. Known as the "hooch highway," the easy border crossings around Detroit led organized crime to buy the bulk of Macomb County where narrow Lake St. Clair (the sixth of the five Great Lakes) became another favored entry point.

Dalitz also oversaw the labor racketeering most famously associated with Teamster President Jimmy Hoffa and labor lawyer Sydney Korshak whose *consigliere* role in positioning Ronald Reagan for the presidency will be chronicled in the *Criminal State* series. Dalitz also oversaw Gus Greenbaum, a key figure in organized crime in Arizona. A Lansky colleague in New York, Greenbaum migrated to the Midwest where he worked for the Chicago Outfit before moving to Phoenix in 1928.

The 1929 Atlantic City conclave also discussed the lucrative racing wire service and its delivery of real-time horse race results to bookie joints nationwide. The wire service became a key organizing mechanism around which syndicate operations coalesced not only nationwide but also in Canada, Mexico and Cuba. Bugsy Siegel ran the wire service in Las Vegas and Los Angeles while Greenbaum oversaw the Arizona operation. By 1941, Siegel became enamored with Nevada as an attractive center for gambling and prostitution. With the help of Siegel's childhood friend Meyer Lansky, syndicate operatives advanced the funds needed to build the Flamingo, a gambling and vacation resort named after Virginia Hill, an Alabama-born dancer, mob courier and Siegel consort.

By 1947, Lansky realized that, in addition to suspect cost overruns, Siegel was skimming the casino skim and using Hill to transport the funds for deposit in Swiss bank accounts. A Murder, Inc. operative killed Siegel in Los Angeles using a high-powered rifle fired through a window from 15 feet away. Confirming by his presence it was a syndicate-approved hit, Greenbaum was on hand in Las Vegas to take over the Flamingo. With Greenbaum's relocation to Nevada, the syndicate named Kemper Marley as his replacement to run the Arizona operation. Marley was by then a land and liquor magnate prospering as a statewide distributor of Bronfman-provided liquor in the post-Prohibition era. According to *Rumrunners and Prohibition*, a popular History Channel account of the era:

> During the 1920s, the Bronfmans made a bonanza in bootlegging. The company may have accounted for half of the illegal liquor crossing the border. Some claimed that Bronfman had a distribution deal for his booze with the infamous Jewish mobster Meyer Lansky...When the morally intentioned Prohibition finally ended in 1933, it left a legacy of bloodshed, racketeering, and one of the wealthiest family dynasties in the world, the Bronfmans.[7]

Marley escaped indictment on federal liquor law violations in a case that led to the March 1948 conviction of James Hensley for black-market liquor sales. He was also charged with conspiracy to conceal the names of those involved in rackets involving the liquor industry. Hensley's six-month sentence was suspended. At the time, Marley's United Liquor had a virtual statewide liquor monopoly dating from soon after the repeal of Prohibition. Al Lizanetz, Marley's public relations specialist, conceded that the Bronfman family founded Marley's liquor operation.

By the mid-1950s, Hensley controlled one of the nation's largest Anheuser-Busch distributorships, a franchise reportedly directed to him by a grateful Marley who escaped indictment in both the 1948 case and in a subsequent case despite his dominant role in statewide liquor distribution. By 2000, Hensley & Co. was the nation's fifth-largest wholesaler of beer with annual sales exceeding $200 million in his closely held firm.[8] On his death in June 2000, his daughter Cindy became controlling shareholder and chairman of the board.[9]

Two decades earlier Jim Hensley had hired his son-in-law, John McCain, as vice-president for public relations—a post he soon vacated, as anticipated, to begin a political career. A 1982 gift of $689,000 from a Hensley & Co. affiliate to Cindy McCain eased the son-in-law's ability to lend his campaign $167,000.[10] A pre-nuptial agreement ensured that McCain's financial records would omit his wife's business interests. She reported $6 million in income for 2007 ($16,400 per day). By 2008, Hensley & Co. had become the nation's third largest Budweiser distributor with more than $300 million in annual sales.[11]

The Arizona Connection

When Kemper Marley died in 1990 at age 83, his *New York Times* obituary highlighted his Phoenix police-reported connection to the 1976 murder of *Arizona Republic* investigative reporter Don Bolles. Articles published by Bolles reportedly persuaded Marley to resign his position on the three-member Arizona Racing Commission soon after his appointment. Bolles was assassinated while investigating statewide corruption. Mortally injured by a bomb concealed beneath his car, Bolles lost both legs and an arm. He died eleven days later.

Before lapsing into unconsciousness, Bolles mentioned, "Adamson, Emprise, Mafia." John Harvey Adamson served a 20-year prison sentence after confessing that he had lured Bolles to a Phoenix hotel parking lot and placed a bomb under his car. Emprise has numerous connections to organized crime in Arizona. Emprise is the corporate name of the Jacobs family operation in Buffalo, New York, known nationwide as "the Godfather of sports." After Eugene Hensley, brother of James, entered a federal prison in Texas in 1969 to serve a sentence for tax evasion, he sold his interest in Ruidoso Downs, a racetrack in New Mexico from which he'd been banned due to his conviction. After the sale, the buyer signed a 20-year concession with Emprise.[12]

The Emprise connection remains relevant to this latest presidential candidate from a state that has long been a magnet for organized crime. It was from the Jacobs' law firm in Buffalo that Bill Miller emerged to run as the vice-presidential nominee along with Arizona Senator Barry Goldwater in his losing race against Lyndon Johnson in the 1964 presidential election.[13] Miller knew that he and Goldwater were not going to win so he often directed the pilots of his campaign plane to circle a few more times if he had a good poker game going.[14] Had the Goldwater/Miller ticket not lost, Lyndon Johnson would not have been in the White House when Israel staged its preemptive land grab in the June 1967 Six-Day War. The response to that U.S.-backed provocation triggered foreseeable outrage throughout the predominantly Muslim region, preparing minds worldwide for the plausibility of *The Clash of Civilizations.*

Johnson was the right president at the right time and under just the right circumstances to perform as a pliable and reliable asset in the lead-up to that war. Profiling of that Oval Office occupant included the well timed servicing—in the White House—of the personal needs of a U.S. commander-in-chief by an attractive blonde former Irgun operative the same night that the 1967 war began. [See Chapter 4.]

Committee on the Present Danger

Organized crime in Arizona also features Jon Kyl, another key component in this transnational syndicate. Second-ranking in the Republican leadership, Kyl serves as honorary co-chairman of the Committee on the Present Danger.[15] Joe Lieberman, the other co-chair, serves as McCain's inseparable political companion and is poised to become a senior appointee in a McCain administration. Within days of wrapping up the Republican presidential nomination in March 2008, McCain announced that he and Lieberman would travel together to Israel.

The Committee on the Present Danger (CPD) was founded in 1950 with a grant from David Packard of Hewlett Packard. Envisioned as a "citizen's lobby," its initial goal was to alert Americans to the danger of the communist threat. To that end, CPD generated support for the military build-up advocated in NSC-68, a National Security Council blueprint for America's Cold War strategy written in 1950 by Paul Nitze, an adviser to Dean Acheson. Truman named Acheson his secretary of state after a surprise victory over New York Governor Tom Dewey in the November 1948 presidential election. That appointment followed former Secretary of State George C. Marshall's adamant opposition in May 1948 to Truman's recognition as a legitimate sovereign state an enclave of Jewish elites and fundamentalists.

By 1951, CPD was sponsoring a weekly broadcast on NBC warning of the dangers of the Soviet threat. That same year saw New York investment banker Donald Stralem fund the production of *Duck and Cover*. The Stralem-produced film directed teachers to train their students how to duck under their desks and cover their heads with their hands in case of an "atom attack" by the Soviet Union. Shown to mandatory attendance in schools nationwide, Stralem's brief film struck terror in the national psyche with a Truman-era Civil Defense education program tailored to the "emotion management" needs of the Cold War.

Soon thereafter, Americans began building bomb shelters and debating how best to exclude their fallout-infected neighbors should they become a target of communist Evil Doers, the present danger of that era. CPD was disbanded in 1953 but only after its leaders were given policy-shaping positions in the Eisenhower Administration. CPD II emerged in March of 1976 to influence the presidential race between Gerald Ford and Jimmy Carter. After Carter's victory, CPD II members lobbied the "missile gap" for the next four years, the present danger of that era.

Prior to President Ford's 1976 electoral loss, the former Michigan Congressman ordered the formation of "Team B" as an alternative threat assessment to the National Intelligence Estimate provided by the Central Intelligence Agency ("Team A"). On the recommendation of neocon Richard Perle, neocon Paul Wolfowitz was made a member of Team B. That appointment provided the future deputy secretary of defense an entry point into the upper echelon of national security politics.

Richard Pipes emerged as the primary intellectual force in compiling Team B assessments. In retrospect, it is now known that Team B exaggerated the risk to national security of Soviet military and economic strength.[16] Team B also set the precedent for what emerged 25 years later as a Pentagon operation (the Office of Special Plans) that "fixed" the intelligence to induce the invasion of Iraq. As with the inflated Soviet threat, policymakers were induced to *believe* that Iraq posed a far greater threat to national security than the facts warranted.

Two decades earlier, Team B's hawkish input influenced intelligence reporting as well as Pentagon spending as its "worst case" scenarios routinely worked their way into Ronald Reagan's campaign speeches and into administration policies. Following his election as president in November 1980, 33 members of CPD II were given policy positions, gaining this neoconservative network the power to shape legislation.

Fixing the Intelligence

The insider influence wielded by CPD II operatives ensured a highly profitable, deficit-financed binge of defense spending during the Reagan era. Revised intelligence estimates after the collapse of the Soviet Union in 1989 confirmed overstatements both in the CPD-II "missile gap" and in Team B claims of the Soviet threat. With the election in November 2000 of George W. Bush, members of CPD II and Team B moved inside the Pentagon where their operations turned to overstating the threat of Iraqi weapons of mass destruction (WMD).

Intelligence agency flaws in assessing the Soviet threat had by then fueled skepticism in the post-9/11 policy environment. When official intelligence estimates of the WMD threat posed by Iraq proved inconsistent with the present danger assessed by pro-Israelis in the Pentagon's Office of Special Plans, the "intelligence" provided by that office was given the benefit of the doubt.

With the perceived authority of a Pentagon intelligence operation overseen by neocon Defense Under Secretary Douglas Feith (a co-author with Richard Perle of *A Clean Break*), pro-Israeli operatives exploited a direct intelligence conduit into presidential decision-making, bypassing legitimate intelligence agencies (subject to Congressional oversight) with the aid of Lewis "Scooter" Libby, the Ashkenazi chief of staff for Vice President Dick Cheney.[17]

Indicative of how an ideologically aligned network can leverage a few people into "virtual" control over national security decision-making, note how few operatives were required to preempt legitimate intelligence operations that cost taxpayers more than $50 billion per year.[18] That insider influence required lengthy pre-staging so that members of this pro-Israeli network were positioned to serve in the right place at the right time and under just the right circumstances.

The CPD emerged again after the March 2003 invasion of Iraq relied on the fixed intelligence provided through the Office of Special Plans. In its third incarnation, members of CPD III again acted as a self-appointed "citizen's lobby" for the latest present danger: terrorism and the need for Pentagon appropriations to protect America—from "Islamo-fascism."[19]

With the prodding of CPD operatives, the costly Cold War

morphed seamlessly into a costly, borderless and endless "global war on terrorism." As terrorists displaced communists as consensus Evil Doers, CPD III chose two high-profile Zionists as honorary co-chairs: Senator Jon Kyl, a Christian Zionist Republican, and Joe Lieberman, a Jewish Zionist Democrat/Independent. In lockstep, both lawmakers lobbied for military action against Iran as the latest present danger.

One co-chairman of CPD III is former CIA Director Woolsey, purveyor of the discredited notion that 9/11 hijacker Mohammed Atta met in Prague with an Iraqi intelligence officer. The other is George Schultz. A former president and director of Bechtel Group, a major defense contractor, Schultz was a key promoter of the discredited missile gap while serving as Ronald Reagan's secretary of state (1982-89).

After losing the 2006 Democratic primary in Connecticut, Joe Lieberman was re-elected to the Senate as an independent. In January 2007, his Democratic Party colleagues named him chairman of the Senate Committee on Homeland Security, enabling them to maintain their slim 51-49 majority in the Senate by granting him that position. Aided by Schultz and Woolsey, Senators Kyl and Lieberman have proven themselves reliable advocates in marketing the profitable "terrorism gap" and calling for vast expenditures in homeland security.

For example, since anthrax-laced letters were sent to Congressional offices and news organizations in late 2001, almost $50 billion has been spent to build new laboratories, develop vaccines and stockpile drugs.[20] The source of that military-grade anthrax remains an open issue.[21] The cost of using private contractors in Iraq will surge past the $100 billion mark before the end of 2008.[22] Contractors in Iraq employ at least 180,000 people, larger than the U.S. military force.

The Phoenix Connection

Evidentiary trails in this area seldom run in straight lines, a fact that will become increasingly apparent in later chapters. Also, "prepare-the-minds" incidents, events and relationships are often pre-staged over lengthy time periods, making barriers to transparency even more daunting. Yet the evidence becomes robust once the reader grasps *how* this syndicate operates across generations with a common criminal focus coordinated around a shared ideology.

For example, when Bugsy Siegel was murdered and Gus Greenbaum took over his role in Las Vegas, the syndicate required a Jewish operative to fill Siegel's role to oversee the racing wire service in Los Angeles. That job fell to Mickey Cohen who became a reliable fundraiser for Richard Nixon, an up-and-coming Congressional candidate. In addition to helping fund Nixon's 1946 race for the California Assembly, Cohen sponsored a mobsters-only fundraiser for his 1950 U.S. Senate race in the Banquet Room of the Hollywood Knickerbocker Hotel. The quota for the 250 members of the "gambling fraternity" was $75,000 ($544,000 in 2007 dollars).

When Cohen first asked for donations he was $20,000 short of his goal from what he described as a crowd consisting of "all gamblers from Vegas, all gambling money; there wasn't a legitimate person in the room." He closed the three doors to the banquet room and informed the attendees, "nobody's going home till this quota's met."[23] The "fraternity" suddenly rediscovered their generosity. Nixon made a short thank-you speech and left with his campaign coffers flush with cash. As Cohen biographer Brad Lewis explains:

> Not only did Mickey raise considerable sums of money for Nixon, he also 'leased' him his campaign headquarters in the downtown Pacific Finance Building on Eighth and Olive streets, prime business real estate. Attorney Sam Rummel handled the arrangements, and Mickey bankrolled the operation. Nixon's people didn't have to pay a nickel for any printed materials. Aside from the large fundraisers, Mickey arranged to funnel money to Nixon on a consistent basis. To avoid scrutiny, the money came through a variety of sources including Artie Samish, who was still one of the most powerful lobbyists in California.[24]

The following text offers an example of the overlapping relationships that typify how syndicate operations are diffused and sustained in "fields within fields...within fields" of relationships that stretch across time, distance and both major political parties. This field-based structure enables *systemic criminality* to proceed in plain view and oftentimes with only modest coordination around shared goals.[25] This brief yet wide-ranging account is included at this point to illustrate *how* this transnational phenomenon has long been deeply imbedded in American politics and how it operates without regard to political affiliation.

Fields within Fields. . .within Fields

In the mid-1950s, Gus Greenbaum managed and then sold the Riviera Hotel and Casino in Las Vegas, one of the premier properties controlled by the Chicago Outfit. The buyer was Meshulam Riklis, a resident of Cincinnati and a former member of the Haganah, a Jewish paramilitary organization active in Palestine from 1920 to 1948 when it evolved into the Israel Defense Forces. Riklis tutored "junk bond king" Michael Milken, then a young bond broker, and reportedly was Milken's first customer.

Fellow Cincinnati resident Carl Lindner emerged as a father figure to Milken, who operated out of the Beverly Hills office of Manhattan-based Drexel Burnham Lambert. Milken oversaw a control fraud at Phoenix-based Lincoln Savings and Loan led by Charles Keating[26] who previously was general counsel to Cincinnati-based American Financial Group, controlled by Lindner.

As mentioned above, Lindner boasts on the firm's website that he is the "largest non-Jewish contributor to Jewish causes in the U.S."[27] Keating was a major contributor to McCain's early Congressional career. As McCain wrote to Keating in 1983 after his first Congressional victory: "Of the many things to be grateful for in this world, the friendship of the Keating family is certainly among the most meaningful."[28] McCain's top-tier contributors included Keating, father-in-law James Hensley and Don Diamond, a real estate developer, to whom we will return.

In the 1970s, Lindner and his American Financial Group began investing in United Fruit whose name was changed to United Brands and then Chiquita Brands International to escape its notorious past. After CEO Eli Black fell to his death from his 44th floor office in New York's Pan Am Building in 1975, Lindner assumed control. In 1977, Black's son Leon emerged as head of mergers and acquisitions and co-head of corporate finance at Drexel Burnham Lambert where he collaborated with Milken.[29]

United Fruit became a key conduit for moving Israeli arms into covert wars throughout Latin America, culminating in the Iran-Contra scandal of 1987. That scandal discredited the presidency of Ronald Reagan when he was forced to concede that his administration sold arms to Iran, an avowed enemy, and used the funds to arm Nicaraguan rebels despite a Congressional ban. The term "Banana Republic" stems from the corrupting influence of United Fruit over multiple decades as the U.S. was discredited throughout Latin America by the firm's bribery of foreign officials and its use of armed force to discipline workers.

Along with insurance firms owned by Riklis and Saul Steinberg,[30] Lindner's American Financial Group was an early investor in Drexel's high-yield ("junk") securities packaged by Milken in deals coordinated with Leon Black.[31] Riklis' Rapid-American Corp. became an acquisition vehicle for Lerner Shops, Playtex and other companies such as RKO film studios, previously owned in part by Joseph Kennedy, father of John F. Kennedy. In 1967, in one of the first junk bond-financed leveraged buyouts (LBOs)—when Michael Milken was still an undergraduate at Berkeley—Riklis acquired Lewis Rosenstiel's shares in Cincinnati-based Schenley Industries.

The Istanbul-born Riklis paid for Schenley with high-interest junk bonds issued by Rapid-American Corp., a firm that Riklis owned with Lindner. Under Lindner's leadership, United Fruit's purchase of 40% of Rapid-American reportedly provided majority owner Riklis and his pro-Zionist colleagues with sufficient resources to purchase for General Ariel Sharon his ranch in the Negev Desert.[32]

Rosenstiel's wife, Leonore, left him to marry Walter Annenberg, Ronald Reagan's "best friend for 50 years" (according to Nancy Reagan) and Nixon's ambassador to Great Britain. Son of Chicago mobster Moses "Moe" Annenberg, Walter laundered profits from the family's racing-wire service through Triangle Publications, publisher of *T.V. Guide* and *Seventeen*. As he distanced himself from organized crime, he steadily gained legitimacy and influence in Republican politics through his ownership of *The Philadelphia Inquirer*.

In 1989, Annenberg liquidated $3 billion of his wealth, including

The Racing Form, in a sale to Rupert Murdoch, donating $150 million each to Annenberg communication schools at the University of Pennsylvania and the University of Southern California. While president, Ronald and Nancy Reagan routinely spent their New Year's vacation at Sunnylands, Annenberg's estate in Rancho Mirage, California near Palm Springs.

When Queen Elizabeth visited Palm Springs in February 1983 her co-hosts for dinner were Leonore Annenberg and Jean Lehman Stralem, wife of Donald Stralem and niece of New York Senator Herbert Lehman. Lehman first emerged on the national political scene in 1928 as lieutenant governor to New York Governor Franklin Delano Roosevelt. As noted earlier, Stralem, manager of Rothschild funds in the U.S., invested $350,000 to produce the 1951 film, *Duck and Cover*, the atomic bomb defense film shown in schools nationwide as an emotion-management component of that era's present danger.[33]

Leonore Annenberg was raised by her uncle, Harry Cohn, head of Columbia Pictures. First married to Belden Kattleman, a Las Vegas businessman, she then married Rosenstiel. During Prohibition, Rosenstiel bootlegged liquor from England, Europe, and Canada via Saint Pierre and then by truck into Cincinnati (Lindner's hometown), building what became Schenley Distillers. Bronfman and Rosenstiel reportedly met often during Rosenstiel's frequent trips to Canada, where they became card-playing friends.

America's Mobsters Go Legit

At former bootlegger Joseph Kennedy's request, the Chicago Outfit's Sam Giancana, with help from the United Mine Workers, arranged for Kennedy's son John to win the 1960 presidential primary in West Virginia. West Virginia was a crucial venue for demonstrating that a Catholic could be a viable American presidential candidate. The Outfit then helped fix the general election results in Chicago, ensuring that JFK was elected president over Richard Nixon with the slimmest-ever popular vote margin in presidential politics (118,550 out of 69 million votes cast).[34]

That brings us back to Buffalo, New York's Jacobs family members ("the Godfather of Sports"). Members of the Jacobs clan were associates of Michael Weinberg, an upstate New York bingo parlor operator whose son, Steve Wynn, has since become synonymous with Las Vegas. Michael Milken provided $160 million in junk bond financing to build Wynn's Golden Nugget casino in Atlantic City, New Jersey.

Before that, however, Wynn became known in Las Vegas as the "adopted son" of Mormon banker Parry Thomas who served as a key conduit for labor union pension fund monies pumped into Vegas during the era of Teamster president Jimmy Hoffa. Thomas backed Wynn in several land deals and set him up in a liquor distributorship.[35] Milken also helped with junk bonds to finance the $630 million required to build The Mirage, one of the first luxury hotel/casinos. In 2008, *Forbes* ranked Wynn the world's 277th richest with $3.9 billion.

The first investment in Las Vegas by Thomas ("the Mormon banker to Vegas") assumed a $475,000 loan ($2.9 million in 2007 dollars) to acquire Paradise Valley, a golf course admired by Hank Greenspun. A casino investor, developer, publisher and ardent Zionist, Greenspun introduced the Israelis to Saudi Adnan Khashoggi ("the biggest high roller to ever hit Las Vegas"), who then was the world's best-known arms dealer.

With support from Meyer Lansky, Greenspun had become a gunrunner for Israel in 1948 and thereafter performed as an Israeli operative. Bugsy Siegel reportedly gave $50,000 to support Irgun while "celebrity gangster" Mickey Cohen sponsored an Irgun fundraiser in 1947. *The Jerusalem Post* insisted of Greenspun, "He's like God in Israel...his contribution to the establishment of the Jewish state is widely considered to be greater than any other American." Compared to what Greenspun did for Israel, "Jonathan Pollard's act was pure innocence." In October 1961 Kennedy pardoned Greenspun who was caught smuggling U.S. military hardware to Israel and convicted of violating the Neutrality Act of 1950.[36]

Nevada's Riviera Hotel and Casino should not be confused with its counterpart, the Riviera Havana, owned by Meyer Lansky until its expropriation by the Fidel Castro government. Largely due to the influence of Moe Dalitz, the man who truly built Vegas (vs. Bugsy Siegel), the Teamsters lent vast sums to Nevada casinos. Dalitz later emerged as a key fundraiser for Nevada Governor and Senator Paul Laxalt who chaired Reagan's presidential campaigns.[37]

Gus Greenbaum and Moe Dalitz remained an influential force in Arizona where they were close to Bob Goldwater, the late Senator's brother who, as a director of the Valley National Bank, helped finance the Flamingo.[38] After the 1981 opening of a branch of Goldwater's department store in The Fashion Show, a $74 million shopping mall opposite the Desert Inn Casino, the Goldwater family traveled even more frequently to Vegas where Senator Barry Goldwater was known as a swinger. In 1958, Greenbaum and his wife were found in their Phoenix home with their throats cut. Barry Goldwater attended the funeral.

The Arizona State Republican Party presents the Harry Rosenzweig Award to the state's top Republican fundraiser. As a child, Harry Rosenzweig's family lived on the same street as the Goldwater family and Harry and Barry remained close throughout their lives.[39] Harry persuaded his best friend to make his first bid for public office in 1949[40] on the Charter Government Party to which "Greenbaum donated lots of money."[41] Rosenzweig served for 10 years as Arizona's Republican state chairman.[42] Uncle Morris Goldwater was one of the founding fathers of the Arizona Democratic Party.[43] With the help of Eisenhower's popularity in the 1952 presidential election year, Goldwater won a Senate seat as a Republican by 7,000 votes in what was then a Democratic state.[44]

To solve this systemic criminality requires that a broad base of Americans understand *how* this "fields-within-fields" *modus operandi* operates unseen yet in plain sight, and how its operations progress by working through people whose profiled needs become the means for influencing their behavior. With that goal in mind, the next chapter turns to the role played in the Keating Five by Senator John McCain who succeeded to Barry Goldwater's Senate seat in 1986 upon the retirement of "the conscience of the Republican Party."

Chapter 3

John McCain and Financial Frauds

People matter in part because they vary in their concepts of duty, integrity and courage. Morals matter, but people are capable of doing immoral acts while believing they are morally superior.

—William K. Black,

The Best Way to Rob a Bank is to Own One (2005)

John McCain was one of the "Keating Five" Senators who stalled the reform of laws governing the U.S. thrift industry on behalf of Phoenix resident Charles H. Keating, Jr. Keating, the chairman of Lincoln Savings and Loan of Irvine, California, relocated to Arizona from Cincinnati in 1976 and, along with McCain's father-in-law, sponsored McCain's first campaign for Congress in 1982 after the high profile former prisoner of war moved to the state in search of a political career.

The first memo that John McCain received from his campaign consultants was filled with instructions that did not quite rise to the level of strategy: Make sure to register to vote, obtain an Arizona driver's license, and open a bank account in the state. "To achieve your immediate goal of establishing yourself in the community, you should join at least one veterans' organization and one service organization such as Kiwanis or Jaycees," Jay Smith and Mark Harroff advised their client on April 13, 1981. "The last step in this initial phase is to join a church, as well as its men's auxiliary."[1]

Arizona was at the core of the nationwide savings and loan (S&L) fraud and no one among the Keating Five was closer to Keating than McCain. Arizona Senator Dennis DeConcini was another member of the Keating Five, along with John Glenn of Ohio, a former astronaut, and Senators Don Riegle from Michigan and Alan Cranston of California. The Senate Ethics Committee censured Cranston in 1991, citing the others for questionable conduct and McCain for poor judgment though some of the political support McCain provided to Keating came while he was in the House and escaped scrutiny by the Senate.

The five senators' campaigns and causes received a combined $1.3 million from Keating,[2] including $112,000 in McCain campaign contributions. That figure understates Keating's role in McCain's political success and ignores the fact that there were two infamous meetings with S&L regulators and McCain attended both.[3] Keating family members and employees made 40 donations to his first Congressional campaign, at least 32 to his second (in 1984) and at no less than 45 contributions when he ran for the Senate in 1986. Within five months of his election to Barry Goldwater's seat in the Senate, McCain attended two meetings with S&L regulators to plead Keating's case. The result became the nation's largest bank fraud with the failure of over 1,000 federally insured institutions.

Accompanied by their daughter and a baby sitter, the McCains made nine vacation trips aboard a jet owned by Keating's company, including numerous trips to Keating's posh retreat in the Bahamas. Only after the S&L scandal surfaced years later did McCain reimburse Keating for the flights. McCain's wife and father-in-law also invested $359,100 in a Keating shopping mall deal. Their profit remains unknown.

In the lead up to Lincoln's collapse, Keating hired a law firm that retained Alan Greenspan, then a consultant, to certify the financial soundness and prudence with which Keating was managing the S&L. Though Greenspan has since conceded he is embarrassed by his failure to foresee what transpired, he also claims that his conclusions today would be the same as then if confronted with the same evidence.[4]

The lessons to be drawn from this scandal extend well beyond the questionable conduct of a few senators and consultants. Understanding the role of these five high profile "assets" in a 20-years ago fraud is less important than grasping the relationships at work in the shadows and seeing *how* criminality can proceed in plain view obscured by a combination of lengthy pre-staging and trans-generational relationships known only to the participants.

The S&L fraud illustrates how this syndicate operates in a nonlinear fashion. The paucity of straight-line evidentiary trails makes it difficult to detect, much less indict and prosecute. Thus the need to describe, if only in summary, the overlapping relationships shared by this massive fraud's most visible members: the Keating Five.

Pillaging a Financial Sector

From their origins in the 1800s, savings and loans could make only home mortgage loans. In federally chartered thrifts, depositors' accounts were insured at a low threshold. During the Carter presidency, stagflation caught S&Ls borrowing at high interest rates (to attract depositors) and lending at low rates—due to mandatory ceilings on interest rates. When oil prices doubled in response to the Iran hostage crisis of 1979, inflation drifted into double digits.

In response, Carter repealed the interest rate ceiling, expanded the types of loans S&Ls could make and raised the limits on federal deposit insurance to $100,000 from $40,000 per account. Regulators then reduced the net worth requirements for S&Ls and removed limits on brokered deposits—the "hot" money S&Ls attracted by offering high interest rates to depositors.

Reagan's subsequent enactment in 1981 of tax incentives for real estate investment catalyzed a lending boom that led to overbuilding. The resulting bubble led to more S&L loans secured by inflated values. Not only did regulatory changes mask the insolvency of troubled S&Ls but relaxed ownership rules disconnected S&Ls from the communities and the local owners they were originally meant to serve.

By December 1982, a bill sponsored by Utah Senator Jake Garn gave S&Ls even greater latitude, allowing them to lend for commercial mortgages and make business loans. In response, key states such as California, Texas and Florida allowed state-chartered S&Ls to invest in *any* venture. As this "race to the bottom" gained momentum, bad loans surged along with taxpayer liabilities on federally insured deposits.

By April 1987, when the Keating Five met with bank examiners who sought to shut down Keating's operation, taxpayer liabilities were soaring as insolvent S&Ls continued to accept taxpayer-insured deposits while making bad loans. During the two years that Lincoln stayed open after that McCain-arranged meeting, the cost of paying off its federally insured depositors grew to more than $2 billion.

Did this Fraud "Just Happen"?

Just as Congress sought to contain the spiraling losses of S&Ls, Keating's law firm retained Alan Greenspan in late 1984 to appraise Lincoln. A former chairman of President Gerald Ford's Council of Economic Advisers, Greenspan portrayed Lincoln as "a financially strong institution that presents no foreseeable risk to depositors or the government." At that point, he was probably correct, assuming he had no knowledge of the control fraud then being pre-staged by Milken, Keating and their co-conspirators.

More than 21,000 U.S. investors lost $285 million when the parent corporation of Lincoln S&L went bankrupt. Most of those defrauded were elderly pensioners who found they held worthless junk bonds that they *believed* were deposits in a federally insured thrift. Some who lost their life savings committed suicide while Keating, a staunch Catholic, donated $1,250,000 to Mother Teresa in India. She later provided a character reference to the presiding judge in Keating's trial. Congressman Jim Leach of Iowa, a member of the House Banking Committee, had a different opinion, calling Keating a "financiopath."[5]

Taxpayers were stuck with nearly $3 billion in Lincoln's losses on the Greenspan-obscured, McCain-enabled, Keating-led, Milken-controlled fraud.[6] Those losses were recognized only after the future Federal Reserve chief wrote an opinion lauding Lincoln's managers for bringing the S&L "to a vibrant and healthy state, with a strong net worth position." The Keating Five, in turn, cited Greenspan's assessment when arguing Keating's case.[7] As the senators' success deepened the S&L crisis, bailout costs grew, worsening the nation's fiscal condition.

Prior to his retention in late 1984, Greenspan had amassed a reservoir of political goodwill that he drew on for his Keating assignment. In 1983, the Greenspan Commission took the political heat off Congress by recommending changes to Social Security, the "third rail" of American politics that few elected officials dared touch. Greenspan's formula for reform, since enacted: Work longer and pay higher payroll taxes.[8]

At the urging of Michael Milken, Keating also retained Dan Fischel who rated Lincoln's risk of bankruptcy at less than one in a million. In retrospect, Lincoln's insolvency was assured because it was designed from the outset as a control fraud by Milken.[9] Fischel praised Greenspan's help in recruiting the Keating Five as "a model of how democracy is supposed to work." Mirroring Greenspan's belief in the flawlessness of financial markets, Fischel assured legislators, regulators, depositors and the public that fraud in the S&L industry was not just improbable but impossible.[10]

Viewing the world through a Greenspan-Fischel mindset, it becomes easy to see *how*, once again, criminality becomes systemic by displacing facts with what people can be induced to *believe*. The combination of deception and self-deceit makes for a particularly potent form of fraud when imbedded in academia, endorsed by think tanks, promoted in the media and written into law. When Fischel gave a clean bill of health to Keating's operations, he screened his analysis through his belief in the innate perfection of financial markets.

From Fischel's perspective, firms auditing S&Ls would never risk their reputations by issuing fraudulent reports. That belief, of course, has often been proven false by massive frauds at Enron and elsewhere.[11] In Fischel's perfect-market world, stockholding by executives like Keating perfectly aligned the motives of managers with shareholders, excluding any possibility of executive fraud, a belief disproven by executives at Worldcom, Tyco, Adelphia and elsewhere. Lastly, any losses found by regulators were irrelevant in appraising a firm's value because that information was already taken into account in financial markets' assessment of risk and perfectly reflected in the share price.[12]

That textbook "consensus" analysis would be comical were its results not so tragic—and were that market fundamentalist mindset not shared by a well-placed cadre of True Believers (such as Greenspan) who deploy that worldview when wielding influence over the lives of others. The gap between facts and beliefs could not be more transparent as beguiling theory trumped real-world results. That gap—that *domain between facts and beliefs*—is where *the people in between* wage unconventional warfare.

With the 1988 election of George H.W. Bush as president, new S&L oversight agencies were created along with the Resolution Trust Corporation (RTC) to handle insolvent S&Ls. As this real estate investment "pump" turned into a financial liquidation "dump," the RTC readied for sale more than $400 billion in distressed properties. Of the $153 billion in S&L losses, taxpayers covered $124 billion with funds that Washington borrowed—backed by taxpayers' full faith and credit.[13]

As typified by the S&L fraud, this gap—between facts and theory— is the realm where *the people in between* inflict serial financial frauds on a trusting public led to *believe* in a consensus worldview hyped by academia, think tanks, media and policy makers. Those frauds have now been internalized (through education) and institutionalized (by law) as this perfect-market mindset expanded to scale under the guise of globalization overseen by the World Trade Organization (WTO). As consensus beliefs became systemic, so did the criminality they enable.

Fischel went on to publish *Payback* in 1995. His premise was simple: the federal prosecution of swindler Michael Milken was "anti-Semitic." A discreet few years later, Fischel was appointed Dean of the University of Chicago School of Law. It was there that the dominant "Chicago model" emerged before morphing into a "law and economics" policy environment known worldwide as the fast-globalizing "Washington" consensus. As this belief-enabled financial fraud grew to global scale, the U.S. was portrayed as guilty by association. [See Chapter 6.][14]

The Ohio Connection

Keating and Greenspan also recruited Ohio Senator John Glenn to help obscure this fraud behind a veneer of self-serving economic theory. Comparable to McCain's status as a war hero, Glenn's political capital became apparent after he was given a Manhattan ticker-tape parade in February 1962 as the first American to circle the Earth aboard the Friendship 7 spacecraft. Six weeks after the Kennedy assassination in November 1963, Glenn retired from the National Aeronautics and Space Administration (NASA) to enter politics. First elected to the Senate in 1974, he served four terms before retiring in 1998, including an election victory after the Keating Five scandal.

In keeping with the *modus operandi* by which this systemic corruption is sustained (through fields-within-fields of relationships), we find here a relationship between Glenn and Cincinnati's Carl Lindner. for whose financial services firm Keating served as general counsel before moving to Arizona. In addition to aiding the Lindner-associated fraud at Lincoln, Glenn joined Kansas Senator Bob Dole in demanding that Mickey Kantor, President Bill Clinton's trade representative, initiate a trade investigation on behalf of Lindner-controlled Chiquita Brands International. Kantor authorized the investigation in October 1994. By year's end, Lindner and his executives had contributed $250,000 to the Democratic Party.

On the surface, the trade dispute involved Chiquita's desire to halt a European program favoring the import of bananas from former colonies in Central/South America and the Caribbean. That trade preference not only assisted the poor in underdeveloped countries such as Jamaica, Belize and Surinam, but also helped dissuade their residents from turning to drugs as a more profitable cash crop.

The Lindner initiative was notable as the first U.S. trade dispute filed with the World Trade Organization (WTO). Known worldwide as "the banana war," the dispute involved a product exported not from the U.S. but from third world countries where Chiquita's predecessor, United Fruit, had a notorious reputation for political bribery and human rights abuses. That record remains well known in Europe and was widely cited in news reports to associate U.S. trade policy (and the Washington consensus) with the company's notoriety.

The fact that Lindner was a member of the *Forbes 400* richest Americans—*Forbes* put Lindner's 2008 wealth at $2.3 billion—only made the dispute all the more damaging to America's stature. Washington's insistence on protecting Lindner's financial interest offered a high-profile example of successful influence-peddling. The Lindner-championed dispute showed that the U.S. had no regard for the impact on the poor that accompanies the perfect markets theory underlying the WTO and its enforcement of trade policies based on the market fundamentalism known as the Washington consensus.

In November 1998, U.S. Trade Representative Charlene Barshefsky proposed 100% tariffs on various European imports to the U.S. unless restrictions were eased on the import of Lindner's bananas. During that period, Lindner emerged as a business partner at American Heritage Homes, a Florida builder, with Terry McAuliffe, co-chairman of the 1996 Clinton-Gore re-election committee and the Democratic Party's "greatest fundraiser in the history of the universe" according to then Vice President Al Gore.[15]

Despite Lindner's Democratic connections he, along with Richard and Robert Lindner, in 1995 and 1996, gave $332,000 to Republicans in "soft" money not subject to limits on amounts given directly to candidates. The Lindners also made more than 450 additional contributions.[16] Such "double giving" to candidates of both parties is a sign not of political activism but of outright influence peddling.

Lindner-related political contributions illustrate how, by doubling the dollar limit on individual campaign contributions, McCain-Feingold "reform" enhanced the influence of the most influential such as John Glenn constituent Carl Lindner. According to Federal Election Commission reports on the 1996 election cycle, Lindner, his extended family and his executive corps gave to House and Senate campaigns in no less than 35 states.[17]

The list of people with the surname Lindner who made political contributions during this trade dispute include, in alphabetical order: Alan, Alan B., Betty, Betty J., Betty Johnston, Betty R., Carl, Carl H., Carl H III, Charlene, Charlene W., Courtney, Courtney O'Neal, Courtney O'Neil, Craig, David, Edith, Edith B., Edyth B., Frances, Frances R., Keith, Keith E., Martha, Martha S., Paul, Paula, Richard, Richard F., Robert D., Robert D. Jr., Robert J., and S. Craig Lindner.[18]

Though John Glenn assisted a constituent with what was ostensibly a trade dispute, the facts suggest that the long-term strategic impact was even more successful. Lindner's high-profile "banana war" portrayed America abroad as a bully willing to deploy its superpower status to benefit a politically well-connected few (with operations outside the U.S.) to the detriment of the poor in the world's poorest countries. The Lindner dispute also showed that U.S. insistence on WTO rulemaking could be deployed for a price that only the most well-to-do could afford.

The Michigan Connection

Elected to the House in 1966 and to the Senate 10 years later, Don Riegle chaired the Senate Banking Committee during the Keating Five fraud. After the scandal became public, he declined to stand for reelection. The nonlinear trail involving Riegle's role requires that one begin at the end of the fraud and examine who benefitted from repossessed S&L properties sold at distressed prices.

A primary purchaser was Sam "The Grave Dancer" Zell of Chicago. The Blackstone Group, a private equity firm led by Stephen Schwarzman, acquired Equity Office Properties, Zell's Real Estate Investment Trust (REIT),[19] in November 2006 for $36 billion. At the time, it was the largest-ever leveraged buyout (leverage means that the buyer used borrowed money). By then, Zell's REIT owned 590 buildings and 105 million square feet of office space in major metropolitan markets. Many of those properties were either built or bought with tax subsidies provided by the deficit-financed policies of the Reagan era. [See Chapter 6.]

Zell used part of his proceeds to buy control of the Tribune Company, owner of the *Chicago Tribune*, the *Los Angeles Times* and 30 other newspapers and television stations.[20] The company was "put in play" following a joint bid by Los Angeles billionaires Eli Broad, a Michigan native, and supermarket investor Ron Burkle. Broad was the co-founder of Michigan's Kauffman & Broad (now KB Home), a publicly traded homebuilder that annually constructs 40,000 modestly priced homes. None of the three bidders (Broad, Burkle or Zell) had previously shown any interest in media properties.

Broad diversified his home construction portfolio in the 1960s when he took KB Home public and moved to Arizona where he sold retirement plans through SunAmerica Insurance. He then relocated to California where he became chairman of Alan Cranston's first campaign for the Senate in 1968. Since 1995, Don Riegle has been an adjunct professor at the Eli Broad School of Business at Michigan State University.

Zell pioneered "securitization" of the REIT industry by bundling mortgages into mortgage-backed securities and selling them like bonds. That financial innovation catalyzed a trend that took REITs from $6 billion to $150 billion during the 1990s.[21] In the real estate downturn, developers fared best "who went public and paid down their debt with investor capital."[22] Frequently those investors were retirement plans.

Zell emerged in the early 1990s as a primary purchaser of Resolution Trust Corporation (RTC) properties. As the RTC unwound the S&L crisis, the Grave Dancer earned his nickname by acquiring distressed properties at fire-sale prices while using his REIT to raise acquisition capital. In January 2000, he conceded "You've seen the beginnings of oligopolization in our industry."[23] As chairman of the Senate Banking Committee, Don Riegle enabled that oligopolization.

> *Oligopoly*—an economic condition in which there are so few suppliers of a particular product that one supplier's actions can have a significant impact on prices and on its competitors.

Fields of Overlapping Relationships

In October 1973, Vice President Spiro T. Agnew resigned. His replacement, Michigan Congressman Gerald Ford, became president in August 1974 when Richard Nixon resigned as part of the Watergate scandal that ended his presidency. The back-to-back Agnew-Nixon resignations made Ford the second unelected president in 11 years, following Lyndon Johnson in November 1963.

Ford's domestic policy adviser was William Seidman, former finance director for Michigan's Mormon Governor George Romney. A decade later, in 1985, President Reagan appointed Seidman chair of the Federal Deposit Insurance Corporation (FDIC), the oversight agency for S&Ls.[24] President George H.W. Bush then appointed him chair of the Resolution Trust Corporation where Seidman oversaw the sale at knockdown prices of more than $400 billion in S&L assets—a key source of the real estate fortune amassed by Sam Zell.

When Ford became president, Mormon Warren Rustand became his appointments secretary and cabinet secretary.[25] Ford and his wife, Betty, routinely vacationed at Rustand's home in Tucson, Arizona.[26] Rustand's home adjoined the residence of Jim Click, son-in-law of Holmes Tuttle who, as head of Ronald Reagan's Kitchen Cabinet, supported the actor's 1966 campaign for governor of California.

Other key beneficiaries of the nationwide S&L fraud included bankruptcy lawyer David Bonderman who had recently succeeded Richard Rainwater as chief adviser to Texas S&L investor Robert Bass. In 1986, when George W. Bush's bid for the Texas Rangers baseball team was in trouble, baseball commissioner Peter Ueberroth stepped in to broker a deal with Rainwater who was asked to assist the deal "out of respect" for former President Bush. In return for 1.8% of the funds invested, the future President Bush received 10% of the team's equity, eventually converting a $606,000 investment into a $15 million gain when the team was acquired for $86 million in 1989.

Of the amount invested, Bush borrowed $500,000 from a Midland, Texas bank where he served as a cameo director. That loan was repaid after Harken Energy Corporation, with no experience either overseas or in offshore drilling, signed an offshore oil exploration contract with the government of Bahrain. That deal raised eyebrows in the industry because Harken had neither the skills nor the equipment for the job. Bush sold his stock at the pumped-up value, leaving other investors to suffer the downside when the deal fell through and the value of the stock plummeted.

In 1988, Bonderman brokered an S&L deal for Robert Bass. By investing $150 million in American Savings Bank, Bass made billions when they sold it. As Bonderman conceded, "The government absorbed all the losses."[27] Bonderman has since emerged as a founder of Texas Pacific Group, a private equity firm. In 2006, "TPG" topped the nation's leveraged buy-out firms with 17 deals worth $101 billion.[28] The Chinese State Administration of Foreign Exchange entrusted TPG with $3 billion to manage, giving TPG $25 billion to invest in leveraged deals.[29]

Forbes estimated Bonderman's 2008 wealth at $3.3 billion. Prior to having joined the Robert M. Bass Group in 1983, he was a bankruptcy specialist in the Washington, D.C. law firm of Arnold & Porter (previously Arnold, Fortas and Porter). Don Riegle serves as a senior strategist for APCO Worldwide, a public relations firm founded by Arnold & Porter with 23 offices worldwide.

The California Connection

Senator Alan Cranston was the only member of the Keating Five censured by the Senate Ethics Committee for "improper conduct." Initially elected to statewide office as California controller in 1958, he was elected in 1968 to the first of four six-year terms in the U.S. Senate. Popular among his fellow senators, Cranston served as Senate Whip (assistant leader) from 1977 until 1991, when he was censured.

When California experienced a surge of S&Ls after the Reagan-era reforms sponsored by Jake Garn, Cranston pressured federal regulators on behalf of Irvine-headquartered Lincoln S&L. In searching for the connective threads in this nonlinear phenomenon, the most obvious candidate was Californian Eli Broad. A home-builder in his native Michigan, Broad amassed a second fortune selling pension plans in Arizona in the mid-1960s.[30] He then relocated to California where he befriended Alan Cranston and chaired his first Senate race.[31]

In 1998, Broad sold SunAmerica Insurance to American International Group, then led by Maurice ("Hank") Greenberg, for $18 billion, netting $3.4 billion for his 19% stake. With Henry Kissinger chair of its international advisory board, A.I.G. saw a $40 billion surge in its market capitalization in the wake of 9/11. As capital markets recalibrated for risk following that event, investors dumped stocks and sought bonds. A.I.G. had apparently been sufficiently prescient to invest 93% of its $700 billion-plus portfolio in bonds, compared with the portfolios of its three primary competitors which were invested 55-60% in bonds.[32]

In 2008, the *Forbes 400* ranked Broad 42nd on its list of richest Americans and 145th among the world's billionaires with $6.5 billion.[33] The bid by Broad and supermarket magnate Ron Burkle for the Tribune Company enabled its purchase by Sam Zell who reinvested a portion of the proceeds from his sale (to the Schwarzman-led Blackstone Group) of properties acquired years earlier from the Seidman-led Resolution Trust Corporation.

Two decades after the Keating Five became only a footnote in financial history, *the people in between* again emerged unscathed operating, as Zell aptly put it, as a national real estate oligopoly. Multiple decades of steady financial concentration have been parlayed into what is fast becoming a national media oligopoly dominated by *the people in between* that may succeed in placing in the White House another pro-Israeli asset.

In the intervening years between the S&L fraud and the Zell sale to Schwarzman, in 1987 Ronald Reagan appointed Keating consultant Alan Greenspan chairman of the Federal Reserve. Known for oracle-like utterances that roiled financial markets, Greenspan will be remembered not for the $8.5 million he received for his memoirs but for his insistence on maintaining the low interest rates that triggered a global credit crisis. That crisis is expected to generate $1 trillion-plus in financial losses worldwide, ensuring a lucrative investment opportunity for the next generation of Grave Dancers.

As *Guilt by Association* went to publication, more than 15 million American homeowners faced mortgage debt greater than the equity in their homes. As this latest pump-and-dump unwinds, the same network of syndicate operatives is emerging again to profit from both the upside and the downside. Keating remains unrepentant, claiming it was not he but government regulators who were responsible. A 2004 compilation of essays agrees: *The Savings and Loan Crisis: Lessons from a Regulatory Failure.*[34] The book is available on the Milken Institute website for $175.

William Black offers a different perspective. Former general counsel to the Federal Home Loan Bank Board during the S&L crisis, he documents Keating's conduct as a "control fraud" engineered by Milken. Now a professor at the University of Missouri, Black published a 2005 book featuring a title more consistent with the known facts: *The Best Way to Rob a Bank is to Own One*, available on Amazon.com for $15.[35] The Milken Institute does not offer Black's book.

Chapter 4

McCain Family Secret: The Cover-up

America is proud to be Israel's closest ally and best friend in the world.

—President G.W. Bush, May 15, 2008, Jerusalem

John McCain's father covered up the Israeli killing of 34 Americans aboard a U.S. Navy ship during the Six-Day War of 1967. As senior naval officer for Europe and the Mediterranean, Admiral John S. McCain, Jr. helped President Lyndon Johnson deceive Americans about that little known incident involving the *USS Liberty*. This chapter reveals that family secret.

On June 8, 1967, Israeli jets attacked the *USS Liberty*, a 455-foot vessel, firing 30 mm aircraft cannons and rockets and dropping napalm. Three Israeli torpedo boats then attacked the ship with 20 mm cannons, 50-caliber machine guns and torpedoes. One torpedo blew a 39-foot hole in a former cargo hold of this refurbished WWII Liberty ship that had its cargo space converted to research facilities for an intelligence team. The blast killed 25 and left the ship listing nine degrees to starboard.[1]

Liberty crewmembers testified that Israeli torpedo boats fired on firefighters and stretcher-bearers. Israeli machine gunners also strafed the ship's fire hoses and destroyed its life rafts at close range as survivors sought to douse fires and evacuate those most grievously wounded. The attackers killed 34 and wounded 174 of a crew of 294 for a 70% casualty rate.[2]

Insight into the motivation for this presidential cover-up began with identifying how Lyndon Johnson allowed himself to be manipulated. The first clue emerged after a discussion with former Congressman Paul Findley, an 11-term Republican from Illinois (1961-1983). During his 11th term, Findley suggested that, if there was to be peace between Israelis and Palestinians, Tel Aviv should talk to the Palestine Liberation Organization.

Upset by that proposal, the American Israel Public Affairs Committee (AIPAC) targeted Findley for defeat in 1982. Richard Durbin, Findley's AIPAC-recruited successor, has since been elected to the Senate where he is second ranking in the leadership. AIPAC has since evolved into a 100,000-member, $60 million per year political powerhouse now embroiled in a spy scandal involving Pentagon analyst Lawrence Franklin who provided two senior (and now former) AIPAC officials with classified U.S. military intelligence on Iran.[3]

> AIPAC evolved from the American Zionist Council when, in 1959, Isaiah "Si" Kenen adopted that nondescript name for an international network of political operations organized to shape U.S. policies critical to Israel, including influencing key U.S. elections. Kenen served as executive director from 1951 to 1954, guided and funded by the Israeli government.[4] From 1947 to 1948, Kenen had served as the Jewish Agency's information director at the U.N.
>
> The Council was restructured as the American Zionist Committee for Public Affairs when Council leaders became uncomfortable using tax-exempt overseas funds to sway elections in the U.S. The Committee registered with the Justice Department as a foreign agent for Israel. To date, AIPAC has resisted registration as a foreign agent.[5]

In response to a question, Findley identified Arthur Krim as the Jewish adviser and fundraiser closest to Lyndon Johnson. Research quickly uncovered published materials on Krim written by the late Grace Halsell, a speechwriter for LBJ and later an author of books chronicling the political influence of Christian Zionists such as Jerry Falwell. Johnson personally hired Halsell, a native Texan, who, importantly for this analysis, was inside the White House Situation Room during the Six-Day War.

With that war, Israeli security became a priority of U.S. foreign policy and a focal point of Pentagon coordination as Tel Aviv became a favored recipient of U.S. military technology.[6] After that 1967 conflict, the U.S. also emerged as a major Israeli arms supplier.

Pro-Israeli advisers surrounded Johnson in the decision-making that led to the 1967 war. "Everyone around me, without exception was pro-Israel," Halsell recalled. She identified more than a dozen close advisers to Johnson, including Walt Rostow, his national security adviser,[7] and brother Eugene Rostow serving as under secretary of state for political affairs, and former Supreme Court Justice Arthur Goldberg, then serving as U.S. Ambassador to the United Nations.

White House counsels Leo White and Jake Jacobsen were likewise pro-Israel as were two key speechwriters: Richard Goodwin, husband of biographer Doris Kearns Goodwin, and Ben Wattenberg whose parents moved to the U.S. from Palestine. Likewise domestic affairs adviser Larry Levinson and John Roche, an avid Zionist and Johnson's intellectual-in-residence.

It was the role of Arthur Krim, however, that confirmed the lengthy pre-staging of the 1967 war and explained the orchestration that led to LBJ's cover-up of the Israeli attack on the *USS Liberty*. A New York attorney and president of United Artists,[8] Krim also served as finance committee chairman for the Democratic Party when Johnson was its leader and Jewish contributors accounted for more than half the funds raised.[9]

> A series of Jewish males chaired the finance committee for the Democratic Party at critical junctures. Those men include August Belmont, a Rothschild financial agent after whom the New York horseracing track is named. Belmont's

financial backing matured into his chairmanship of the National Democratic Committee, 1860-1872.[10]

Henry Morgenthau, a naturalized German Jew, chaired the finance committee of the Democratic National Committee during Woodrow Wilson's successful presidential campaigns of 1912 and 1916.[11] In 1913, the same year Wilson appointed him U.S. Ambassador to the Ottoman Empire, Henry Morgenthau, Jr. acquired a farm near Franklin D. Roosevelt's Hyde Park estate.

In 1914, Morgenthau Senior arranged for Jacob Schiff of Kuhn, Loeb & Company to raise $50,000 to rescue Jewish settlements in Palestine. Absent this Morgenthau/Schiff alliance: "Palestinian Jewry almost certainly would have perished."[12] Morgenthau Senior led one of several elite Jewish delegations to the 1919 Paris Peace Conference where Wilson's 14 Points were scuttled, including Arab self-determination. In its place, a "mandate" system forced long-warring tribes of Sunnis, Shias and Kurds into a single state (Iraq).

As part of the Treaty of Versailles ending World War I, an onerous reparations burden was imposed on Germany.[13] That debt-imposed humiliation provoked an extreme form of German nationalism and a recession-fueled fascism that led to World War II and Germany's embrace of the National Socialist Party. Under Adolph Hitler, the Nazi government portrayed *all* Jews as complicit in the un-payable debts imposed at Versailles. As President Roosevelt's Secretary of the Treasury during WWII, Henry Morgenthau, Jr. advised that FDR limit Jewish immigration to the U.S.[14]

Deep Insiders

Mathilde Krim, a striking blonde Italian 20 years younger than her husband, was previously married to Davin Danon. Raised in Palestine, her handsome Jewish-Bulgarian husband was exiled by the British for his activities with Irgun Zvai Leumi, the Zionist-terrorist network led by Menachem Begin who emerged as Likud Party Prime Minister in 1977. Mathilde also worked as an Irgun operative, largely in Europe.

The Krims became regular guests at the LBJ Ranch. As Halsell explained: "There were also many instances in which Arthur and Mathilde were guests at the White House, and other times when, for many days running, Mathilde—without her husband—was a guest there. The Krims built a vacation home near the LBJ Ranch known as Mathilde's house, and Johnson often traveled there by helicopter."[15]

As with Morgenthau's proximity to Roosevelt, the Krims' proximity to Johnson ensured that their friendship flourished when the Senate majority leader became John F. Kennedy's surprise pick as Vice President and then succeeded him to the Presidency following Kennedy's assassination in November 1963.[16]

Over the 1967 Memorial Day weekend, the Krims were houseguests at the LBJ Ranch when the commander-in-chief learned of Soviet Premier Aleksei Kosygin's warning that "if Israel starts military action, the Soviet Union will extend help to the attacked party." While waiting for the State Department to draft a response to Israeli Prime Minister Levi Eshkol, Johnson and the Krims drove to a neighbor's home where an aide brought the message for the president's review.

Halsell described the changes that LBJ made to the message (in italics below)—while in the Krims' company—to explain America's perspective on the pending conflict:

> After reassuring Eshkol of America's interest in Israel's security, the draft message continued: "It is essential that Israel not take any preemptive military action and thereby make itself responsible for the initiation of hostilities." LBJ restated the warning by adding two key words so that the sentence conveyed a message far more amenable to Tel Aviv, "It is essential that Israel *JUST MUST* NOT take any preemptive military action..."[17]

According to Kennedy Under Secretary of State George Ball, Johnson made it clear both to the Israelis and his Jewish-American supporters that the U.S. would not object if the Israelis took matters into their own hands.[18] Defense Secretary Robert McNamara offers a different account, recalling that Johnson and he "put immense pressure on [Israeli foreign minister Abba Eban] to persuade his government not to pre-empt." Johnson's Kosygin-prompted note to Levi Eskhol, written in the presence of Arthur and Mathilde Krim, suggests that both men are correct: Tel Aviv could preempt provided the American public could be induced to *believe* that Israel was the victim and not the aggressor, a strategy fully consistent with game theory.

Johnson then traveled to New York for a $1,000-a-plate fundraiser on June 3 sponsored by Arthur Krim who chaired the President's Club of New York. Mathilde was seated next to Johnson when Abe Feinberg, the American Zionist community's legendary political fundraiser, leaned over Mathilde's shoulder and whispered: "Mr. President, it [Tel Aviv's attack] can't be held any longer. It's going within the next 24 hours."[19]

The next day, Johnson visited the home of political adviser Abe Fortas for a dinner with Defense Secretary Robert McNamara and New York investment banker John Loeb.[20] Fortas had cemented his confidante relationship with Johnson in 1948 when, in LBJ's first Senate race,[21] the Washington lawyer finessed the extensive vote fraud apparent in the Democratic primary, in which Johnson claimed an 87-vote victory, including 200 votes tallied in alphabetical order.[22] Fortas' legal strategy ensured that Johnson's name appeared on the November 1948 ballot as the Democratic Party candidate. In what was then a strongly Democratic state, that Fortas-enabled result assured the ambitious Texan a seat in the U.S. Senate.[23]

In October 1965, as president, "Landslide Lyndon" appointed Fortas to replace Arthur Goldberg on the Supreme Court after persuading Goldberg to serve as U.N. Ambassador. Fortas became embroiled in scandal when it was discovered that stock swindler Louis Wolfson offered to pay Fortas and his wife $20,000 per year to make up for his lost income as a lawyer.[24] Justice Fortas accepted the first installment in January 1966. The payment was revealed in 1968 as part of a successful Senate filibuster by Republicans and "Dixiecrats" (conservative southern Democrats) when Fortas was denied his Johnson appointment as Chief Justice to succeed Californian Earl Warren.[25]

Pre-staging the Six-Day War

In a scenario reminiscent of Eddie Jacobson tearfully lobbying his friend Harry Truman to recognize the Jewish state in 1948 (chronicled later in the *Criminal State* series), Lyndon Johnson was lobbied in 1967 by Arthur Goldberg to protect the Jewish state in the lead-up to the Six-Day War. When Goldberg deployed heart-rending rhetoric to portray Israeli vulnerability and the pending victimization of Jews at the hostile hands of an Arab "ring of steel," Johnson waved a Central Intelligence Agency report predicting Israel could win *any* war in the region in two weeks. When Goldberg persisted, Johnson ordered the CIA to revisit their analysis. The agency returned with a revised report concluding that Israel could win any war in the region in one week.[26]

On June 4, as the Fortas dinner party was winding down, Fortas cautioned Johnson that war might soon erupt in the Middle East. When LBJ turned to Defense Secretary McNamara for his opinion, the Pentagon chief said there would be no war. Johnson confirmed that U.S. intelligence agencies agreed with McNamara's assessment.[27] Johnson left for the White House at 10:58 p.m.

At 4:30 a.m. on June 5, Walt Rostow called LBJ to inform him that Israel had attacked Egypt. Mathilde Krim, the former Irgun operative, was Johnson's guest at the White House that night. Before informing anyone else, LBJ stopped by the blonde beauty's bedroom to tell her, "The war has started." Not until more than three hours later, at 7:45 a.m., did Johnson speak with Soviet Premier Kosygin who expressed his hope and expectation that the U.S., as Israel's closest ally, would restrain Tel Aviv.

In the war's first few hours, the "victimized" Israelis destroyed the Egyptian Air Force while its aircraft were still on the ground. By evening, the Jordanian Air Force was also largely destroyed. Walt Rostow sent Johnson a memo describing Tel Aviv's military success as "the first day's turkey shoot." LBJ also received a memo that day from Arthur Krim that read, "Many arms shipments are packed and ready to go to Israel, but are being held up. It would be helpful if these could be released." Johnson ordered the arms shipped. By the evening of the second day, two-thirds of Syria's air force had been destroyed.

According to Halsell, the glee in the State Department Operations Room was palpable, leading Eugene Rostow to caution, "Gentlemen, gentlemen, do not forget that we are neutral in word, thought and deed." At the State Department's mid-day press briefing, spokesman Robert McCloskey repeated Rostow's official "neutrality" lie.[28]

White House counsel Harry McPherson arrived in Tel Aviv enroute to the U.S. from Vietnam the night before the war broke out. In *A Political Education*, he describes arriving at the foreign ministry for a brief meeting with Abba Eban the first day of the war before conferring with Israel's chief of military intelligence. In response to the repeated question, "Did the Egyptians attack?" McPherson and U.S. Ambassador Walworth Barbour received only evasive answers.[29] As air raid sirens wailed, McPherson recalls:

> Barbour suggested that we might continue the discussion in the underground bunker. The general studied his watch. "No, that won't be necessary. We can stay here." Barbour and I looked at each other. If it wasn't necessary, the Egyptian air force had been destroyed. That could only have happened so quickly if it had been surprised on the ground. We did not need to ask for confirmation, but left at once to cable the news to Washington.[30]

Israel was neither under attack nor under threat of attack as Israeli commanders later conceded. The air raid sirens were props in the stagecraft of waging war by way of deception. The circumstances were stage-managed to make both Israelis and foreign observers *believe* the Jewish state was endangered while Tel Aviv annexed land belonging to its neighbors that it still occupies four decades later.

The Non-Separation of Powers

In the lead-up to the Six-Day War, Fortas emerged as a back channel between the Israeli embassy and the White House. He had known Israeli Ambassador Avraham Harman since the ambassador's arrival in Washington in 1959. During Prime Minister David Ben-Gurion's visit to the U.S. in March 1960, Fortas sponsored a breakfast at his home attended by Harman and Johnson who was then Senate Majority Leader.

Fortas' biographer conceded: "For several weeks before the crisis erupted into war, the Israeli ambassador was 'in very frequent contact' with Fortas and regularly visited the justice at his chambers or his house." Fortas also attended a critical White House strategy meeting on the Middle East on May 26, 10 days before the war began. When it came to Israel, Fortas was far from a neutral adviser. "When they get back from Egypt," a law clerk in his office overheard Justice Fortas say, "I'm going to decorate my office with Arab foreskins."[31]

Throughout the six days of war, Near East experts met daily with Johnson in the Cabinet Room. Justice Fortas attended each meeting.[32] Reflecting on comments by Fortas to Johnson at their June 4 dinner party, John Loeb wrote to Fortas on June 6: "You were prophetic about the Middle East. Thank the Lord the President has you as a friend and counselor." In the summer of 1970, *The New York Times* reported that Fortas had registered as a lobbyist for Kuhn, Loeb & Company.[33]

> Abraham Kuhn and his brother-in-law, Solomon Loeb, made their first fortune in Cincinnati during the Civil War selling trousers to Union troops. They opened their first New York store as an outlet for men's trousers. According to biographer Ron Chernow: "The color-blind Solomon seemed strangely placed in the textile trade. In 1867, flush with their wartime profits, Kuhn and Loeb inaugurated a New York banking house."[34]
>
> In 1873, Jacob Schiff joined Kuhn, Loeb & Company in Manhattan and, two years later, married Therese Loeb, Solomon Loeb's daughter.[35] According to Chernow, "Schiff came from a family that had befriended the Rothschilds and that counted six centuries of scholars, rabbis and businessmen." Paul Warburg married Nina Loeb, daughter of Solomon Loeb of Kuhn, Loeb & Co., then chief financial agent of the Rothschilds in the U.S. Felix Warburg, who moved to the U.S. in 1895, married Frieda Schiff, daughter of Jacob Schiff, then best known for managing bond issues to finance railroads, including a reorganization of the Union Pacific Railroad in 1897.[36]

Orchestrating Realities on the Ground

On June 6, the day after Israel launched its attack, Walt Rostow urged that the Israelis not be forced to withdraw from territories they were then seizing unless they first had peace treaties in place with the Arab states. In a memo since made public, Johnson's national security adviser proposed a strategy similar to today's proposed strategy for East Jerusalem and the West Bank featuring then, as now, Israeli claims about "realities on the ground."

> If the Israelis go fast enough and the Soviets get worried enough, a simple cease-fire might be the best answer. This would mean that we could use the *de facto* situation on the ground to try to negotiate not a return to armistice lines but a definitive peace in the Middle East.[37]

In other words, peace was possible provided everyone agreed that Tel Aviv could retain land seized with a preemptive attack that was still ongoing. In a memo, Ben Wattenberg and Larry Levinson cautioned Johnson that the U.N. may attempt "to sell Israel down the river." By then, pro-Israeli supporters had gathered in Lafayette Square across from the White House demanding a statement of presidential support for Israel and insisting on a repudiation of the official White House stance of avowed neutrality.

Though Johnson retired for the night at 11:30 p.m., White House records show he received a call at 11:59 p.m. from Mathilde Krim who had traveled to New York earlier in the day though only after leaving LBJ a personal note supportive of Israel and urging that he deliver her message "verbatim to the American people."[38] Johnson declined to relay her message in a presidential address. He did, however, recommend her comments to Secretary of State Rusk.

On the night of June 7, the naval intelligence ship *USS Liberty* approached within sight of the Gaza Strip. Cruising in international waters more than 12 miles off the coast of the Sinai Peninsula, the vessel monitored communications in that sensitive area, particularly activity by aircrews assigned to Soviet bombers in Egypt.[39] As Egypt was a Soviet client state, any Egyptian attack on America's ally Israel could drag the U.S. into a nuclear war. The U.S. had a need to know.

Under the command of General Moshe Dayan, Israel was preparing for an attack the next day that would complete this stage in Israel's territorial expansion for Greater Israel by capturing Syria's

Golan Heights.[40] Those seeking a reason for Israel's attack on the *USS Liberty* suggest it was to prevent Washington from learning that the Israeli offensive was continuing despite calls for a ceasefire by the Syrians, the Soviets and the U.S.[41]

When news of the Israeli attack on Americans reached the U.S., the Israel lobby shifted into high gear along with its Congressional contingent and its media counterpart. Wattenberg assured Johnson that if he supported Tel Aviv's account of the *USS Liberty* incident as a case of "mistaken identity" and ignored the 208 American casualties,[42] including 34 killed, influential Jews in the U.S. media would tone down their criticism of his policies in Vietnam.[43] In return for his defense of Israel and a presidential cover-up,[44] the shift in mainstream media opinion provided a temporary political respite for the war-weary president who, less than a year later, declined to run for reelection.

By then Clark Clifford had replaced Robert McNamara, who had grown sour on the war, as Secretary of Defense. On March 22, 1968, Johnson convened a meeting of his senior informal advisory group on Vietnam. To his surprise, only Abe Fortas and General Maxwell Taylor, chairman of the Joint Chiefs of Staff, continued to support a hard-line approach. The rest were either lukewarm or opposed to the war.

In his memoirs,[45] Clifford recalls how, nine days later, after LBJ announced he would not stand for reelection,[46] the president "wandered around the White House talking to people and viewing, with evident pleasure, the bewildered analysis of the commentators on television" who failed to anticipate his decision.[47] Then Clifford and Johnson returned to the West Hall of the White House where they joined a few others with whom the commander-in-chief enjoyed a special relationship, including the Rostows and Arthur and Mathilde Krim.

Precedents and Repercussions

As the *USS Liberty* came under attack, Navy fighter jets were launched from nearby aircraft carriers *USS Saratoga* and *USS America*. Defense Secretary McNamara had them recalled on Johnson's direct order. Never before in U.S. military history had a rescue mission been cancelled with a U.S. Navy ship under attack. Richard Parker, former U.S. political counselor of the U.S. Embassy in Cairo in 1967, recalls an initial assumption that the attackers were Egyptian and that the jets were recalled when it was learned that Israel was the attacker.

The *Liberty* incident also remains the only peacetime attack on a U.S. Navy vessel not investigated by Congress.[48] The cover-up would have been impossible but for the complicity of Admiral John S. McCain Jr., father of the Arizona Senator, who was then stationed in London as Commander-in-Chief, U.S. Naval Forces, Europe. After the incident, Admiral McCain allowed a court of inquiry just one week to complete an investigation—a crippling limitation in light of the complex nature of the event and the dispersion of the witnesses.[49] He also instructed the court to investigate only the ship's response to the attack. As the court's senior legal counsel later explained: "Admiral McCain was adamant that we were not to travel to Israel or contact the Israelis concerning this matter."[50]

Nor did the court consider written testimony from any of the 60 medical evacuees who were unable to testify in person,[51] including James Ennes who was officer of the deck when the attack began.[52] Even before the court convened, Admiral McCain framed the findings to support Tel Aviv's claim that, in the fog of war, its forces mistook a sophisticated U.S. Navy intelligence vessel for a dilapidated Egyptian freighter. Tel Aviv claimed that a clearly marked U.S. Navy ship bristling with 40 special purpose antennae had been mistaken for *El Quseir*, an Egyptian horse cavalry transport roughly half its size that was then berthed in Cairo waiting to be scrapped. The torpedo depth set by Israeli torpedo boats was perfect for tearing a hole in the *USS Liberty*. A torpedo set for that depth would have run under the Egyptian ship, due to its shallow draft.

Admiral McCain's order provided Johnson the "fixed" record required to conceal an Israeli attack on a U.S. Navy vessel that, the evidence suggests, was meant to kill all 294 Americans aboard. Conversations recorded between the pilots and Israeli ground control confirm they not only knew the ship was American but were also frustrated at the difficulty in sinking it quickly and completely with no survivors.[53]

This McCain family secret helps explain the Senator's support for Tel Aviv no matter how extreme its position—and his close ties with Joe Lieberman, an Orthodox Jew and ardent Zionist. Within days of 9/11, Senators McCain and Lieberman and other pro-Zionists inundated the airwaves with calls to attack Iraq. Three months after 9/11, Lieberman and McCain appeared together on the aircraft carrier *USS Theodore Roosevelt* where McCain, striking a commander-in-chief pose, waved an admiral's cap and proclaimed, "On to Baghdad."

> John McCain's grandfather was known as Slew by his fellow officers and, affectionately, as Popeye by the sailors who served in his command. A native of Mississippi whose grandfather owned slaves, he played the horses, sipped bourbon and water and rolled his cigarettes with one hand. Admiral McCain was commander of all land-based aircraft in the South Pacific during WWII. A 1906 graduate of the Naval Academy, the aircraft carriers under his command once shot down 49 Japanese planes in a single day and destroyed 3,000 grounded enemy planes in a 35-day period. Planes under his command took part in action over Leyte Gulf, Luzon, Formosa and the Japanese Homeland. Admiral McCain died September 2, 1945, less than three weeks after the victory over Japan (VJ Day) on August 14, 1945.
>
> John McCain's father, a 1931 graduate of the Naval Academy, served as a submarine commander during WWII. He too became a navy aviator and also rose to the rank of four-star admiral, the first family in U.S. military history to achieve that father-son distinction. In July 1968, one year after aiding Johnson with the cover-up, he was named Commander-in-Chief of the Pacific Command (CINCPAC) during the Vietnam War, a position he held until 1972. Admiral McCain died March 24, 1981.
>
> Lieutenant Commander John S. McCain III, a 1958 graduate of Annapolis (894th in an academic class of 899), served as a navy pilot assigned to the aircraft carrier *USS Oriskany* when his A4E Skyhawk aircraft was shot down by a surface-to-air missile over Hanoi. He retired a captain after

> serving from 1958-1981. He was elected to the Congress in 1982 and to the Senate in 1986 to a seat vacated by Barry Goldwater.

Two civilian lawyers scrubbed the official report on the *USS Liberty*, diverting attention away from Tel Aviv. After the report was redrafted (by *the people in between*), the official record left no reference to the Israeli machine-gunning of life rafts, a clear war crime. In effect, the McCain cover-up granted plausibility to an implausible claim: Israel Defense Forces mistakenly attacked a U.S. Navy ship with an estimated 30 sorties flown over the 455-foot vessel by a minimum of 12 aircraft, leaving 821 holes, more than 100 of which were rocket-size, while also jamming all five of its emergency radio channels.

Richard Helms, CIA Director from 1966 to 1973, conceded that "few in Washington could believe that the ship had not been identified as an American naval vessel." Presidential counsel Clark Clifford (who had advised President Truman to recognize Israel in 1948) was among those few:

> "Having been for so long a staunch supporter of Israel, I was particularly troubled by this incident; I could not bring myself to *believe* that such an action could have been authorized by [Israeli Prime Minister] Levi Eshkol."[54] (emphasis added)

Despite an interim CIA report favoring Israel's account, Helms noted, "there could be no doubt that the Israelis knew exactly what they were doing in attacking the *Liberty*."[55] "It was no accident," Helms reported.[56] Admiral Thomas Moorer, former Chairman of the Joint Chiefs of Staff (1970-74), called it "one of the classic all-American cover-ups."[57] Helms recalled: "It was the world's good fortune that the hostilities on the Golan Heights ended before that day was out." Early on June 10th, Soviet Premier Kosygin utilized the hot line between Moscow and Washington to warn of a "grave catastrophe" and promised "necessary actions, including military" should Israel fail to halt operations within the next few hours.[58]

Even now, few Americans realize that Israel's 1967 war of expansion in the Middle East resulted in the two nuclear-armed superpowers squaring off just five years after the Cuban missile crisis. In the midst of this conflict, Moscow threatened an "independent decision" if the U.S. failed to bring Israeli aggression to a speedy close.[59]

War by Deception

Captain Ward Boston, counsel to the U.S. Navy Court of Inquiry, belatedly confirmed his concerns about the cover-up. Acting as a "good soldier" who followed his orders to remain silent, he waited more than three decades to go public. In October 2003, he admitted that Johnson and McNamara ordered that the inquiry conclude the attack was a case of "mistaken identity."[60] "It was the most sophisticated intelligence ship in the world in 1967," according to Admiral Moorer. "With its massive radio antennae, including a large satellite dish, it looked like a large lobster and was one of the most easily identifiable ships afloat."[61]

After keeping quiet about his firsthand knowledge for 36 years, Boston published a sworn affidavit stating he was "outraged at the efforts of apologists for Israel" who "claim this attack was a case of 'mistaken identity.'" He singled out for particularly harsh criticism the 2002 publication of *The Liberty Incident* by A. Jay Cristol,[62] a federal bankruptcy judge, who dismissed as "conspiracy theorists" those who challenged the official court report.[63] Reflecting back on his conversations with Admiral Isaac Kidd, Jr. who served as president of the court of inquiry, Boston recalled, "Admiral Kidd called me two hours after an interview with Cristol and said 'I think Cristol's an Israeli agent.'"[64]

In June 2007, on the 40th anniversary of the attack, Boston published "Time for the Truth about the *Liberty*."[65] From his home in Miami, Cristol responded by dismissing all criticism as "propaganda" by those "whose agenda is to attack the present excellent symbiotic relationship between the United States and Israel."[66]

Rear Admiral Merlin Staring, former judge advocate general for the U.S. Navy, was asked to assess the report of the court of inquiry before it was sent to Washington. The report was taken from him, he says, after he began to question certain aspects. He now describes it as "a hasty, superficial, incomplete and totally inadequate inquiry."[67] In stark contrast, Senator McCain heaped praise on Cristol's analysis supporting the court's findings. Now the senior Republican on the

Senate Armed Services Committee, McCain not only endorsed Cristol's book, he broadcast his support by publishing it in *The Congressional Record*:

> After years of research for this book, Judge A. Jay Cristol has reached a similar conclusion to one my father reached in his June 18, 1967 endorsement of the findings of the court of inquiry. I commend Judge Cristol for his thoroughness and fairness, and I commend this work.

As part of an independent commission to investigate the attack, Admiral Moorer, former commander of the 7th Fleet, described several details confirming why the commission concluded the attack was purposeful:[68]

- After eight hours of surveillance, Israel launched a two-hour air and naval attack against the *USS* Liberty.
- Israel attempted to prevent the *Liberty's* radio operators from sending a call for help by jamming American emergency radio channels.
- Israeli torpedo boats machine-gunned at close range lifeboats that had been lowered to rescue the most seriously wounded.

As a result, our commission concluded that:

- There is compelling evidence that Israel's attack was a deliberate attempt to destroy an American ship and kill her entire crew.
- In attacking the *USS Liberty*, Israel committed acts of murder against U.S. servicemen and an act of war against the United States.
- That due to the influence of Israel's powerful supporters in the United States, the White House deliberately covered up the facts of this attack from the American people.
- That a danger to our national security exists whenever our elected officials are willing to subordinate American interests to those of any foreign nation.

- The truth continues to be concealed to the present day in what can only be termed a national disgrace.

In addition to calling for a new court of inquiry and a congressional investigation, the commission urged that June 8 be proclaimed *USS Liberty* Remembrance Day in order to remind the American people of the threat to U.S. national security inherent in any passionate attachment of elected officials to a foreign nation.

Crime Pays

Eyewitness accounts of the incident conflict with claims of an innocent mistake, including the fact that Israel Defense Forces aircraft flew over the *Liberty* eight times between 6 A.M. and 1 P.M. before opening fire on the easily identified U.S. Navy ship. Israeli requests for secrecy about its role in the attack were delivered to Johnson through Eugene Rostow.[69] Admiral Moorer described the U.S. Navy reaction to the attack on the *USS Liberty* as "the most disgraceful act I witnessed in my military career." He posed the uncomfortable question that no one has yet asked the son of the U.S. Navy admiral who played a leading role in this cover-up: "Does our government continue to subordinate American interests to Israeli interests?"[70]

Much as Admiral John S. McCain, Jr. saw his career advance when, after the cover-up, he was named Commander of the Pacific Fleet, Admiral Kidd advanced from Rear Admiral (two stars) to a four-star admiral and Commander of the Atlantic Fleet.[71] Jim McGonagle, the ship's skipper, received a promotion, command of a newly commissioned ship and the Congressional Medal of Honor. In a break with military tradition, the nation's highest honor for valor was presented not at the White House but at the Washington Navy Yard.

Admiral Moorer, who became Chief of Naval Operations shortly before the award order arrived for McGonagle, protested to Pentagon chief McNamara but the order stood. During the low-profile ceremony, the commander-in-chief was nowhere in sight. Instead the Secretary of the Navy presented the award. Disgusted by the cover-up, Moorer observed, "The way they did things, I'm surprised they didn't just hand it to him under the 14th Street Bridge."[72]

Ambassador Edward Peck, commenting on the "nature and extent of the cover-up," noted that this was "the first time in history the Congressional Medal was awarded for action in the face of an enemy with which the United States was not at war. In fact, Israel, the nation that launched and sustained a two-hour air and sea attack on a US Navy ship was considered a friend." On the 40th anniversary of the attack, this former Chief of Mission in Iraq and Deputy Director of Ronald Reagan's White House Task Force on Terrorism cast this official behavior in stark terms:

> This is obsequious, unctuous subservience to the peripheral interests of a foreign nation at the cost of the lives and morale of our own service members and their families. It should no longer be condoned.[73]

No protest was heard from the Congress for which the medal is named. Before the award was bestowed, the White House consulted the Israelis who gave their permission to proceed. McGonagle's daughter later conceded to a fellow veteran that her father admitted he was pressured to fabricate a pro-Israeli account of the assault.[74] As court counsel Ward Boston summarized Admiral Kidd's assessment: "we've been ordered to shut up."[75] Not until 1982 were gravestone inscriptions changed to name the *USS Liberty* as the ship on which Americans died in what the crew thought was a defense of American interests. For 15 years, the inscriptions read simply, "Died in Eastern Mediterranean." The ship's name was added only after a protest from the *USS Liberty* Veterans Association.

From a game theory perspective, the cover-up enabled by Admiral McCain was essential to preserve Israel's portrayal of itself as a hapless victim residing in an anti-Semitic region. That lie also helped cover up the fact that the 1967 War was not defensive but a pre-planned land grab for Greater Israel. By taking territory while feigning self-defense, that conflict also served as a provocation certain to catalyze a response that could plausibly enable the *next* war (in 1973) to be portrayed as "defensive" when Israel's neighbors sought to reclaim the land taken.

Yitzhak Rabin, Israel Defense Forces chief of staff in 1967 would later concede: "I do not believe that Nasser wanted war. The two divisions he sent into Sinai on May 14 would not have been enough to unleash an offensive against Israel. He knew it and we knew it."[76] Similarly, General Moshe Dayan explained that, "many of the fire-fights with the Syrians were deliberately provoked by Israel." He explained that the kibbutz residents who pressed the government to take the Golan Heights did so less for the security than for the farmland.[77]

In December 1987 the *USS Liberty* incident was officially closed with an exchange of diplomatic letters and Israel's payment of $13.7 million in reparations,[78] including $6 million for a ship then valued at more than $40 million. The *USS Liberty* was dismantled and sold as scrap in 1973 for $110,000. On June 8, 2005, the *USS Liberty* Veterans Association filed a war crimes report with Secretary of Defense Donald Rumsfeld. By law, the secretary is obliged to initiate an inquiry on receipt of such a serious charge.[79] As of September 2008, the report had been forwarded to five separate bureaucracies that declined the challenge the adequacy and integrity of the McCain court of inquiry.[80]

Arming the Belligerent

The Israeli killing of Americans aboard the *USS Liberty* (a premeditated murder according to Admiral Moorer) marked a strategic milestone for the Jewish state. No one in the Israeli government or military received even a reprimand. Tel Aviv suffered no political repercussions either for its preemptive seizure and continued occupation of Arab lands or for the murder of Americans. Instead, Lyndon Johnson increased U.S. financial, military and political support and the Pentagon was directed to include security of the belligerent Zionist state as a strategic objective of U.S. national security.

By advancing the careers of senior Naval officers complicit in the cover-up up, Johnson signaled future generations of military leaders that they can expect promotions if, following orders, they abandon their tradition of duty and honor. Much as AIPAC intimidated Members of Congress by removing from office Paul Findley and others who challenged Israeli policies, LBJ set a precedent for rewarding military commanders who subordinate their honor to Israeli interests.

> As a senior member of the Senate Armed Services Committee, John McCain heard the February 2003 testimony of Army Chief of Staff General Eric Shinseki when he warned that

> "several hundred thousand" troops would be required to invade and secure Iraq. Deputy Defense Secretary Paul Wolfowitz assured the committee that 50,000 troops would be sufficient.
>
> McCain did not object when General Shinseki was rebuked by war-planner Wolfowitz. Instead, he told the *Hartford Courant* in a March 5, 2003 article, just before the invasion: "I have no qualms about our strategic plans." Later he claimed credit for advocating a "surge" in U.S. troops to quell a deadly sectarian insurgency that could have been prevented by heeding Shinseki's call for more troops. Candidate McCain cites that surge as a key qualification to serve as commander-in-chief.
>
> It is difficult to imagine a presidential candidate less qualified to restore the honor of the U.S. Navy in light of the McCain-enabled cover-up of the *USS Liberty* incident.

Soon after the Six-Day War, France canceled an Israeli contract for the delivery of 50 Mirage jet fighters. That led to U.S. negotiations for the delivery to Israel of 50 Phantom F-4 jet fighters beginning in 1969.[81] Within two years of the Six-Day War, the Pentagon was training Israeli pilots on U.S.-made fighter jets. With that step, any future Israeli aggression in the region would be perceived as enjoying the approval of U.S. foreign policy and the enthusiastic support of Americans.

Israel soon emerged as a major arms supplier worldwide as a sizeable portion of its workforce became dependent on the perception of Israel as a weak and vulnerable state under siege by a hostile world of anti-Semites, Jew haters and Holocaust deniers.[82] Yet it was only after Israel's 1967 land grab that such charges were deployed in the U.S. to intimidate and discredit Americans who criticize Israeli policies.[83]

Israel suffered no consequences for killing 34 Americans. Instead, Tel Aviv again proved its prowess at waging war by way of deception based on its mastery at manipulating a U.S. President by servicing not only his personal and emotional needs (Mathilde Krim) but also his political and financial needs (Abe Fortas, Abe Feinberg, Arthur

Krim, Arthur Goldberg, *et.al.*). In addition, Israel again confirmed the success of a long-term strategy for Greater Israel that pre-stages supportive personnel (agents, assets and *sayanim*) for key political positions inside the U.S. government: the Rostow brothers, Fortas, Goldberg, Jacobsen, Goodwin, Levinson, Wattenberg, etc.

An Invitation to Game Theorists

When Johnson declined to make delivery of nuclear-capable F-4 Phantom jets contingent on Israeli compliance with the Nuclear Non-Proliferation Treaty, he not only signaled that the U.S. had no objection to Tel Aviv's nuclear weapons program, he also opened the way for Israeli firms to distribute nuclear components worldwide and signaled the U.S. was not serious about non-proliferation.[84]

When Johnson chose not to pursue John Kennedy's efforts to shut down the Zionist state's nuclear weapons program, he enabled Israel to use the fear of nuclear weapons as a means to provoke, without fear of retribution, the regional frictions that made plausible *The Clash of Civilizations.* That conflict-of-opposites emerged seamlessly as a successor to the nuclear terrorism of Mutual Assured Destruction (MAD) that dominated an earlier conflict-of-opposites: the Cold War era. The 1967 war pre-staged the regional dynamics that made plausible the latest present danger: the global war on terrorism.

By providing Tel Aviv with an arsenal of modern offensive weapons along with an agreement limiting their use for *defensive* purposes, Johnson further emboldened Israeli game theorists. With access to America's state-of-the-art weaponry, Israel became better equipped to provoke reactions to which Israel Defense Forces could respond in "self-defense." In effect, LBJ gave game theorists the military means and motive to wage *agent provocateur* warfare against which Tel Aviv could then defend, justifying Israeli requests for more U.S. military assistance.

The history of weaponry confirms that each advance in defensive weaponry catalyzes an advance in offensive weaponry (and vice versa). In the midst of the SALT talks (Strategic Arms Limitation Treaty) in Reykjavik, Iceland in 1986, Ronald Reagan and Soviet Leader Mikhail Gorbachev were on the verge of overruling their advisers and reaching an agreement to eliminate all strategic nuclear weapons. At the time, Reagan sought to pursue development of a missile defense program.

Gorbachev proposed that the U.S. program be limited to laboratory work for 10 years for fear that Reagan's Strategic Defense Initiative (SDI) might catalyze an arms race in space while jeopardizing steps to eliminate vast arsenals of land- and sea-based nuclear weaponry. Had Reagan agreed to that one-decade limitation two decades ago, nuclear weapons might now be eliminated in their entirety, removing the threat of that weapon of mass destruction.

Richard Perle, an exemplar of *the people in between*, boasted how he undermined that potential Reagan-Gorbachev agreement when he persuaded Reagan that, by accepting Gorbachev's proposal, the SDI program would be endangered.[85] Had an agreement been reached in 1986 to eliminate all nuclear weapons, Israel's "opaque" nuclear weapons program would have been affected as well, negating a key game theory advantage that Tel Aviv has since deployed with success.

In the oft-recurring conflict-of-opposites manipulation chronicled in this account, each new offensive weapon evokes a new defensive weapon, just as each new defense catalyzes a new offense. Thus the focus in this account on identifying those who catalyze serial conflicts-of-opposites while profiting off the misery of both sides.

An Invitation to Terror

From a game theory perspective, by covering up the murder of Americans aboard the *USS Liberty*, a U.S. President (with the aid of Admiral John McCain, Jr.) confirmed that Israeli extremists could kill Americans without endangering U.S. support. The encouragement of Israeli extremism was further enhanced by the discouragement Americans experienced during the 1960s. The debacle in Vietnam and a decade of high-profile murders (the Kennedy brothers and Martin Luther King, Jr.) laid the mental and emotional threads for Americans to *believe* four decades later that it was their elected government (vs. an unelected government *inside* their government) that was responsible for the debacle in Iraq.

The war in Iraq—destined to become a quagmire—was certain to catalyze another round of skepticism, cynicism, self-doubt and disillusionment. As with the Vietnam war in the 1960s, events in Iraq four decades later were guaranteed to erode confidence in government and to heighten distrust of the U.S. by other governments, particularly in the Middle East. Secretary of State Rusk was in the White House Situation Room with Lyndon Johnson when word came of the attack on the *USS Liberty*. In his autobiography, Rusk put the Israeli attack in geopolitical perspective by describing the discrediting effects of that land grab on Israel's loyal ally:[86]

> I was never satisfied with the Israeli explanation. Their sustained attack to disable and sink *Liberty* precluded an assault by accident or by some trigger-happy local commander. Through diplomatic channels we refused to accept their explanation. I didn't believe them then, and I don't believe them to this day. The attack was outrageous.
>
> What followed was just as bad. For 20 years, since the creation of Israel, the United States had tried to persuade the Arabs that they needn't fear Israeli territorial expansion. Throughout the 1960s the Arabs talked continuously about their fear of Israeli expansion. With the full knowledge of successive governments in Israel, we did our utmost to persuade the Arabs that their anxieties were illusory.
>
> And then following the Six-Day War, Israel decided to keep the Golan Heights, the West Bank, the Gaza Strip, and the Sinai, despite the fact that Israeli Prime Minister Levi Eshkol on the first day of the war went on Israeli radio and said that Israel had no territorial ambitions. Later in the summer I reminded Abba Eban [Israel's Foreign Minister] of this, and he simply shrugged his shoulders and said, "We've changed our minds." With that remark, a contentious and even bitter point with the Americans, he turned the United States into a 20-year liar.

The Six-Day War pre-staged today's geopolitics. Following that 1967 conflict, America discredited itself by allowing its values to be associated with Israeli duplicity. By its entangling alliance with a duplicitous state, the U.S. was seen as a partner in the same treachery and deceit for which Israel was already infamous.[87]

Israeli offenses against international law were routinely covered up by U.S. vetoes of U.N. Security Council resolutions. In the U.N. General Assembly, American diplomats routinely defended Israeli violations of norms of civilized behavior. As American values of moderation, tolerance and candor became identified with Israeli extremism, racism and deceit, the U.S. emerged guilty by association. Meanwhile U.S. policymakers continued to deceive themselves that Israel was a democracy and an ally.

With America seen as its defender, Zionist extremists concluded they could ignore international law with impunity.[88] To date, they have been correct, as 39 U.N. resolutions urged that Israel vacate territories occupied since 1967. With each U.S. veto, the credibility and moral standing of the U.S. declined, along with the authority and effectiveness of the U.N. as it too became guilty by association.

Nation State as Agent Provocateur

The region-wide resentments provoked by Israel's 1967 aggression ensured an enduring anger that Tel Aviv periodically rekindled, reinforced and refocused as part of a long-term emotion-management *modus operandi*. Post-9/11, regional animosities were again inflamed by reports confirming what those in the region had already surmised: The intelligence that induced Israel's ally to invade Iraq was false, flawed and "fixed" around an agenda advanced by those notorious for their mastery of strategic deceit.

Such strategic duplicity may come as a surprise to misinformed Americans. It comes as no surprise, however, to those who have long lived in close proximity to a state known for routinely waging war by way of deception. Even now, many Americans *believe* that Israel was the victim in the 1967 conflict and not the aggressor, confirming the key role of self-deceit in sustaining this entangling alliance.

Israeli Air Force commander Motti Hod boasted that Tel Aviv's destruction of the Egyptian Air Force had been planned and rehearsed since 1951, five years before Israel invaded Egypt to catalyze the Suez Crisis (one week before the 1956 U.S. presidential election) and 16 years before the Jewish state launched its preemptive war of 1967.[89] That war, in turn, fed regional dynamics that would make plausible *The Clash of Civilizations* as the latest present danger, catalyzed by the emotionally wrenching provocation of September 11, 2001.

Lengthy pre-planning ensured that, on a bright June day in 1967, it took only 80 minutes for Israeli jets to destroy 309 of Egypt's 390 aircraft and kill a third of its pilots. The assault was planned for 7:45 a.m. Tel Aviv time because Israeli intelligence knew Egyptian pilots would be relaxing from early morning patrols and Egyptian commanders would be caught in rush hour traffic enroute to their offices.[90]

According to George Ball, President Kennedy's Acting Secretary of State, the fiction that a defenseless Israel was playing David to an Arab Goliath was "mythmaking for the ill-informed American public"[91]dispensed by a pro-Israeli media. The saga of the oft-threatened underdog fighting for its survival required, then as now, a combination of national scale psy-ops and geopolitical pre-staging. Had an unbiased media inquired how, if Arabs were the aggressor, they were surprised with their air forces on the ground, Israel's victim status would have proven a far more difficult sell. Then, as now, a complicit media was essential to sustain the myth.

Tel Aviv continues to stage serial provocations as part of a psy-ops strategy designed to portray Israeli extremists as sympathetic victims. Even now, American lawmakers continue to *believe* the U.S. enjoys a "special relationship" of trust with a faithful ally. Yet the facts suggest that alleged friend drew on America's post-WWII stature to vouch for an extremist enclave's status as a legitimate sovereign state. Then as now, America's leadership was susceptible to deception and self-deceit.

Israeli mythmaking was granted additional credence when, in August 2000, the Clinton-Gore Administration awarded a former Irgun operative the nation's highest civilian honor. For her public service on AIDS-related research and policies, the Presidential Medal of Freedom was bestowed on Mathilde Krim in August 2000 for her "extraordinary compassion and commitment."[92] No mention was made of her well-timed special relationship with an earlier commander-in-chief.

LBJ Library photo by Frank Wolfe (October 27, 1968)

Lady Bird Johnson, Arthur, Mathilde and Daphna Krim, President Lyndon B. Johnson.

LBJ Library photo by Yoichi R. Okamoto (June 23, 1967)

Mathilde Krim, President Lyndon B. Johnson.

LBJ Library photo by Yoichi R. Okamoto (June 23, 1967)

Lynda Bird Johnson, Arthur and Mathilde Krim, Lew Wasserman, President Lyndon B. Johnson, Mrs. Wasserman.

AP Photo/PabloMartinez Monsivais

President Clinton awards the Presidential Medal of Freedom to Mathilde Krim, Ph.D., during ceremonies in the East Room of the White House, Wednesday, Aug. 9, 2000.

Chapter 5

The Presidency and Russian Organized Crime

Privatization is now starkly revealed as a massive plunder of public property.

—Michael Meacher[1]

Rather than engage the Russians, John McCain seeks to enrage them.[2] In May 2006, he and Joe Lieberman sought to embarrass President Vladimir Putin by calling for a U.S. boycott of the July 2006 G-8 summit of industrial nations. That meeting was convened in Putin's hometown of St. Petersburg, an historic showcase newly refurbished by the Putin government and a city where he served as deputy mayor during the reform era of Mikhail Gorbachev.

In an effort coordinated with the late Congressman Tom Lantos to discredit Putin, McCain portrayed as a "political prisoner" Mikhail Khodorkovsky, the most infamous of Russia's corrupt oil oligarchs. When, without further explanation, he also charged that the indictment of Russian media oligarchs Boris Berezovsky and Vladimir Gusinsky was "politically motivated," it became clear that the candidate was either ignorant about—or complicit in—Russian organized crime. As Russian media moguls in the 1990s, Berezovsky and

Gusinsky played critical roles in rigging the 1996 re-election of President Boris Yeltsin. During Yeltsin's first term as president, a handful of Ashkenazi oligarchs financially pillaged Russia's post-Soviet economy under the guise of Glasnost (openness) and Perestroika (restructuring).

Russia's "Big Seven" oligarchs invested an estimated $500 million in Yeltsin's re-election,[3] enabling them to hold onto privatized assets long enough that public assets stolen from the Russian people could plausibly be portrayed as private and hence subject to the protection of post-Soviet law. Six of the "Big Seven" qualify for Israeli citizenship. This chapter identifies the syndicate operatives that a McCain presidency would protect at the risk of U.S.-Russia relations—and to the great detriment of the Russian people.

Though Boris Berezovksy frequently travels to Tel Aviv with an Israeli passport, he resides in London where he enjoys political asylum—a status Moscow aims to see revoked. Gusinsky relocated to Tel Aviv from Moscow where he was a vice-president of the Bronfman-led World Jewish Congress and chairman of the Russian Jewish Congress.

By the time oil oligarch Khodorkovsky was jailed for fraud and tax evasion, his lieutenant Leonid Nevzlin had already fled to Israel to escape an arrest warrant on charges that he organized a series of contract killings from inside Yukos, a Russian oil company over which he and Khordorkovsky gained control in 1995 in a Yeltsin-era fraud known as "loans for shares."[4] When he fled Russia, Nevzlin was also the sole beneficiary of a trust that controlled voting rights in Yukos. When Moscow sought his extradition, Tel Aviv refused.[5]

Until his October 2003 arrest, Khodorkovsky was actively discussing his planned presidential campaign in which he would have invested a portion of his massive oil wealth. Had he succeeded (quite likely given the Ashkenazi-oligarch control of Russian media at the time), he would have gained political control of a nation that he had already financially plundered in partnership with a network of predominantly Ashkenazi operatives.

Though campaigning for president on his national security credentials, McCain has misdiagnosed issues of profound consequence not only to ordinary Russians but also to Americans systematically defrauded by the same transnational syndicate. With regularity, the candidate has favored those complicit in the criminal network chronicled in this account. Thus the skepticism with which Moscow must have viewed John McCain's May 2008 campaign proposal for a new arms pact with Russia.[6]

This chapter also describes the *modus operandi* by which Russia was looted by organized crime operatives sharing the same ideological bias as those operating in the U.S. In addition to chronicling a U.S. presidential candidate's relationship with this syndicate, this chapter also describes the suspect political dynamics behind the "Orange Revolution" in Ukraine. The consistency with which John McCain has associated with this transnational network raises the sensitive issue whether his candidacy enjoys syndicate support.

Mega-Thief Mikhail Khodorkovsky

To claim that Khodorkovsky is a "political prisoner" requires a closer look at how, at 32 years of age, a single Russian-Ashkenazi citizen amassed state-owned assets worth more than $30 billion. A description of this politically facilitated fraud demonstrates just how few well-placed operatives are required to sustain this criminality across borders and across generations.

Bank Menatep, founded by Khodorkovsky in 1990 when he was 27, pre-staged the fraud used to gain a controlling interest in Yukos, which was privatized in 1995.[7] In 1993, Khodorkovsky became deputy to Vagit Alekperov (aka "the Don") who was then minister of fuel and energy charged with reorganizing the Russian oil industry for privatization. After brokering corrupt transactions between bureaucracies and industries, Menatep emerged as a conglomerate of Khodorkovsky-controlled enterprises.[8]

Under the 1995 "loans for shares" scheme, the cash-strapped Yeltsin administration pledged shares in state-owned oil companies to oligarch-controlled banks as collateral for loans to the government. When the government defaulted on the loans, the oil company shares were "auctioned" to the oligarchs by the same oligarch-controlled banks.[9] Participation in the auctions required not only an invitation, typically by seeking approval from Yeltsin's daughter, Tatyana, but also a registration approved by oligarch-owned banks.

Bank Menatep managed the Yukos auction, enabling Khodorkovsky, Nevzlin and their partners initially to take control of Yukos by acquiring 45% of its shares for $159 million with 11.5 billion barrels of proven reserves—less than three cents per barrel.[10] Two years later, Yukos was listed on the Moscow stock exchange at a value of $7 billion. By 2004 its value topped $34 billion.

Even the funds used to bid in the government auctions came largely from the government. Favored banks (owned by the oligarchs) were given loans by the central bank at negative interest rates, and government funds were kept on deposit at below-market interest rates. Not only were the banks also allowed to seize profits of certain Russian traders and avoid paying tax on their windfalls, but they could also participate in the government bond market where annualized yields ranged from 60 to 200 percent in dollar terms, 1995-98.[11]

Self-Made Fortunes

To grasp the role played in this criminality by personal relationships, it helps to understand the role of intermarriage, including that of Ashkenazi oligarch Oleg Deripaska, Russia's richest oligarch. According to *The New York Times*:[12]

> His marriage to Polina V. Yumasheva, the daughter of a presidential speechwriter to President Yeltsin, Valenin Yumasheva, was the closest to a dynastic wedding in the new Russia… Eighteen months after they were married, Mr. Yumasheva married Mr. Yeltsin's daughter Tatyana, making Polina the stepdaughter of Mr. Yeltsin—and Mr. Deripaska a member of the Yeltsin family through marriage.[13]

Sibneft, another major oil company, owned reserves equivalent to Texaco before its merger with Chevron. The shares of Sibneft sold at auction for $100.3 million to Yeltsin insiders Roman Abramovich and Boris Berezovsky.[14] Known as the "Grey Cardinal" and "The Godfather of the Kremlin,"[15] Berezovsky introduced Abramovich to Yeltsin's inner circle and later sold out to him when Berezovsky fled to London in 2000 to escape fraud and embezzlement charges brought by the Putin government.

Like other oligarchs, Abramovich also began his criminal career with corrupt export schemes that acquired state-owned commodities at low state prices and sold them abroad at far higher prices. These early oligarchs (operating as *the people in between*) exploited that difference to amass fortunes across an array of commodities. Abramovich and his mentor, Boris Berezovsky, specialized in the theft of oil and aluminum.

In 2004, Abramovich sold his stake in Russian Aluminum to Deripaska.[16] In its 2008 listing, *Forbes* ranked Abramovich, age 41, the world's 15th richest billionaire with personal wealth of $23.5 billion.[17] In February 2008, *The Moscow Times* estimated Deripaska's wealth at $40 billion placing him, at age 40, among the world's top 10 billionaires as rising prices for oil and metals boosted his net worth (*Forbes* ranked him ninth in 2008 with wealth of $28 billion).[18]

Without explanation, *Forbes* describes as "self-made" the vast fortunes amassed by Russia's oligarchs in a process that senior *Forbes* editor Paul Klebnikov characterized in 2000 as "the biggest disaster (economically, socially and demographically) since the Nazi invasion of 1941."[19] In early 2008, 74 billionaires lived in Moscow. With an average wealth of $5.9 billion, the Russian capital eclipsed New York City as home to the world's greatest number of billionaires. In both cities, the billionaire population is predominantly Ashkenazi.

In July 2004, Klebnikov, then editor-in-chief of *Forbes Russia*, was murdered as he left his Moscow office. He had just published a profile of Russia's Top 100 richest featuring many of the newly rich who would be hard pressed to explain how they legitimately acquired their self-made fortunes. The subtitle of Klebnikov's 2000 book, *Godfather of the Kremlin*, captured the scope of the criminality that John McCain defends: *Boris Berezovsky and the Looting of Russia*.

McCain charged that Putin's opposition to the oligarchization of Russia is "a creeping coup against forces of democracy and market capitalism." By associating the stature and authority of his position as a U.S. Senator with opposition to the indictment of Berezovsky and Gusinsky, McCain helped dash the dreams of ordinary Russians who aspire to be governed by the rule of law rather than by oligarchs and the rule of in-laws such as Deripaska. To restore a credible legal system after looting on such a scale requires leaders willing to expose those who defrauded the Russian public by inducing *belief* in the corrupted authority of law.

According to *The Washington Post*, McCain campaign manager Rick Davis twice arranged for the candidate to meet with Oleg Deripaska whose links to organized crime are sufficiently compelling that a visa to visit the U.S. was revoked in July 2006.[20] Their first encounter was arranged at the annual World Economic Forum in Davos, Switzerland in January 2006. They met again in Montenegro seven months later during an official U.S. Senate trip to that eastern European country.[21]

> *Fields within Fields.* On March 20, 2008, after John McCain secured the Republican nomination for president, Nathan Rothschild and his father, Lord Jacob Rothschild, sponsored a fundraiser for McCain in London.[22] A principal adviser to Oleg Deripaska, Nathaniel is a descendent of Nathan Mayer Rothschild who helped finance Britain's victory over Napoleon at Waterloo.[23] In addition to providing financial advice to the Russian oligarch on the aluminum giant Rusal, Nathanial Rothschild also advises Indian steel magnates.[24]

The New Russian Royals

Along with the Big Seven oligarchs, Berezovsky and Gusinsky donated the money and media time required to re-elect Yeltsin in 1996. Also known as "Russia's Rupert Murdoch," Gusinsky launched *Sevodnya*, a newspaper that threw its unqualified support behind Yeltsin's presidential campaign. Yeltsin promptly rewarded Gusinsky with Russia's first private television network (NTV). That key asset anchored Gusinsky's creation of a media conglomerate that included print, radio and television.

Roman Abramovich became a business partner of Yeltsin's son-in-law, Leonid Dyachenko, and also served on the board of Sibneft, Berezovsky's primary oil holding. Soon after Putin succeeded Yeltsin as president on New Year's Eve of 1999, Berezovsky sold to his protégé Abramovich his interest in Signeft (oil) and ORT, Russia's largest television network. Abramovich promptly conveyed ORT's voting rights to Vladimir Putin.

In 2003, Abramovich purchased Chelsea, Britain's leading soccer club, for $300 million and has since reportedly spent $500 million on player transfers. In addition to his lavish home in Moscow, his six-story house in London's Eaton Square, formerly part of the estate of the Duke of Westminster, is reported to be worth more than $46 million. With proceeds from their plundering, Russia's criminal elite now own an estimated one in five homes in London's posh Mayfair district.

In September 2005 Abramovich cashed out a 73% stake in Sibneft in a $13 billion sale to Gazprom, Russia's state-owned energy conglomerate. He owns multiple mansions and at last count three mega-yachts of more than 300 feet in length with two more under construction, including *Eclipse*, a super luxury yacht that measures more than 525 feet, the world's largest.[25]

In April 2008, the Kensington and Chelsea council approved plans for Abramovich to build the United Kingdom's most costly residence at an estimated expense of £150 million ($298 million). The eight-bedroom mansion is expected to be eight floors, three of them underground.[26] In July 2008, he announced the purchase of a villa on the French Riviera for $500 million to honor his upcoming marriage to model Daria Zhukova, 25. The estate requires a full-time staff of 50 gardeners to maintain the grounds.[27]

Though he resides primarily in London, Abramovich saved an estimated $1 billion in Russian taxes by investing several hundred million dollars in Russia's Far East region of Chukotka.[28] Impoverished residents call the young Ashkenazi oligarch a "messiah" for lavishing a portion of his stolen wealth on their destitute region where he served as governor from 2001 until recently. His grateful constituents may not realize that his political status protected him from prosecution in Russia. In November 2005, he was sworn in for a new five-year term but resigned in July 2008.[29]

> Abramovich attends services in Russia of the Orthodox Lubavitch Hassidic movement headquartered in Brooklyn, New York—the Jewish equivalent of fundamentalist evangelical Christians. Abramovich provided funding for Italian-American Rabbi Berel Lazar who relocated to Russia in the early 1990s to promote the Lubavitch movement. In June 2000, one day after meeting with Putin in the Kremlin,

> Lazar convened a meeting of Hassidic rabbis and their emissaries from 45 Russian regions where they voted Lazar chief rabbi of Russia, replacing Adolph Shayevich, a rabbi recognized by the World Jewish Congress.
>
> Lazar's position was arranged by Putin (reportedly advised by Abramovich) so that the Russia government could bring corruption charges against media czar Gusinsky without being subjected to the charge of anti-Semitism, damaging Russia's reputation in world affairs. As head of the Russian Jewish Congress (to which Gusinsky made a $10 million annual contribution), the Gusinsky case had to be handled with care. Once Rabbi Lazar became chief rabbi, there was less concern that pursuing Gusinsky would provoke that charge.[30] Gusinsky relocated to Spain and then to Israel where he remains.
>
> Putin invited Lazar to a special dinner at the Kremlin during the January 2001 visit to Moscow of Israeli President Moshe Katsaw. A special cleansing (koshering) of the Kremlin kitchen was ordered for the first time in Russian history. To escape charges of anti-Semitism, Putin pit two Jewish factions against one another. Yet he also exchanged the (relative) moderates of the World Jewish Congress for extremists of an Orthodox Hassidic sect known to enjoy financial support from at least one of Russia's richest oligarchs.[31]

When Gusinsky fled to Israel, his NTV television station was taken over by Gazprom, the state gas monopoly led by Dimitri Medvedev until his March 2008 election to succeed Putin as president. During his heyday in Moscow, Gusinsky maintained a close relationship with Yuri Luzhkov, an Ashkenazi *khozyain* (boss) appointed mayor of Moscow by Yeltsin in 1992 and since elected three times.[32]

The Moscow Mob

Luzhkov helped Gusinsky gain control of Channel 4, a major Moscow television station, as well as other media properties. Gusinsky, in turn, helped re-elect Luzhkov who designated Most Bank, controlled by Gusinsky, the primary bank for financing Moscow real estate projects and infrastructure. When Luzhkov became mayor, Elena Baturina emerged as a key beneficiary of Moscow construction contracts. By 2007, her net worth of $2.3 billion ranked her 335th on the *Forbes* 2008 list of the world's billionaires.[33] Baturina is Luzhkov's wife.

As the world's fourth-most-expensive city behind Tokyo, Osaka and London, Moscow is notable for its staggering social divide. In a city where the official sustenance wage is less than $170 per month and homelessness is rampant, Luzhkov directed an estimated $250 million to rebuild the 19th century Cathedral of Christ the Savior, the world's largest Orthodox church, destroyed on the order of Stalin's chief administrator Lazar Kaganovich in December 1931.[34] Luzhkov's assessment of Moscow's steadily widening social divide: "It's normal, the city is working."[35]

Gusinsky now divides his time between Tel Aviv and Joe Lieberman's home state of Connecticut where he maintains a home in the upscale town of Greenwich. Gusinsky and Luzhkov toured the U.S. together, meeting with their American counterparts who wanted to enter the Russian media market.

As the predominantly Ashkenazi operatives in this transnational syndicate staged privatization frauds, the Russian public endured a dramatic five-year decline in life expectancy, the most dramatic reversal in human welfare recorded in a developed nation other than in wartime.[36] At least 12.5 million men "disappeared" in the former Soviet Union due to suicide, alcoholism, a failing healthcare system and destructive behavior.

Life expectancy in Russia fell to 66 years, 14 years below the European Union average. As yet, no one has proposed how to factor such costs into the oligarchization of Russia. Nor has anyone explained why a candidate for the U.S. presidency would protect those who financially pillaged Russia unless his candidacy enjoys syndicate support—or unless he considers oligarchies consistent with democracy and market capitalism.

As poverty swept a nation never known for its prosperity, Khodorkovsky and his colleagues undermined the Russian tax base by shipping Yukos oil to a tax haven at a small markup and paying tax only on the difference. The oil was then sold at world prices and no tax paid on the real profit. When, in response, lawmakers sought to raise taxes on the oil sector, he blocked the legislation by using his tax savings to fund opposition political parties.

Khodorkovsky's deep-pocket philosophy of democracy bears a striking resemblance to the McCain-Feingold campaign finance reform that allows America's well-to-do to invest unlimited amounts in their pet political projects. Had McCain's reforms been operative in Russia, Khodorkovsky could have funded his political opposition to tax reform through tax-exempt "527" organizations, all the while citing freedom of speech, freedom of the press and even freedom of religion by portraying as anti-Semitic anyone who opposed his political campaign.

While ordinary Russians were coping with the effects of this criminality, Khodorkovsky was negotiating the sale of a large block of Yukos shares to ExxonMobil or ChevronTexaco and proposing to use the proceeds to fund his own presidential campaign. If successful, Russia's "piratization" would have financed in Russia an Ashkenazi-oligarch system of governance with wealth defrauded from the Russian public. Yeltsin predecessor Mikhail Gorbachev charged in July 2005 that $1 trillion had been hidden abroad by those "plundering" Russia.[37] The facts suggest the total may be considerably more.

The all-pervasive influence of the Russian Mafia was well known before the Yeltsin government enabled an Ashkenazi elite to take organized crime to national scale. In *The Piratization of Russia*, Marshall Goldman, emeritus professor of Russian economics at Wellesley College, provided a glimpse of the political realities inside the Kremlin prior to the Gorbachev era:

> Brezhnev's daughter was having an affair with a circus clown who was also a diamond smuggler while her husband, Yuri Churbanov, deputy head of the national police, was on the payroll of the Uzbek Mafia. Even more amazing, the head of the Uzbek criminal organization paying Churbanov was Sharal Rashidev, who in his day job was the Secretary, or leader, of the Uzbek Communist Party. No wonder few of the efforts to attack crime in the waning days of the communist era were successful.[38]

Birds of a Feather

Why does an aspirant for the White House (John McCain) allege that those countering this criminality are mounting "a creeping coup against forces of democracy and market capitalism"? Why attack Putin while defending Berezovsky and Gusinsky? Why, unless his candidacy enjoys syndicate support, describe mega-thief Mikhail Khodorkovsky as a "political prisoner"? If not a Kremlin overseen by an Ashkenazi oligarchy, what sort of government would a McCain administration envision for the Russian people?

Prior to his arrest, Khodorkovsky transferred voting control of Menatep, a Yukos holding company, to deputy chairman Leonid Nevzlin whose 2004 wealth *Forbes* estimated at $2 billion. Nevzlin fled to Israel shortly after Russian authorities indicted a former Yukos security chief for four murders including the death of the mayor of Nefteyugansk, a Siberian oil town at the center of the Yukos empire.[39]

Two fellow Yukos billionaires, Mikhail Brudno and Vladimir Dubov, fled with Nevzlin where they now live as his neighbors in Herzilya, an exclusive seaside community north of Tel Aviv. The Yukos security chief was sentenced to twenty years in prison for murders that Nevzlin is alleged to have ordered[40] and Khordokovsky reportedly approved.[41] In 2005, Israeli Prime Minister Ariel Sharon declined Putin's personal appeal to extradite Nevzlin for prosecution on a murder charge in Moscow dating from when Nevzlin led the Russian Jewish Congress, a Bronfman affiliate.

Russian law enforcement officials claim that the murder of a city official was but one of many that Nevzlin ordered. In March 2008 the Russian government began a murder trial for Nevzlin *in absentia.* Moscow cites evidence that he oversaw an operation resembling Murder, Inc. that ordered the assassination of Russian business executives and officials from 1998 to 2004.[42]

Despite these charges, Nevzlin traveled freely in the U.S. after his Christmas Eve 2006 arrival in Newark, New Jersey under State Department protection championed by Congressman Tom Lantos. Nevzlin's pro-Israeli supporters claim that the charges against him are political payback for his alliance with Khodorkovsky. Lantos assured *The Jewish Week* that Nevzlin is "as honest as they come," adding, "To accuse him of murder is about as absurd as my being charged with murder."[43] In August 2008 a Russian court, trying Nevzlin *in absentia*, found him guilty of ordering four murders and attempted murders.[44] Alexei Pichugin, the former head of Yukos security, was sentenced to 24 years in prison in 2006 for carrying out those murders.[45]

During Nevzlin's visit to the U.S., he met with (predominantly Jewish) members of Congress and with hedge fund operator Michael Steinhardt, a key financial supporter of the Democratic Leadership Council (DLC). The "centrist" DLC was founded after a "leftist" campaign dominated by organized labor ensured Minnesota Senator Walter Mondale's loss to Ronald Reagan in the 1984 presidential election. The DLC was led by Senator Joe Lieberman when he commenced his failed 2000 campaign for vice president with presidential candidate Al Gore, Jr. Eight years earlier, Bill Clinton resigned as DLC chairman to begin his successful Clinton-Gore presidential campaign. As Steinhardt boasted in a March 2006 televised interview: "I was president of the DLC when we brought Bill Clinton to office."[46]

Michael Steinhardts's father, Sol "Red" Steinhardt, was a prominent jewel fence for New York's crime syndicate during the 1930s. He was particularly close to Arnold Rothstein,[47] the acknowledged head of organized crime and an inspiration to Meyer Lansky who emerged as chairman of the National Crime Syndicate and its enforcement affiliate, Murder, Inc., following the 1929 crime conclave in Atlantic City. As a hedge fund operator, Michael Steinhardt paid 75% of the $70 million in civil fines required to settle a Securities and Exchange Commission/Department of Justice case in the early 1990s when he sought to corner the market in short-term Treasury notes. Steinhardt was estimated to have made $600 million on his Treasury positions.[48]

In 2000, Steinhardt and Charles R. Bronfman founded Taglit-Birthright Israel to pay for young Diaspora Jews to travel to Israel to discover their Zionism.[49] As of May 2008, 165,000 participants from 53 countries had traveled to Israel under a program that the Israeli government sponsors by covering a third of the costs.[50] In 2007, casino mogul Sheldon Adelson donated $30 million. He gave $36 million more in 2008.[51] In 2007, he also contributed funds for a lavish new office building in Washington, D.C. for AIPAC.[52]

Influence, Submission and Control

Could Vladimir Putin be seeking to protect the Russian people from any further deprivations at the hands of this oligarchy? Does he aim to correct a nationwide control fraud inflicted on Russia by a transnational criminal syndicate?[53]

Of particular concern to a fledgling democracy should be efforts by this predominantly Ashkenazi network to purchase—as it did in 1996—the presidency of Russia (or any nation) with a combination of stolen public assets and control of the public's airwaves. Russia's leadership can take little comfort in the fact that a similar challenge faces America, a mature democracy.

In response to Russia's systemic criminality, John McCain charged that the widely popular Russian president was seeking to "create an empire of influence and submission, if not outright control." Future research will identify who persuaded the candidate to issue a series of similar statements. Without more facts, it is impossible to know whether he is complicit, incompetent or naïve—or whether someone in his office routinely releases such statements in his name.

At the annual Munich Security Conference in February 2007, President Putin portrayed as "very dangerous" the current U.S. approach to global relations. Based on Putin's experience with this syndicate's operations in Russia, it is reasonable to conclude that he was referring to the influence of an unelected (Ashkenazi) government operating with impunity inside the U.S. government—as *the people in between.*

> *Fields within fields.* McCain campaign manager Rick Davis lobbied for Imagesat, an Israeli firm that sells satellite imagery. He also consulted to Pegasus Capital Advisors, a private investment firm with a financial stake in Imagesat. Pegasus offered Davis and his partner in the Davis Manafort firm a chance to participate in one of its investments. In November 2005, Pegasus acquired a stake in Traxys, a transnational company that trades in industrial metals, a business where Oleg Deripaska made his initial fortune by stripping assets from state-owned enterprises and selling them abroad.[54] Aluminum was an early target.

The criminal network identified in this account typically influences both sides in political contests. Davis Manfort worked in Ukraine for Rinat Akhmetov, the richest man in Ukraine and the principal financial backer of Viktor Yanukovych, the Moscow-backed candidate for the Ukraine presidency. In 1996, Davis served as deputy campaign manager for Republican Bob Dole. Both Dole and Democrat Bill Clinton used Carl Lindner-provided aircraft during their 1996 presidential campaigns.

A consultant to Michael Bloomberg's New York mayoral campaign, Davis joins others in the McCain campaign who lobbied for telecommunications companies, including Verizon, Comsat and SBC Communications—firms with a direct interest in matters before the Senate Commerce Committee, chaired by McCain in 2001 and again from 2003 to 2005.

Two initial exceptions to the McCain campaign's conflict-of-interest guidelines benefited Davis' firm. The first allowed lobbying not in excess of a specified threshold. The second allowed lobbying overseas on behalf of foreign firms and politicians.[55] The campaign's ethics guidelines, crafted by Davis, were tightened only *after* McCain secured the nomination.[56]

Davis also draws a salary as president of the Reform Institute, a group McCain helped found to reduce "the influence of special interests" in politics and government. In marketing his lobbying services both domestically and abroad, Davis described himself as someone who has "operated at the highest level of decision and deal making." As senior campaign manager, he controlled the use of McCain's campaign bus, the Straight Talk Express. In early July 2008, Davis' responsibilities as campaign manager were reduced.[57]

Trans-generational Orchestration

Revenues from Russia's financially pillaged enterprises were recycled into corrupt privatization auctions only after rampant inflation (2,500% in 1992 alone) destroyed the savings of ordinary Russians, leaving only syndicate operatives with the funds to bid. "Shock therapy" fiscal discipline (sharp cutbacks in social spending) further ensured that only those Russians complicit in this nationwide fraud could afford to participate in purchasing the wealth of their nation.[58]

Anatoly Chubais, the Ashkenazi politician with the most influence over privatization, is widely considered the most hated man in Russia. He earned it. He cites as evidence of the success of privatization the fact that "there was no civil war." He means it. "This is the true value of our reforms," Chubais boasts, "not the fact that oligarchs are worth billions today. I couldn't care less about that."[59]

As a key architect of Yeltsin's 1996 re-election campaign, Chubais concedes that Yeltsin did not understand his own administration's privatization methods ("not the economic intricacies but certainly the political and economic big picture"). Chubais justifies his role in the massive frauds that created Russia's oligarchs by pointing to the robber baron era of American capitalism, arguing "Russia is already in the process of liberating itself from the same thing."[60]

Chubais' assessment fails to distinguish between America's early-stage capitalists—who created great wealth—and Russia's 20th century oligarchs—who defrauded their fellow citizens of the nation's great wealth, plunging the most vulnerable into abject poverty. With few exceptions, those enriched by Chubais built nothing new. Oftentimes the oligarchs forced their employees to sell them the few shares they had gained in the privatization process.[61] More than two-thirds of the top 100 richest Russians claim "self-made" fortunes from their ownership of natural resources and raw material firms that belonged to the Russian people.[62]

The mindset voiced by Chubais may be influenced by Vladimir Potanin, his neighbor in the Russian countryside. As a Kremlin insider, Potanin got an early start in this massive fraud when he created a foreign trading company to export state-owned natural resources and raw materials. His outsized profits capitalized a Yeltsin-favored bank where state enterprises and municipalities kept their cash (Potanin served as Yeltsin's first deputy prime minister for seven months). His bank (Oneximbank) was both an originator and a beneficiary of the 1995 loans-for-shares scheme. As one of the Big Seven, he was also a major force in Yeltsin's reelection in 1996.

Through Oneximbank, Potanin acquired more than 20 firms.[63] With a 2008 net worth of $19.3 billion, he ranks 25th among the world's billionaires.

In defending the indefensible, Chubais acknowledges University of Chicago economist Milton Friedman as both inspiration and guide for an ostensibly "legal" process that, by 2003, led to a handful of oligarchs controlling 85% of Russia's leading private companies.[64] Confirming that this crime is poised to continue, Thomas Mirow, the newly appointed president of the European Bank for Reconstruction and Development, announced in July 2008 the "encouraging signs" that Chubais could play an influential role in negotiating a new accord between Russia and the European Union.[65]

To orchestrate a fraud of such magnitude in plain sight required the appearance of good faith and legality along with some semblance of intellectual authority. Each of those components was furthered by U.S. Treasury Under Secretary Lawrence Summers who in the mid-1990s had just completed two years as chief economist at the World Bank. Backed by the perceived authority of those institutions, Summers dispatched to Russia a handpicked advisory team from Harvard University that lent this larceny the appearance of good faith legality and academic legitimacy.

Associating this systemic criminality with Harvard's historic credibility eased the enactment of legislation required to perpetrate fraud under the authority of law. The Harvard team of predominantly Ashkenazi advisors crafted much of the legislation (at the request of Chubais) that enabled the oligarchization to proceed "lawfully," in plain view and with impunity. With Yeltsin's re-election, the Ashkenazi-ation of Russia gained the legal protections allowed private property in post-Soviet Russia even as the perpetrators moved much of their ill-gained wealth out of the country.

Under Cover of Democracy

An acclaimed economist, Summers resigned in 2006 as president of Harvard. When pressed at a February 2006 faculty meeting for his opinion of scandals surrounding Harvard's advisory team to Russia, Summers claimed he did not know the facts. That lie sealed his fate with a dismayed faculty, ending the shortest term served by a Harvard president in 144 years.[66]

While syndicate operatives were stripping assets from the Russian economy and impoverishing the Russian people, Yukos CEO Mikhail Khodorkovsky was modeling his Open Russia foundation after Open Society activities funded by George Soros in Eastern and Central Europe. Research suggests those activities provide Soros a handy means for gathering in-country intelligence while recycling his hedge fund profits back into his "pro-democracy" operations.[67] Open Society operations also offered this Hungarian-American investor a plausible reason to insist on an early presence in post-communist economies—in plain view, with protection of the authority of law and under cover of democratic principles. As in the U.S., the openness of democratic societies became the means by which duplicity could operate with impunity in plain view.

At the February 2007 Munich Security Conference, President Putin opposed the deployment in Russia of foreign organizations as channels for funding by foreign governments. "This is not about democracy," he argued. "This is about one country (he did not specify which) influencing another" while the inflow of funds is "hidden from our society." As Russia screened pro-democracy organizations for ulterior motives, Putin was portrayed as "anti-democratic."

The Orange Revolution

John McCain describes himself as a strong supporter of Ukrainian Viktor Yuschenko whose "Orange Revolution" presidential campaign of November 2004 gained worldwide media coverage as Kiev became a rallying point for pro-democracy groups. Such groups are now under attack as officials fear they incite crises to catalyze regime change.

Soros-funded Open Society efforts joined forces in Ukraine with the National Democratic Institute (NDI), a government funded U.S. operation chaired by Madeleine Albright, former Clinton administration Secretary of State.[68] Also active in the Ukraine was NDI's Republican counterpart, the International Republican Institute—chaired since 1993 by John McCain.[69] Both organizations are taxpayer-financed through a neoconservative-favored project known as the National Endowment for Democracy. The Endowment's activities are coordinated with the State Department's Agency for International Development.

The role played by those organizations in Ukraine's presidential election helps explain why nations are reasserting their sovereignty to resist this form of foreign intervention. Often that resistance involves charges of outside interference by the U.S. to incite riots and work stoppages and encourage coups d'etats.[70] A guilt-by-association *modus operandi* utilized in this election suggests a pro-Israeli rather than a pro-democracy agenda, and points to a nontransparent motive.

In a high-profile election in this widely watched venue, dioxin poisoning disfigured the face of Yushchenko, Ukraine's pro-democracy presidential candidate. Widely published before-and-after photos of the handsome Orange Revolution candidate made Viktor Yanukovych, the Moscow-backed opposition, appear "ugly" by comparison—and guilty by association.

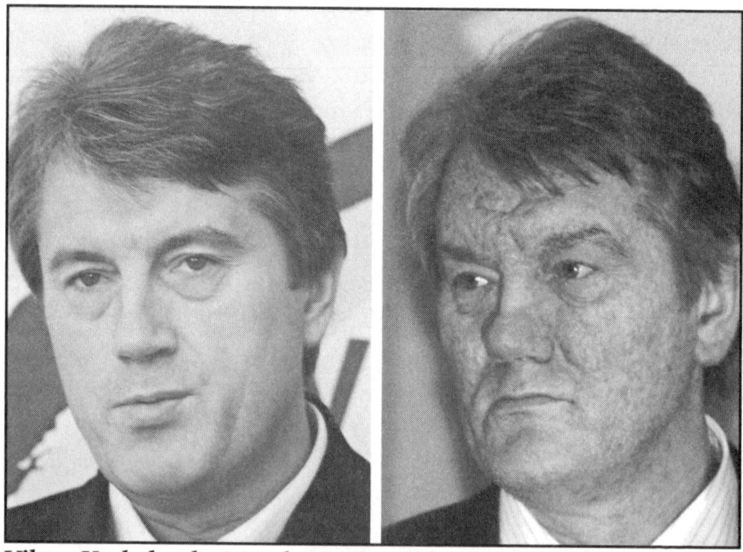

Viktor Yushchenko March 28, 2002, left, and Dec. 6, 2004, right. (AP Photo/Viktor Pobedinsky/Efrem Lukatsky)

With sustained media coverage, that poison-induced power of association evoked the dark ghosts of Russia's Stalinist past. News reports routinely referenced a 1978 incident when a ricin-poisoned pellet was fired from a pneumatic umbrella into the leg of Bulgarian dissident Georgi Markov on London's Waterloo Bridge.[71] Markov died four days later. As news reports repeatedly referenced the Markov incident, the Moscow-backed candidate was discredited.

The poisoning of a popular presidential candidate also fueled the plausibility of a resurgence of a Cold War conflict of opposites — pro-democracy vs. pro-Moscow. In that media-stoked morality play, the disfigured Yushchenko was cast as the freedom-seeking hero victimized by Moscow's Evil Empire, and featured a steady stream of references to Putin's suspect past as a colonel in the Soviet-era KGB.

Specialists in exotic poisons know that dioxin is generally not deadly. Its defining property is its capacity to create disfiguring cysts on the upper torso. The evidence suggests that the poisoning worked its intended effect on the candidate, on the election and on politics in the region. After his election victory Yushchenko soon proved that he was both corrupt and incompetent. By September 2005 he had sacked his entire coalition government when its own members accused one another of corruption and cronyism. He acknowledged that ordinary Ukrainians had come to see the Orange Revolution as a means of transferring wealth from an old to a new elite.[72]

Ukraine has since endured a series of unstable power-sharing arrangements. With Yushchenko's approval, Nathaniel Rothschild, in line to become the fifth Baron Rothschild, is now prospecting for oil in Ukraine.[73]

> Mikhail Fridman, a Russian Ashkenazi oligarch born in Ukraine, founded Alfa Group in the 1990s as a commodities trading firm whose shadow economy profits enabled him to capitalize Alfa Bank, one of Russia's largest, along with a conglomerate with interests in oil, telecommunications, electricity, chemicals, pharmaceuticals, cement, glass, construction and retail sales. His role in the 1995 loans-for-shares fraud enabled him to later merge TNK, an oil company he controlled, with British Petroleum to create TNK-BP, Russia's third largest oil producer.[74] In 1996, Alfa Bank also reaped large profits on government treasury bills.
>
> As one of the original Big Seven bankrollers of Yeltsin's 1996 re-election campaign, Fridman joined an elite group who then "controlled half of Russia's economy" according to

former Security Council Deputy Secretary Boris Berezovsky.[75] Though Berezovsky exaggerated, it would be accurate to say that 20 oligarchs controlled half the Russian economy. Both Berezovsky and Fridman owned a stake in ORT television, a major media outlet that backed Yeltsin's re-election. *Forbes* ranked Fridman 20th on its 2008 list of the world's billionaires with a personal net worth of $20.8 billion.[76]

With a personal wealth of between $5 and $10 billion, Victor Pinchuk is Ukraine's second richest oligarch. Married to the only daughter of Leonid Kuchma, Ukraine's former president, Pinchuk describes George Soros and Bill Clinton as his friends as he became a donor to the foundations of both. Soros called him an "enlightened capitalist" as Pinchuk acquired a $160 million London estate and financed programs in Washington at the Brookings Institution.[77]

Guilt by Association Redux

John McCain's conduct suggests he is naive about *how* unconventional warfare is waged by *the people in between*. The timing of the high profile poisoning in London of Alexander Litvinenko in November 2006 should have raised McCain's suspicions as an *ex officio* member of the Senate Intelligence Committee. Alarms should have sounded when media reports immediately sought to link the murder of a former KGB colonel (Litvinenko) to former KGB colonel Vladimir Putin—with no plausible motive for Putin to order such a murder.

Rather than kill Litvinenko quickly and quietly, did *the people in between* stage that "theater of assassination" for a strategic purpose? Why then? Could it be because President Putin was then engaged with members of the Quartet (Russia. the U.S., the European Union and the U.N.) to end the 40-year Israeli occupation of Palestine as an essential step toward stability to the Middle East? From a game theory perspective, it would have been *perfectly predictable* that Litvinenko's murder would create friction between two key players—Russia and the U.K.—and distract the leaders of both (aka entropy).

During the first week of December 2006, an analysis of this Putin-discrediting, power-of-association entropy strategy (titled "Khodorkovsky's revenge") was distributed widely, with a copy to the Russian embassy.

Who, if not the syndicate profiled in this account, had the means, motive and opportunity to murder Litvinenko in London? Two days after Khodorkovsky lieutenant Leonid Nevzlin arrived at Newark airport on Christmas Eve 2006, Russian Prosecutor General Yury Chaika issued a press release identifying Nevzlin as a murder suspect in the Litvinenko poisoning and seeking his extradition. Litvinenko met with Nevzlin in Israel just weeks before his death.[78]

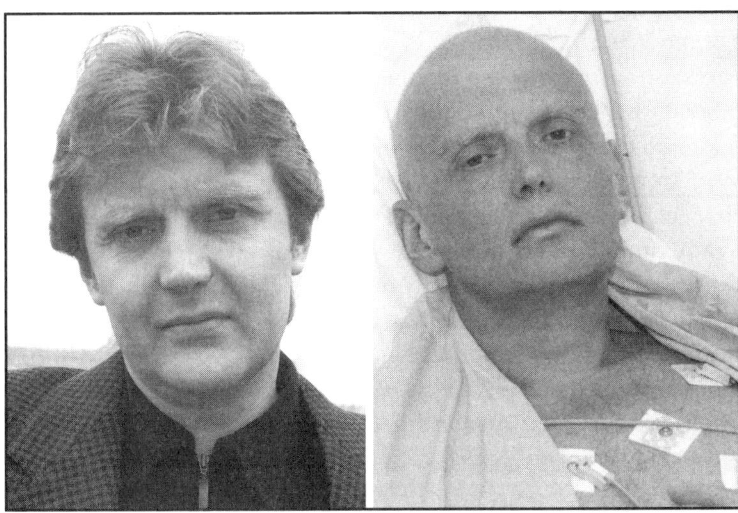

Former KGB Colonel Alexander Litvinenko, photographed at his home in London Friday, May 10, 2002. (AP Photo/Alistair Fuller). Litvinenko photographed in London hospital, November 20, 2006 (Getty Images/Natasja Weitsz).

By early January 2007, Time Warner had bought the rights to a film version of the Litvinenko murder that will be produced by Hollywood star Johnny Depp and in which he may play the lead role.[79] In mid-January 2007, Chaika protested the refusal of U.S. authorities to extradite Nevzlin, citing the principle of reciprocity between law enforcement bodies.

When Nevzlin traveled to the U.S. in July 2005, he criticized Putin in a Yukos-related Helsinki Commission briefing where he urged that Russia be expelled from the G-8.[80] Tom Lantos and John McCain championed Nevzlin's proposal in the Congress. Why would a candidate for the American presidency advocate a proposal by a Russian fugitive complicit in international organized crime and reportedly active in a Russian version of Murder, Inc.?

Throughout the Litvinenko incident, London-based oligarch Boris Berezovsky continued to plead his innocence in the murder in London of a man who had worked for him. Litvinenko also provided testimony that helped Berezovsky persuade British authorities that the godfather of the Kremlin merited political asylum. Litvinenko assured Whitehall that the Kremlin (i.e., Putin) had ordered Berezovsky's murder.[81] While Litvinenko was slowly dying, Berezovsky funded a public relations campaign to inject Putin-discrediting storylines into the global media marketplace.

Moscow wants to bring Berezovsky to trial for fraud and embezzlement. Berezovsky's hatred for Putin remains palpable as evidenced by the funds he invested in a guilt-by-association public relations campaign that sought to link Putin to the Litvinenko murder. Media outlets used the murder as an opportunity for another flurry of stories claiming that Khodorkovsky, like Litvinenko, was the victim of an abusive state.[82] From Tel Aviv, Nevzlin funded an anti-Putin public relations campaign that ran parallel with Berzovsky's campaign from London.[83]

> Was this high-profile murder with an atomic-age poison (polonium-210 is deadly in microgram amounts) meant to reinforce another mental thread: the threat of Iran's nuclear program? The choice of murder weapon is consistent with the power-of-association *modus operandi* chronicled throughout this account. Was the associative effect meant to reinforce the threat of nuclear terrorism?

Another indication of this global syndicate's hand at work in Russia is Khodorkovsky's enlisting of Henry Kissinger and Jakob Rothschild as Open Russia board members. Yukos also retained U.S. attorney

Stuart Eizenstat to market its former CEO as the embodiment of post-Soviet democracy and free enterprise modernity. Using guilt-by-association marketing, the Yukos public relations campaign compared Khodorkovsky's imprisonment with Russia's Stalinist past and portrayed the conduct of mega-thief Khodorkovsky, to use McCain's phrase, as the apex of "democracy and market capitalism."

That associative "bleed-over" sought to discredit Putin while portraying Eizenstat's client as the hapless victim of an oppressive state reverting to its Stalinist past. Like a toxic fog, hints of anti-Semitism hung ever present in the background, intimated but never clearly stated. Had that accusation been made, might an inquisitive public have realized that history's greatest heist remains largely an Ashkenazi operation?

Wielding the power of association as a media-deployed weapon, the Yukos public relations campaign portrayed Putin's KGB past as evidence of an oppressive police state intent on victimizing an innocent oil company executive. John McCain obligingly cast the Yukos chief as a "political prisoner" as though he were the innocent victim in a good versus evil morality play. While McCain rushed to the defense of Khodorkovsky and Berezovsky, Russian general Aleksandr Lebed offered an appraisal consistent with the known facts:

> Berezovsky is the apotheosis of sleaziness on the state level; this representative of a small clique in power is not satisfied with stealing—he wants everybody to see that he is stealing with impunity.[84]

Unless John McCain enjoys the support of this transnational syndicate, why would he join Tom Lantos, Joe Lieberman, Boris Berezovsky and Leonid Nevzlin in an effort to discredit Russia's leadership?

President McCain and the Godfather of the Kremlin

John McCain's support for Boris Berezovsky demands an explanation. The range of criminality in which "the Godfather of the Kremlin" engaged is a testament both to his genius and his psychopathy:

- Berezovsky first mastered the ability to strip state-owned assets (oil, timber, aluminum), avoid taxes and hide that wealth offshore—the root cause of the destruction of the ruble.

- At Avtovaz, the most mobster-ridden of any large Russian company, police identified no fewer than 65 contract murders involving Avtovaz managers and dealers in a firm where Berezovsky wielded substantial influence.[85]
- His control fraud at Aeroflot offers a case study in how an oligarch could loot a company without owning it by directing 80% of the airlines' global revenues to foreign accounts that he controlled.[86]
- His grasp of labor racketeering was on display when he financed a miners' strike and bragged about it as he profited from the conflict.
- His corruption of Russian media was legendary, particularly in rigging Yeltsin's re-election with the help of media oligarch Vladimir Gusinsky.
- After he and Gusinsky raised Boris Yeltsin from 10% approval to a 1996 election victory, Yeltsin appointed him deputy secretary of the Security Council.
- He then financed Chechen organized crime by arranging ransom payments for kidnappers while simultaneously discrediting (and endangering) the entire Chechen people.
- When Chechen President Aslan Maskhadov announced that Berezovsky was financing organized crime, one month later, in December 1997, the severed heads of four kidnapped British telecom workers were found lined up on the side of a highway in Grozny.[87]

A master of the technique of waging war through *the people in between*, Berezovsky was notorious for appointing agents of the oligarchs to government staffs. Following his appointment to the Security Council, *Izvestia* revealed that Berezovsky was both Israeli and Russian. After repeated denials, he was forced to admit that he held an Israeli passport, declaring, "Any Jew in Russia has a double citizenship"—a comment that outraged Russian Jews loyal to Russia.

Berezovsky then complained that he was the victim of "a rising tide of anti-Semitism." If not for that claim (and his stolen fortune), why would the British grant him asylum? Why would a candidate for the U.S. presidency support a gangster whose behavior turned democracy into a profanity for ordinary Russians? Berezovsky's blatant criminality played a key role in discrediting both markets and democracy. Russians now speak of privatization as "grab-it-ization" (*prikhvatizatsiya*) and refer to democracy as "shitocracy" (*dermokratizatsiya*).[88]

Americans should be concerned when a presidential candidate lends his support to key figures in transnational organized crime. The Russian experience confirmed that this global syndicate is masterful at committing nationwide frauds by corrupting a nation's lawful authority, *including the office of the president*—as with "asset" Boris Yeltsin, a notorious alcoholic.

With the pro-Israeli bias of mainstream media, the political environment—both in the U.S. and abroad—is ripe for frauds on an unprecedented scale. As in Russia, those frauds include a presidential election in which the public's airwaves can be deployed to induce Americans to *believe* that a candidate would put America's interests first—despite what the confirmed facts suggest.

Media and Nonlinear Criminality. In the course of a July 27, 2008 interview with CNN's Wolf Blitzer, presidential candidate John McCain agreed to answer several call-in questions. Without identifying the caller, Blitzer asked, "If you were president, would you move the U.S. embassy from Tel Aviv to Jerusalem?" McCain immediately answered "Yes." Blitzer then clarified his answer by asking, "Like, as soon as you were inaugurated, right away, you would order the State Department to do that?" McCain responded, "I've been committed to that proposition for years." The next morning Prime Minister Ehud Olmert announced it was unlikely Israel and the Palestinians would reach a peace accord by the end of 2008, considering the volatile issue of Jerusalem.[89]

Chapter 6

Money, Democracy and the Great Divide

The issue of economics is not something I have understood as well as I should. I've got Greenspan's book.

—John McCain[1]

Like many others, John McCain fails to grasp the harm done in the name of "economics." Nor does he comprehend what other nations have endured at the hands of our "Chicago" model of economics. A lack of understanding by ordinary citizens is reasonable. That failure in a presidential candidate is frightening.

This chapter shows why—with the authority granted "economics" during the second half of the 20th century—Americans experienced record-breaking levels of inequality:

- From 2003 to 2005 the *increase* in combined income for the top 1% of Americans exceeded by 37% the *total* income of the poorest 20%.[2]
  - Incomes for the top 1% grew an average $465,700 (42.6%) each.
  - Incomes for the bottom 20% grew an average $200 (1.3%).

- By 2005 Americans claiming more than $1 million in annual income (less than one quarter of 1% of U.S. taxpayers) claimed 47% of total annual income gains.[3]
- By 2006 the top 1% of U.S. families pocketed the largest share of national income since 1929.
    - Adjusted for inflation, from 2002 to 2006, incomes of the bottom 99% grew at less than 1% annually.[4]

A review of the past quarter-century shows *how* the current brand of "economics" was guaranteed to make the rich richer. Professing his *bona fides* as a "true conservative," John McCain proposes another Reagan presidency featuring "supply-side" economics. Consistent with game theory, the financial results—then, now and in the future—are *perfectly predictable*, as we shall see.

The *Criminal State* series chronicles the organized crime origins of that earlier supply-side presidency. A Californian branded a maverick Republican, Reagan succeeded Arizona maverick Barry Goldwater as "the conscience of conservatism." As the successor to Goldwater's Senate seat, the maverick McCain promises a replay of Reagan's maverick economics.

Deficit-Catalyzed Cash Flow

With Reagan's election in 1980, belief in *supply side* economics displaced the belief in *demand side* economics that had guided policymaking since the 1930s. That shift was catalyzed a half-century later by advocacy featured in *The Wall Street Journal*,[5] America's premier financial news daily.[6] In the 1930s, Washington turned to deficit spending to stimulate consumer spending *(demand)* in a Depression-era economy. Those borrowed funds enabled Roosevelt's New Deal to pay people for work on public works projects. It was not the New Deal, however, but warfare that brought an end to joblessness.

World War II drew on deficit financing to defeat Nazi-era fascism as the U.S. deployed its *full faith and credit* to pay people to wage war. In effect, Americans extended themselves credit to address that threat to American values. By war's end, our credit was the world's best and our bonds were the most secure—because the U.S. was by then home to half the world's post-war productive capacity.

Washington again turned to deficit spending in 1981. This time, however, the nation's credit was deployed to stimulate not consumer spending (demand) but investment spending (supply). *Stagflation* was headline news along with the *misery index* measuring the combined agony of inflation and unemployment. When Jimmy Carter lost the presidency in 1980, federal debt totaled $900 billion. Reagan's supply-side "economics" was enacted in 1981 at a projected fiscal cost of $872 billion over five years.[7] Though portions were later pared back, he proved that a maverick "true conservative" could double the national debt with just one tax bill—provided he *believed* in the model.

Left unmentioned was *how* those supply-side deficits were certain to enrich the few while indebting the many. To grasp *how* requires a look at how tax policy affects finance, and how today's globally dominant "closed system of finance" delivers *perfectly predictable* results—as any financially savvy game theorist could foresee.

"Free Cash Flow"

"Reaganomics" allowed more rapid tax write-offs for the cost of investments. When an office building can be written off in 15 years instead of 45, for example, more buildings are built. By allowing more write-offs, more cash became available to invest in the nation's supply of office buildings. A former S&L official likened those real estate incentives to "dropping napalm on a forest fire."[8] To afford those supply-side incentives, the Reagan treasury pledged *our* full faith and credit to cover the shortfall in tax revenues.

More cash, of course, also meant more capacity for companies to repay debt. As that public subsidy passed through private hands, the leveraged buyout (LBO) began its steady rise as financiers applied those deficit-financed funds to purchase companies with borrowed money ("leverage"). Twenty-five years later, LBO firms in the U.S. raised $254 billion in a single year (2006). Private equity funds in Europe raised another $101 billion.

With companies able to afford more debt, a debt-free company came to signify inattention to how financial leverage could boost shareholder returns. Finance-ability became the new performance norm and "free cash flow" the new collateral for securing and repaying record-level debt. More cash made LBOs more feasible as the U.S. Treasury pledged *our* national credit capacity (our "full faith and credit") to pay for Reagan's maverick economics. In effect, *we* got the mortgage (the deficits) while *they* got the house. The deficits became ours while the wealth financed with our deficits became *theirs*—as the already wealthy grew rapidly more so, as did financial sophisticates (*the people in between*).[9]

Reagan's "maverick" supply-side era also saw the rise of Wall Street campaign contributors determined to see more public subsidies for private-sector finance. That demand was met with a deficit-financed surge in defense spending, a rewrite of rules governing the thrift industry, and tax cuts for those few who pocketed the bulk of this debt-financed wealth. Those changes also catalyzed the first nationwide financial fraud, the S&L crisis, in which Alan Greenspan played a key role. [See Chapter 3.]

Thus too the dramatic change in composition of the *Forbes 400,* as 100 of America's richest now trace their wealth to financial services—up from 30 when the list was first compiled in 1982 at the outset of the supply-side era. With public sector deficits as the lubricant, private sector debt could run amok. With the availability of deficit-financed "free" cash flow, financial markets sent executives a clear message: either load up your company with debt or someone else will. As debt became the new imperative, financial leverage became addictive, as did government deficits.

The pace of LBOs quickened as it became apparent this free cash could be used not just to expand the *supply* of new investments, but also to fund buyouts of existing investments.* In neither case was there any concern that the benefits were *certain* to flow largely to a few. So long as the firm was creditworthy, debt itself was indifferent whether it was used to finance new assets or transfers of old assets. Yet, as we shall see in the "closed system" analysis (below), the rich-get-richer result was foreseeable in either case.

That deficit-financed cash flow also helped afford the high yield interest rates paid on corporate bonds used to finance LBOs. Beverly Hills bond broker Michael Milken emerged as the "junk bond king" when, five years after supply-side economics took effect, his bond commissions for 1987 alone totaled $550 million.

Two decades later, loan brokers adapted the Milken model to bundle subprime mortgages ("junk loans") for sale as high yield

* *The author was then counsel to the U.S. Senate Committee on Finance (1980-1987).*

securities—and to bundle auto loans, student loans and credit card loans into collateralized debt obligations (CDOs). Batches of CDOs, in turn, were bundled for sale as the latest debt-fueled financial innovation. Applying "Chicago" math, each transaction was tallied as a sign of more "economic" growth as "financial creativity" became the legacy of the supply-side era.

As with junk bonds, commissions on junk loans were generous. The end results were of no concern to those originating the loans or repackaging them for sale as high yield securities. "Easy credit" (aka easy debt) lured debtors to assume obligations they often could not afford. Investors, in turn, were attracted by the high yield interest. Pension plans offered a reliable market for junk loan securities, enticed by Triple-A ratings that led pension fund managers to *believe* the financial risk was low.[10]

Local Gains, Globalized Losses

By keeping interest rates low for a lengthy period (2002-2006), Fed Chairman Alan Greenspan drove up home equity values—providing collateral against which homeowners could borrow. The resultiing household version of deficit spending made it *appear* that "economics" were booming. As a greater *supply* of home equity loans stimulated more consumer *demand*, leveraged-up firms could apply consumers' cash to retire their junk bonds and pay down their LBO debt, further enriching the well-to-do and the financially sophisticated (*the people in between*).

In the 18th century, the Dutch believed that money-lending schemes (debt) could replace declining industries as an engine of growth. The U.S. drifted in the same debt-disabled direction as Great Britain when the British Empire became guilty of imperial overreach.[11] As London emerged as a global financial center, the "economics" of the U.K. grew dependent on servicing the appetites of a globalized carriage trade. The British now find themselves held captive to the capital market whims of a worldwide financial elite, reduced to offering amnesty to Ashkenazi mobsters such as Boris Berezovsky and coddling Russian mega-thieves such as Roman Abramovich.

Though Alan Greenspan was told that deception was increasing in mortgage markets and unscrupulous practices were spreading, he placed his faith in "financial innovation" and "the ownership society."

As he explained in his memoirs, "I believed then, as now, that the benefits of broadened home ownership are worth the risk." But as a financial sophisticate—and one of *the people in between*—the Federal Reserve Chairman knew better.

In 1998, Greenspan oversaw the Fed-coordinated rescue of Long Term Credit Management (LTCM). With $4.7 billion in equity and $124.5 billion in borrowed funds, LTCM leveraged its operations into investments in financial derivatives totaling $1.25 trillion.[12] When LTCM's position turned sour, triggered by a default on Russian government bonds, the New York Fed, fearful that a misstep might destabilize global financial markets, brokered a bailout by the major banks and investment banks. When the smoke cleared around this debt-dependent scheme, LTCM's investors still realized a 17% return.

A decade later, the 2007-2008 subprime mortgage meltdown reignited similar fears of systemic disorder as the credit crisis spread worldwide, facilitated by a "Chicago" consensus that ensured the globalization of debt-induced contagions. Those who recall the S&L crisis view this latest debt-fueled "pump-and-dump" as another opportunity to buy distressed properties at knockdown prices. As the winners and losers were sorted out, two clear winners emerged: the top executives of Lehman Brothers and Goldman Sachs.

Lehman, the nation's largest underwriter of mortgage-backed securities, counterbalanced its high-risk holdings with hedging strategies. Likewise Goldman Sachs, whose staff divided a $20 billion year-end bonus pool in December 2007, after the firm announced it made more from hedging against subprime losses than it had lost on its subprime investments. Goldman's CEO was paid $67.9 million for 2007; Lehman chairman and CEO Richard Fuld received a $35 million bonus.

As brokers, Lehman Brothers and Goldman Sachs profited by selling junk loans to others. As investment bankers, they protected the value of their own holdings with what critics called the "Houdini hedge" against potential losses. Their success came because, as financial sophisticates, they positioned themselves to profit off the debt-induced travails of others, a common tactic deployed by *the people in between.*[13]

After personally pocketing more than $40 million for 2007, Lehman's Fuld announced for the first quarter of 2008 a $2.8 billion loss for the publicly traded firm.[14] By August 2008, the firm had lost 76% of its value.[15] In other words, the gains were privatized (or "piratized") while the losses were born by the public, largely by Baby Boomer retirement plans as the dominant holder of publicly traded securities. And by taxpayers because tax subsidies for retirement plans now exceed $150 billion per year.[16]

Our Debt, Their Equity

Throughout the debt-entranced epoch since the maverick "economics" of the first Reagan administration, more firms became the target of LBOs, fueling more cutbacks in jobs, pensions and health care. Expenses were further reduced by moving production offshore. Those savings helped repay LBO debt while retaining access to the U.S. economy for its financial features:

- Purchasing power (*demand*)—to repay debt,
- Capital markets (a *supply* of funds)—to buy junk bonds, and
- Fiscal subsidies—to repay debt and retire junk bonds.

Catalyzed by supply-side economics, wealth concentrated at a record pace as the U.S. borrowed abroad to afford tax subsidies for financial sophisticates at home. In 1982, $91 million was required for inclusion on the first annual *Forbes 400* list of richest Americans. Average wealth was then $200 million on a list featuring 13 billionaires. In 1982, supply-side "economics" leveraged America's credit capacity (and its tax base) on behalf of a handful of Americans who, *predictably,* became far, far richer.

By 1986, the average wealth of those on the *Forbes 400* topped $500 million. From 1983 to 1998, 53% of capital market gains flowed to the top 1% of American households. By 2000, $725 million was required for inclusion on a *Forbes* list that by then featured 274 billionaires, with an average wealth of $1.2 billion.

As leveraged buyout debt was repaid, the lower costs required to service that debt drove competitors to lower their costs, too, by further reducing benefits and shifting production offshore. Those trends increased the pressure for freer trade and fewer barriers to international financial flows. It was during this period that Alan

Greenspan emerged to play his enabling role in the S&L crisis prior to being named by Reagan to chair the Federal Reserve Board in 1987.[17] Any competent game theorist (and any competent economist) could foresee the results of loading private sector leverage (debt) on top of public sector leverage (deficits).[18]

To guard against another "true conservative" defrauding the nation, a financially savvy public must grasp the foreseeable impact of again pledging the public's credit to finance private assets. Reagan's maverick "economics" guaranteed results that were *perfectly predictable* to those sophisticated in finance and "economics" (i.e., *the people in between*). The next several pages explain *how* this massive fraud proceeded in plain view.

Closed System Finance

To grasp *how* financial exclusion is *guaranteed* to repeat generation after generation (and *why* "the rich get richer"), it helps to visualize *how* finance operates as a "closed system."[19] As consensus "economics" expanded to global scale, this closed system ensured that oligarchies would become the dominant feature worldwide.[20]

By injecting deficit-financed funds into this closed system, supply-side policies were certain to *hasten the pace* at which wealth and income concentrated. That trend was catalyzed with the help of deficits that saw securitized federal debt ("treasuries") expand from $900 billion in 1980 to a projected $10,000 billion by early 2009.

Sources of Funds—Today's Closed System of Finance

HOW CONSENSUS FINANCE CREATES OLIGARCHIES

INTERNAL FUNDS

- RETAINED EARNINGS AND PROFITS—Reinvested for current owners
- DEPRECIATION RESERVES—Reinvested for current owners

EXTERNAL FUNDS

- DEBT—Repaid on behalf of current owners
- EQUITY—Most affordable by current owners

This chart shows *how* the "operating system" of private sector finance pre-determines ownership patterns—regardless to what use finance is *applied*. This closed system operates in plain sight yet invisibly—except to *the people in between* knowledgeable about finance. This chart also explains why those who specialize in financial services now dominate the *Forbes 400*. This section explains *what* financial sophisticates understand that enabled them to grow rich as the nation sank deeper into debt.

As a general rule, internal funds account for 75% of all monies raised each year. Retained earnings and profits, of course, are reinvested for current owners. Likewise for depreciation reserves. Depreciation protects private property by allowing owners to recover the cost of their income-producing assets (buildings, equipment, machinery, etc.) before paying tax on the income those assets produce.

Tax deductions ("write-offs") for depreciation typically account for 90% of internal funds, or two-thirds of all funds (90% of 75% = 67%). Prior to the supply-side era, the write-offs allowed each year matched the useful life of an asset: the cost of a depreciating asset could be recovered as it wore out or became obsolete. Supply-side economics increased the amount—and hastened the pace—of those deductions.

Stagflation during the Carter era provided the rationale to shift depreciation from the *physical* to the *financial* when property owners testified that inflation had eroded the value of funds set aside to recover the cost of their property. In response, supply-siders shifted depreciation from *useful life* to *cost recovery*, and then shortened the time over which write-offs could be claimed though an accelerated cost recovery system (known as "ACRS").

As confirmed by the "closed system" dynamics, deficits incurred to enhance depreciation were *certain* to most benefit those who were already most benefitted by this system. Financial sophisticates understood that. Why did lawmakers fail to anticipate such foreseeable results?[21] Why would a presidential candidate prescribe another dose of this rich-get-richer medicine?

Any policy that fuels this closed system has the same effect. Whether taxes on profits are raised or lowered, the rich-get-richer dynamics remain unchanged. Likewise for depreciation: large or small, fast or slow, the wealth-concentrating effect remains unchanged. Similarly, interest rates on debt can be high or low—the impact on ownership patterns is identical. The only difference is the pace at which ownership concentrates. Supply-side economics quickened the pace.

Lastly, not since the days of J.P. Morgan (1837-1913), have sales of new equities (newly issued shares) accounted for more than 4% of total funds raised in any year. Those few funds are raised largely by selling shares to those who can best afford them—those already within the closed system. Plus a portion of the proceeds from any sale of new equities is paid to *the people in between* who handle share offerings.[22]

Globalizing a Perfectly Predictable Disaster

After the Fall of the Wall in 1989, this *closed system* expanded rapidly to global scale. As soon as state-owned enterprises were transformed from public to private ownership, the "closed system of finance" began to operate. The results ensured that *future* ownership would be limited largely to those few owners created by the privatization process.

As financial sophisticates, *the people in between* understood that those *initial* owners (such as the Russian oligarchs) would remain the dominant owners *in perpetuity*. With the shift to private property, depreciation (a private property concept) protected the owners' property as well as their income by allowing their income-producing property to be replaced from pre-tax income. Whether financing new assets or acquiring preexisting assets, the oligarchs' wealth is now funded within the same *closed system*—as Harvard's advisers surely understood.

Once Russia's "piratization" fraud was complete, its predominantly Ashkenazi oligarchs could claim the protection of post-Soviet law as public assets attained by fraud assumed the *appearance* of private property. As owners of ostensibly *private* property, the oligarchs immediately gained access to the self-perpetuating closed system of finance. That system's well known capacity for *self-financing* also ensured that their income-producing assets could *pay for themselves*—from the income they produce.

Post-piratization, the oligarchs no longer needed to resort to fraud, they could rely on the closed system of finance and the laws protecting private property. In time, their wealth could even be portrayed as "self made" as public relations campaigns transformed their social status from larcenous to "legitimate" as their sophisticated thievery faded from memory displaced by a *belief* that their vast wealth was due to their brilliance as savvy businessmen.

When Ronald Reagan won his first term as president in November 1980, Republicans also won enough seats in the Senate to become the majority and thereby control the legislative agenda. In January 1981, Bob Dole of Kansas took over chairmanship of the Finance Committee from Russell Long of Louisiana. Dole soon commenced hearings on Reagan's supply-side prescription. The House of Representatives approved a companion bill written in the Committee on Ways and Means chaired by Dan Rostenkowski of Chicago. Within the year, Reagan's maverick "economics" became the law of the land.

Systems' theorists coined an acronym (POSIWID) to separate beguiling beliefs from real-world facts. Rather than being seduced by what a system is intended to do, they focus on what it, in fact, does. Both privatization and supply-side "economics" can be usefully evaluated from a POSIWID perspective: the purpose of a system is what it does.

The perilous role of belief in "economics" is evidenced by the fact that, after the collapse of the Soviet Union, the World Bank by the mid-1990s was advising privatization programs in 95 countries. As the facts of Marxist-era "economics" became apparent, nations sought relief from an earlier misplaced belief. In response, their new belief—in "Chicago" economics—typically led those nations recovering from Marxist economics to embrace a "consensus economics"—at the World Bank's insistence—that was certain to create oligarchies.

Market Theory versus Financial Reality

Regardless of the label put on "economics," broad-based purchasing power (*demand*) remains essential for healthy markets, just as broad-based ownership remains indispensable for healthy democracies.[23] By embracing a *closed system* of finance *certain* to concentrate both wealth and income, democracies are endangered and markets undermined. That's *how* the "Washington" consensus—with its roots in "Chicago" economics—put the health of communities worldwide at risk even as people sought to recover from the perils of state ownership that accompanied their belief in an earlier version of "economics."

It is simply not credible to suggest that financial sophisticates failed to grasp the results certain to accompany these *closed system* dynamics. Nor is it plausible to propose that banks and investment banks failed to comprehend the foreseeable impact of supply-side economics. For example, Reagan Treasury Secretary Don Regan was chief executive of Merrill Lynch before he led the advocacy team for Reaganomics.

As this *closed system* became the global norm behind a façade of privatization, LBOs expanded in size and geographic reach, and oligarchs emerged worldwide. By charging a 2% management fee and pocketing 20% of any increase in value, private equity and hedge fund managers, along with bank operatives (such as Citigroup CEO Sanford Weill), joined the ranks of the super-rich. The closest analogy to this financial phenomenon is the casino skim.[24]

The foreseeable trends now expanding rapidly to global scale include:

- As referenced earlier, the wealth of the *Forbes 400* richest Americans grew by $290 billion in 2006 alone, for a combined wealth of $1.54 trillion in 2007.
- By 2008 the minimum personal wealth for inclusion on the *Forbes* list was $1.3 billion, up form $91 million in 1982.
- The average CEO of a large U.S. company was paid $10.8 million in 2006[25]—364 times the pay of one of their employees, or as much pay each day as an employee takes home in a year.[26]

The merger of finance and politics continues to gain momentum. In April 2008, Kohlberg Kravis Roberts & Co. (KKR), a private equity firm, announced that Ken Mehlman, former chairman of the Republican National Committee, had become head of global public affairs, a new position for a firm that has completed more than $400 billion in LBOs.[27] Manager of G.W. Bush's 2004 re-election campaign, Mehlman now serves as one of John McCain's top fundraisers in the financial sector.[28]

Only as this account was nearing completion did it become clear what agenda the private equity firms meant to pursue through Mehlman's political connections. In this latest pump-and-dump, the major firms are prepared to exploit the desperation of ailing banks and concerned regulators by investing huge amounts in the nation's largest banks. Before doing so, however, they want legislative and regulatory exemptions from rules designed to prevent conflicts of interest and the abuses known to accompany such concentrations of economic power.[29]

As record-breaking public-sector debt was incurred to fund record-breaking accumulations of private-sector wealth, a crisis in infrastructure emerged nationwide as roads, bridges, schools, water treatment and such suffered from financial neglect. With the American Society of Civil Engineers estimating $1.6 trillion needed over the next five years, KKR, Lehman Brothers and other top-tier private equity firms are prepared to profit from the crisis.[30]

As the rich grew vastly richer and *the people in between* skimmed hundreds of billions of dollars, household income stagnated. For the bulk of Americans, weekly earnings in 2007 were the same as in 2000—despite an 18% growth in productivity. Americans work two weeks longer each year than they did in the 1970s, and 350 hours longer per year than Europeans. The income of men in their 30s is 12% lower than it was three decades ago. Households led by someone 65 or under made an average 3.4 percent less in 2007 than in 2000.[31]

As Americans bought Chinese exports, Beijing emerged as a financial superpower with $1,800 billion in foreign exchange as of July 2008. Much of that money came from American shoppers who put their faith in Chicago-inspired "economics" and "consensus" free trade. As wages stagnated in the U.S., that transfer of financial capital continued to gain momentum. For all of 1985, America's trade deficit with China totaled $6 billion. In January 2008 alone, it totaled $61.6 billion, marking a fundamental shift in economic power.[32] For all of 2007, imports outstripped exports by nearly $800 billion.[33]

OPEC countries earned an estimated $690 billion from oil exports in 2006, up from $243 billion in 2000. Members of the Organization of Petroleum Exporting Countries hold petrodollar investments conservatively estimated at $3.6 trillion. In July 2008, with oil at $140 per barrel, Saudi Arabia alone tallied $1.4 billion per day for each day's sale of 10 million barrels, or $511 billion per year. Saudi Arabia's promise to pump 12 million barrels per day in 2009 suggests an annual revenue stream at July 2008 prices of $613 billion. Those petrodollars will need to be invested somewhere.

Belief-Based Results

Fed Chairman Alan Greenspan's inducement of sustained low interest rates persuaded Americans to borrow in order to pull more than $500 billion a year out of their home equity from 2004 to 2006. A sizeable portion of that debt-financed purchasing power (*demand*) found its way abroad, increasing Bejing's *supply* of investment capital.

Today's pattern of narrow "closed system" prosperity alongside widespread insecurity typifies the oligarchization that was *certain* to accompany the globalization of financial markets. To review highlights from these *perfectly predictable* global trends:

- By 2007, India's 40 billionaires had amassed a combined wealth of $351 billion, up from a combined wealth of $170 billion in 2006.
- In 2006, China had 15 billionaires. The following year, their ranks had swollen to more than 100.[34] By January 2008, *China Daily* reported 146 billionaires.[35]
- In 2008, *Forbes* reported 1,125 billionaires worldwide worth $4.4 trillion, up from 946 billionaires worth $3.5 trillion in 2007 (an increase from 476 billionaires worth $1.4 trillion in 2003).
- In Indonesia, 61.7% of the country's stock market value is held by its 15 richest families. The comparable figure for the Philippines is 55.1%, and 53.3% for Thailand.[36]
- Port cities have mobilized to service the marina needs of the super-rich. More than 820 mega-yachts were under construction in 2007. Russian oligarchs have commissioned the most opulent yachts.

- The richest 2% of adults worldwide now own more than 50% of global assets, while the poorest half of the adult population holds 1% of worldwide wealth.
- The U.N. Human Development Report identified 2.6 billion people who lack adequate sanitation and 1.1 billion people who lack access to clean water, while one billion people live on less than $1 per day.
- Key measures of societal health either have stalled at appalling levels or worsened. The U.N. Food and Agriculture Organization announced in December 2007 a serious risk that global hunger will worsen in 2008.
- In the U.S., the number of people living under the poverty line rose by 5.7 million since 2000, to 12.5 percent of the population. The number of impoverished children increased to 18% or almost one in five children nationwide.[37]
- Meanwhile, of the $619 billion growth in America's total income for 2007, 42% went to the one in 400 Americans who made more than $1 million in 2006.[38]

Passage of the North American Free Trade Agreement (NAFTA) unleashed in Mexico the consensus-assured effects of free trade in goods and capital. As imports from U.S. agribusiness undercut Mexican farmers and chain stores squeezed out small shop owners, livelihoods disappeared in Mexico and illegal immigration soared in the U.S. By 2008, the world's second richest person was Mexican Carlos Slim Helu. In a nation of 109 million where one in five live in abject poverty, his personal wealth of $60 billion generates more earnings in a single year than the combined income of three million of his fellow citizens. His wealth surged $12 billion in 2006 alone after Mexico's telecom firm was privatized (i.e., oligarch-ized).

Dollar Democracy

Supply-side policies and post-Cold War privatization coincided with a worldwide surge in funds held by institutional investors, led by assets in U.S. pension plans ($16,600 billion as of March 30, 2007).[39] Mandated by law to pursue only those values measurable in money, pension plans have a predictable need for new investments, making them ready purchasers of junk-loan securities marketed as Triple A-rated securities.

As consensus-educated policymakers enacted laws granting more priority to financial values, less attention was paid to protecting those values essential for healthy communities and democratic societies. Instead of people having an influence over forces that affect them, more deference was granted free-flowing capital by a public induced to *believe* in the wisdom of financial markets—despite the facts.

The "economics" that underlie this analysis retain their seductive allure: no investor seeks a return less than the best, and no money manager can retain his job without producing competitive returns. The result is a globalizing force, backed by international law and the World Trade Organization (WTO), that scours the world 24-7 richly rewarding those who pursue solely those values denominated in money.

In March 2008, Treasury Secretary Henry Paulson applauded the International Monetary Fund's commitment to develop a code of "best practices." That code is meant to guide investments by sovereign wealth funds such as China's foreign exchange reserves or the vast petrodollars held by oil producing nations. Those funds, projected to top $17,000 billion over the next decade,[40] will soon rival pension funds in scale and global influence. By best practices, Paulson, a former co-chairman of Goldman Sachs, meant a commitment to disavow "political motivations" (i.e., any motivation other than financial) and a pledge to invest solely on the basis of "commercial principles."[41]

In the consensus-speak common to Washington and Wall Street, those words signify a commitment to disregard any values other than financial. New York Senator Charles Schumer, a leading advocate of "value investing," touts this practice as an example of "openness" consistent with democratic values. In short, a shared *belief* in commercial values (i.e., financial values) is poised to preempt democratic values worldwide.[42]

At the January 2008 World Economic Forum in Davos, Switzerland, former Treasury Secretary Lawrence Summers proposed an international "code of conduct" limiting investments to "value maximization"—meaning the maximization of *financial* value.[43] With the globalization of a shared mindset *insistent* that lawmakers grant primacy to those values calculated in money, money has gradually become democracy's primary purpose—with *perfectly predictable* results (from a game theory perspective) and to the *foreseeable* detriment of communities worldwide. As this returns-fixated "Washington" consensus expands to global scale, America appears guilty by association.[44]

Complicit in Concept

Is it possible that, having been educated in a shared mindset (a consensus), Americans were deceived to *believe* in an "economics" that imperils their freedom? Were we induced to freely commit our full faith and credit to finance a system of globalization by which we would become dominated by the very forces we freely choose? By Washington's insistence on granting primacy to financial returns, did *we* evoke a global consensus to enact local laws ensuring that democratic principles would be systematically displaced in favor of *financial* principles?

Just as it was *our* "Chicago" mindset that fueled the financial forces now endangering our freedom, it is *our* purchasing power now fueling Beijing's capacity to modernize its military. By inducing us to globalize a money-myopic mindset, did *the people in between* persuade us to make choices that divided Americans from each other—even as we freely advocated the very forces that undermined democracies and markets as other nations followed our lead?

How did this consensus *belief* come to dominate American culture? Originally envisioned as a form of self-governance meant to endure "for the ages," how did American democracy come to grant deference to those values denominated in dollars? How did remote capital markets become a point of reference to which we obligingly sacrificed our democratic values at the cost of our local communities?

By reinforcing behavior measurable in money, that shared mental state has come to represent in the eyes of a bewildered global public the values for which America now stands. Those who recall our role in rescuing the world from the fascism of WWII wonder what happened to *that* America. Instead, claiming the moral authority of international law (and rules enforceable by the WTO), *our* mindset (the "Washington" consensus) is systematically displacing those values—including freedom—not measurable in money.[45]

As this widely shared *belief* became the lens through which we view our world, this shared perspective shaped what America has become. As our narrow search for financial value displaced our concern for that broader array of values essential to healthy communities, *financial* freedom emerged triumphant. Any restraint on financial freedom is now seen as a limit on *personal* freedom and contrary to "best practices." In effect, that "consensus" perspective grant unfettered freedom to *the people in between.*

As "our" consensus expanded to global scale, *we* discredited democracy by our insistence that deference be granted forces that endangered our own liberty. Could this be the *indirect deception* (and domination) that Israel Shahak warned is favored by "totalitarian Judaism"? [See below.] Does Talmudic extremism seek an exclusionary "economics" by inducing those who are its target to freely embrace the forces of their own exclusion? Could the globalization of consensus "economics" be *how* Zionism achieves its exclusivist goals?

Is the allure of this shared mindset meant to induce the "mark" to freely embrace the *perfectly predictable* results chronicled in this chapter? Could this be a form of *systemic* fraud expanding to global scale through our entangled alliance with a nation founded on the principles of fundamentalist Judaism? Is this the *illusion of a common interest* we were cautioned to avoid by America's first president? Is this the enslavement of belief from which our Framers sought to keep us free?

As the demand for financial returns works its way through future generations of technological advance, the *closed system of finance* is certain to create oligarchies worldwide at a steadily accelerating pace. If U.S. lawmakers continue on this course, American foreign policy will be seen as the enabling force that fractured societies and undermined democracies. If, as a nation, we continue on this path, the Adam Smith vision of *community-attuned markets* will be displaced with distant capital markets that systematically undermine those values essential to the long-term health of communities both here and abroad.

If that "economics" is permitted the financial freedom its advocates seek, *the people in between* will gradually displace personal with financial freedom—based on the personal decisions that *we* ourselves feely make.[46]

> In his 1994 book, *Jewish History, Jewish Religion*, the late Israel Shahak described attempts to reimpose the "totalitarian Jewish community and its power…of which Zionism is the most important."[47] In comparing such elite and extremist Jews to the Janissaries of the Ottoman Empire, he noted that the Ottoman regime was based initially on the almost complete exclusion of native Turks from positions of influence: "Thus the position of the Jews was best under a regime which was politically most dissociated from the peoples it ruled."[48]
>
> As a Holocaust survivor and a half-century resident of Israel, Shahak became one of Zionism's most outspoken critics. Placing Jewish extremism in historical context, he cited Talmudic scripture to remind readers that, in fundamentalist Judaism, deception against another Jew is a sin but against a Gentile only *direct* deception is forbidden. Similarly, the Talmud forbids fraud against Jews but not against Gentiles.[49]

Chapter 7

The New Anti-Semitism

The new anti-Semitism appears in the guise of 'political criticism of Israel'…

—Natan Sharansky, Likud Party[1]

I think there is a strain within the pro-Israel community that says unless you adopt an unwavering pro-Likud approach to Israel that you're anti-Israel…

—Barack Obama, Democratic Party[2]

In October 2004, President George W. Bush signed into law the Global Anti-Semitism Review Act directing the State Department to "monitor and combat acts of anti-Semitism" in foreign countries. He announced the signing during a campaign event in Florida whose Jewish population is the third largest in the world after Israel and New York. The State Department opposed the legislation, saying it already compiles such data in its annual reports on human rights and religious freedom. Sponsored by Representative Tom Lantos, the legislation included a finding that "anti-Semitism has at times taken the form of vilification of Zionism, the Jewish national movement, and incitement against Israel."[3]

Both the Lantos legislation and the State Department press release naming Gregg Rickman as envoy for anti-Semitism highlighted an October 2003 incident involving Malaysian Prime Minister Mahatir Mohammad who told the Organization of the Islamic

Conference that Jews "rule the world by proxy."[4] Describing the worldwide Jewish population as between 13 and 14.6 million, U.S. diplomats mocked Mahatir's claim that the world's 1.3 billion Muslims "cannot be defeated by a few million Jews."

Redefining Anti-Semitism

The use of anti-Semitism to discredit critics of Israeli policy dates from the 1967 Six-Day War. Prior to that conflict, the American Jewish community was not much interested in Colonial Zionism with its toxic mix of fundamentalist fervor and an expansionist agenda. A similar phenomenon emerged after the Holocaust. Though the Zionist movement had sought broader support for many years, the Holocaust was the catalyst that rallied the Diaspora around the proposal for a Jewish homeland in the Middle East with Jerusalem its capital.[5]

Soon after the 1967 War, any deviation from the pro-Zionist "party line" was met with harsh criticism. Dissenting Jews were scorned as "self-hating" while non-Jews who criticized Zionism were smeared as "anti-Semitic." After the Six-Day War, critics of Israeli policies faced an added barrier: Policies crafted in Tel Aviv matched those in Washington. That alliance made Zionism appear respectable, particularly with the "echo effect" of those policies being portrayed in a favorable light by mainstream media and pro-Israeli think tanks.

After President Lyndon Johnson (with the assistance of Admiral John S. McCain, Jr.) covered up Israel's killing of 34 Americans aboard the *USS Liberty* on June 8, 1967, it became clear there was no extreme to which Tel Aviv could go that would endanger White House support. From a game theory perspective, the Six-Day War fulfilled its strategic purpose. It not only rallied moderate Jews who were lukewarm to Colonial Zionism but the success of that territorial expansion also confirmed throughout the Middle East that America was firmly on the side of Israeli expansionism, Zionist extremism and fundamentalist Judaism.

As moderate and liberal Jews migrated politically rightward, those involved in the U.S. civil rights movement faced a moral dilemma: How could they promote equal rights for minorities in the U.S. and fail to oppose Israel's treatment of the Palestinians? Rather than pressure Tel Aviv to reform, many of them dropped their opposition to

Zionism. Thus began a paradox for moderate Jews that remains unresolved: How to reconcile a commitment to human rights with the inhumane policies of the Jewish state and its expansionist agenda for Greater Israel?

The Internal Diaspora

Absent the horror of the Holocaust, President Harry Truman could not have recognized Zionism as a legitimate basis for a sovereign state in May 1948 over the vehement opposition of Secretary of State George C. Marshall, the Joint Chiefs of Staff, the State Department's director of policy planning and the Central Intelligence Agency.

Truman was lavish in his praise of Marshall, conceding: "He won the war."[6] Yet in the aftermath of the Holocaust and with the Balfour Declaration having been endorsed by Democrats Wilson and Roosevelt, Truman also felt responsibility for the survivors and their claim as displaced persons to a homeland in Palestine. Critics suggest that Truman risked the welfare of the U.S. in return for pro-Israeli campaign contributions to his cash-starved 1948 presidential campaign, which he was expected to lose.

While the politics of campaign finance clearly played a role, Truman also acted out of humanitarian and moral concerns informed by his Christian Zionist upbringing in rural Missouri where he famously read the Bible cover-to-cover five times by age 15. His decision was also shaped by opinions, sentiments and predispositions developed as a young man steeped in Baptist theology that emphasized the Jews' return to Zion as a prerequisite for the return of the Christian messiah.[7]

In an Oval Office meeting of May 12, 1948, two days before the British mandate in Palestine expired, Marshall assured Truman that, if he followed the advice of White House counsel Clark Clifford and recognized the Zionist state, Marshall would vote against him in the November election.[8] After Truman recognized Israel, Marshall never again spoke to Clifford. Not until 1984 was it revealed that Abe Feinberg and a network of Zionist Jews financed Truman's nationwide whistle-stop campaign for which Feinberg arranged to have Jewish delegations meet and financially "refuel" the train with $400,000 in campaign cash ($2.9 million in 2007 dollars).[9]

In the minds of those who comprise the Diaspora, the Six-Day

War reactivated the psychological insecurity associated with the Holocaust. In combination, those two events catalyzed an *internal Diaspora* based on:

> *Nationalism*—a shared emotional bond among Jews worldwide as a dispersed form of nationalism (the Diaspora) bound to Israel those who may never set foot there. After the Six-Day War, the state of Israel became the Land of Israel based on the more expansive area it occupied and the additional territory it still intends to take.
>
> *Insecurity*—a shared sense of vulnerability and victimhood as Jews worldwide defended themselves against anti-Semites. Whenever Israeli policies came under attack (as now), media campaigns claimed another outbreak of anti-Semitism.[10]

Bound by a common anxiety and the allure of a "promised land" offering refuge through a "right of return," Israel emerged as *a shared mental state* also available as a physical "homeland" for anyone the Jewish state deemed "Jewish." In combination, the Holocaust and the Six-Day War made Zionism a geopolitical possibility. Without the Holocaust, Truman's recognition of Zionism as a legitimate sovereign state would have proven impossible. Absent the 1967 war, moderate Jews would have continued their opposition to a Jewish state as an impediment to assimilation.

The anti-Zionist American Council for Judaism knew that an enclave of Jewish fundamentalists would subjugate the Arabs, provoking cycles of violence. They also understood that recognition of an expansionist Jewish state would imperil their faith tradition worldwide by enabling even anti-Zionist Jews to be portrayed as foreign agents of an aggressor state. Charges of "dual loyalty" could be used to impugn even those Jews most appalled at what Israel has become as pressure from the Israel lobby discredited the U.S. worldwide by ensuring official indifference to Palestinian suffering.

The Holocaust catalyzed the emotional and political reaction required for Truman's recognition of Israel as a sovereign nation. The Six-Day War re-catalyzed the perception of vulnerability required to ensure that Israel became the well-armed ally of a superpower then led by Lyndon Johnson. Tel Aviv's 1967 land grab also enabled the "Israelites"—with support from their Christian Zionist allies—to seize more territory that Jewish fundamentalists had long claimed was theirs because they are Jews.

Thus the strategic motivation fueling charges of a "New Anti-Semitism" to impugn anyone opposing the retention of occupied Palestinian land and the seizure of more territory for the steadily expanding Land of Israel. Or, as fundamentalist Jews maintain, the "redemption" of land that is rightly theirs. Thus also the need for an aggressive strategy meant to discredit, isolate, ostracize or marginalize anyone critical of Tel Aviv's expansionist policies. With the 1967 war, the Anti-Defamation League of B'nai B'rith (Hebrew for *sons of the covenant*) increased its funding and re-focused its operation.

When Jimmy Carter published *Palestine: Peace Not Apartheid* (2006), the ADL was ready. National director Abraham Foxman promptly attacked the former president, a loyal friend of Israel, as "anti-Semitic."[11] Martin Peretz, editor of *The New Republic*, quickly claimed the Christian Zionist Nobel peace laureate "will go down in history as a Jew-hater."[12] As sponsor of the 1979 Egyptian-Israeli peace process, Carter arguably did as much as any U.S. president to improve Israeli security. Yet the Committee for Accuracy in Middle East Reporting (CAMERA), an AIPAC-related media watchdog, published full-page ads in *The New York Times* attacking Carter and urging that readers complain to the publisher whose phone number was included in the ad.

Attack on the Academies

Efforts to shield Israel from criticism routinely target not just policymakers but also professors, authors, columnists and other opinion-shapers. In an irony seldom lost on the target, the attacker typically cites the right to free speech while seeking to silence the critic. Norman Finkelstein, an anti-Zionist Jew, has long irritated the ADL. His 2000 book, *The Holocaust Industry*, merely rankled the ADL.[13] With its extended critique of *Chutzpah* by Harvard-Zionist Professor Alan Dershowitz, Finkelstein's 2005 book, *Beyond Chutzpah—The Misuse of Anti-Semitism,* caused Zionists to hit the panic button.

Dershowitz, a self-described loyal defender of human rights, sought to halt the book's publication.[14] Finkelstein, 55, recently was denied tenure at Chicago's DePaul University following pressure from Jewish organizations and individuals, including Dershowitz. On May 23, 2008, Israel's Shin Bet security service detained Finkelstein for 24 hours at Ben-Gurion International Airport. Akin to behavior found in Soviet bloc countries, entry was denied an outspoken critic of state policy. Though Jews worldwide are assured a right of return to the Jewish homeland, this Jewish son of Holocaust survivors reports he was told that he could not return for 10 years.[15]

None of this is new. In *They Dare to Speak Out* (1985), former Congressman Paul Findley devoted an entire chapter to attacks on academics who criticize Israeli policies.[16] As the target of a successful AIPAC congressional campaign in 1982, Findley is an experienced veteran of such attacks. In detailing coordination among AIPAC, B'nai B'rith and ADL, he described how Hillel Foundation student groups target on-campus speakers known to be critics of Israeli policy.

Findley quotes a professor who encountered the "silent covenant within the academic community concerning Israel" and the costs imposed on those who criticize its policies. He described how a Middle East studies program was discontinued in a campaign organized by ADL, the Jewish Relations Council and Ira Silverman of the American Jewish Committee. One observer compared their intimidation campaign to "the Great Fear sweeping across France during the French Revolution."[17]

In a chilling account of an early 1980s campaign meant to intimidate academics nationwide, a network of pro-Israeli organizations targeted Mazher Hameed, a research fellow at Georgetown University's Center for Strategic and International Studies (CSIS). Though the scholar's report on Saudi Arabian oil field security was widely praised, Tel Aviv sought to discredit the author in order to halt the sale to Saudi Arabia of a high-tech AWACS airplane featuring the U.S. Air Force's most sophisticated airborne radar.

The analysis pointed out the risk that Israel could mount a preemptive attack, roiling world oil markets. Since 1976, Israel Defense Forces had routinely engaged in practice bombing runs over the Saudi airbase of Tabuk, dropping empty fuel cannisters to prove their point. Tel Aviv also let it be known they could create their own "oil embargo" by disrupting Saudi oil operations.

The Airborne Early Warning and Control System (AWACS) offers a plane-mounted radar system designed to detect aircraft from hundreds of miles away. With an AWACS deployed over that theater of operations, it would be far more difficult for Tel Aviv to induce policymakers to *believe* that Israel was not an *agent provocateur* but a perennial victim living in an anti-Semitic neighborhood.[18] Not only did the scholar lose his job, *The New Republic* threatened to publish a series alleging petrodollar donations to CSIS, insinuating the research was biased and "fixed" and challenging its tax-exempt status. In response, CSIS retroactively amended the researcher's contract to withdraw budgeted funds and force his departure.

Shortly after learning that CSIS had been successfully intimidated and his position terminated, Hameed returned to his office to find it had been burgled. The next day his personal post office box was broken into. To ensure he had no doubt that he was being stalked, items that were not his began appearing in his home.[19]

The Intimidation Effect

Intimidation is routinely deployed against critics, whether Jewish or otherwise. Abe Rosenthal, for years the managing editor of *The New York Times*, sought to protect U.S. military technology when, in October 1999, he wrote a column exposing Israeli collaboration with their counterparts in Beijing. Citing "obsequious Israeli speeches praising the Chinese minister of defense," Rosenthal described Tel Aviv's visitor as "one of the ranking Tiananmen killers" who sought Israeli assistance to upgrade Russian-made MiG-21 fighter jets for the Chinese military.[20]

Though a staunch supporter of Israel, Rosenthal cautioned that Tel Aviv's transfer of U.S. military technology to China could endanger U.S. interests and make Israel an American political target. After putting U.S. national security ahead of the Zionist state's geopolitical agenda, he abruptly left the *Times* in a public dispute with Max Frankel, his successor as executive editor.[21] For 17 years, the nation's most influential editor, Rosenthal was a key architect of the modern *New York Times* and was then writing a popular column for the paper.[22]

In the insular media industry, Rosenthal's abrupt departure had the same shot-across-the-bow impact as AIPAC's success in removing Congressman Paul Findley and targeting two chairmen of the Senate Foreign Relations Committee: Democrat William Fulbright of Arkansas in 1974 and, a decade later, Republican Charles Percy of Illinois.[23] Just as the Israel lobby's display of political power intimidated a generation of policymakers, the sudden departure of a legendary newspaper editor served notice on a generation of editors and journalists: *do not* challenge Tel Aviv, period. And *do not* challenge the impact of Israeli policy on U.S. national security or your career will disappear. In the parlance of organized crime: You work for us and we can prove it. Look at Findley, Fulbright, Percy, Rosenthal and others.

On October 28, 1981, the Senate voted 52 to 48 against a resolution that would have blocked the AWACS sale to Saudi Arabia. After that (rare) loss by the Israel lobby, Paul Findley's Congressional seat was targeted in 1982 along with a gubernatorial race by Adlai Stevenson III. Both elections were in Illinois, Barack Obama's home state. Political insiders understood that those losses marked a major victory for Tel Aviv in an electorally critical state.[24]

Following Israel's success with those elections, a conclave convened in Manhattan in 1983 to better coordinate pro-Israeli political operations. That group included James Wolfenson, Martin Peretz, Rita Hauser, Barry Diller and developer George Klein.[25] In 1984, AIPAC targeted a third Illinois policymaker (Percy) and then touted its victory when executive director Thomas A. Dine boasted to a Jewish audience in Canada:

> All the Jews in America, from coast to coast, gathered to oust Percy. And American politicians—those who hold public positions now, and those who aspire—got the message.[26]

The message of electoral intimidation was an inescapable signal from Tel Aviv to anyone interested in public service. The impact of the message was magnified by the fact that Percy was Republican chairman of the Committee on Foreign Relations with a popular Republican president in the White House (Reagan). Dine reemerged during the Clinton administration as a senior Madeleine Albright appointee to the European and Eurasia office of the U.S. Agency for International Development where he oversaw the Harvard-advised Ashkenazi-ation of Russia. He was then appointed president of Radio Free Europe.

For the past 25 years, pro-Israeli influence has been expanding across key industries, including media, popular culture (Diller was then CEO of Paramount Pictures),[27] academia and think tanks (Peretz was then editor of *The New Republic*) and finance (Wolfensohn served from 1995 to 2005 as World Bank president where he focused on globalizing the Washington consensus certain to create oligarchies worldwide). Hauser was appointed to the President's Foreign Intelligence Advisory Board during the war-planning period (2001-2004) when fixed intelligence induced the U.S. to invade Iraq.

The intimidation factor remains robust. As this account neared completion, Palestinian journalist Mohammed Omer was assaulted in June 2008 by eight armed officers of Shin Bet, Israel's security service. Returning from London, he had just received the Martha Gellhorn prize for journalists who expose establishment propaganda. Crossing into Gaza, he was threatened, forced to strip at gunpoint and then dragged naked by his heels after being beaten unconscious, fracturing several ribs and causing internal injuries. Tel Aviv insisted he was a smuggling suspect and that he lost his balance during interrogation.[28]

As the Gaza correspondent for the *Washington Report on Middle East Affairs*, he had just published an assessment of Israel's situation:

> Israel's international support, after all, depends on how it is viewed by the world. Promoting an acceptable image requires thousands of advocates, from editors and journalists to diplomats, politicians, advertising and public relations agencies and a network of grassroots activists dedicated to making sure very little about Israel's policies and actions makes it into the consciousness of the world community.[29]

The Progression of Anti-Semitism

Anyone critical of Israeli policies is now routinely portrayed as an anti-Semite. Even the survivors of Israel's attack on the *USS Liberty* are labeled anti-Semitic for urging a Congressional investigation of the circumstances surrounding the killing of 34 U.S. servicemen by Israel Defense Forces in 1967. The survivors ask: "How does seeking an inquiry become 'anti-Semitism'?"[30]

In February 2006 the Church of England voted to review its investment in Caterpillar, Inc. when the church discovered that Israel uses Caterpillar equipment to destroy Palestinian homes. Concerned at the ethical implications of profiting from that policy, the church resolved to study the issue. Even that expression of moral concern was quickly portrayed as "anti-Zionist—verging on anti-Semitic."[31]

The misuse of that toxic charge is beginning to backfire, however. The court of world opinion has grown weary of Tel Aviv conceding no wrong in its treatment of those displaced and their lands occupied to create a Zionist state—particularly when its behavior has been far different than what was promised and anticipated when Truman recognized Zionism as meriting sovereign status in the heart of the Muslim Middle East. That behavior includes official discrimination reflected in at least 20 laws that disadvantage Arab-Israeli citizens in key areas such as education, housing and employment. For example, an Arab cannot buy a home in the settlement areas. An Arab who marries an Israeli cannot reside in Israel. Arabs are even issued different colored license plates for their cars.

In November 2006 the ADL's Abe Foxman condemned as an "overwhelming failure" efforts to reform the U.N. Commission on Human Rights, claiming it was a tool of Arabs and Muslims.[32] The next day, Foxman attacked the U.N. Human Rights Council (successor to the commission) for appointing Nobel peace laureate Desmond Tutu, Anglican Archbishop of Cape Town, to lead a fact-finding mission to Beit Hanun, a town in the Gaza Strip where Israel Defense Forces shelling killed 19 Palestinian civilians. Claiming the council "has never operated with any moral authority," Foxman helped Tel Aviv justify its denial to Bishop Tutu of any cooperation with the inquiry.[33]

In March 2008 the U.N. Human Rights Council dispatched Richard Falk, an emeritus professor of international law at Princeton University, as special investigator on Israel-Palestine human rights. Israel's Foreign Ministry denied him a visa when Falk, a Jewish critic of Tel Aviv's policies, defended his statements comparing Israel's treatment of Palestinians with the Nazis' genocidal treatment of Jews, claiming Israel had been unfairly shielded from criticism.[34] The council's previous investigator, John Dugard from South Africa, compared that treatment to apartheid, the policy used by South Africa's white regime to disadvantage blacks in key areas such as education, housing and employment.

Over a 17-month period (November 2006 to April 2008), Israeli policymakers progressed from being compared to racist South Africans to being compared to the racial purists of Nazi Germany. Meanwhile Tel Aviv refused to cooperate with an international fact-finding mission led by a black Nobel peace laureate and leader in the Anglican Church. By mid-April 2008, Gaza-based Hamas leader Mahmoud Zahar decried Judaism as having "corrupted itself in the detour into Zionism, nationalism and apartheid." Writing in *The Washington Post* as Jimmy Carter traveled the region urging that peace talks include the elected Hamas government, Zahar likened the plight of Gazans to Jews in the Warsaw Ghetto during WWII, saying Gazans can do "no less" than rise up against Israel.[35]

The day before Zahar's commentary described Gaza as "the world's largest open-air prison," Israeli forces supported by U.S.-provided aircraft invaded central Gaza and killed 14 Palestinians including five under age 16 along with a Reuters cameraman when an Israeli tank fired on his clearly marked "Press" jeep.[36] That same day, while a Hamas delegation was enroute to Cairo to meet with Carter, former Israeli Prime Minister Benjamin Netanyahu described how the mass murder of 9/11 aided Israel:

> We are benefiting from one thing, and that is the attack on the Twin Towers and Pentagon, and the American struggle in Iraq...[These events] swung American public opinion in our favor.[37]

Prior to the 9/11 attack, both Netanyahu and Israeli Prime Minister Ariel Sharon had lamented the seeming inability of Americans to identify with the plight of Israelis and their experience with terrorism.

The Logic of Anti-Semitism

As successive Israeli governments drifted ever further to the political right, the American Jewish Congress, B'nai B'rith and the Anti-Defamation League led a campaign to equate anti-Zionists with anti-Semites, as reflected in the Tom Lantos-sponsored Global Anti-Semitism Review Act. The logic runs like this: In a world where there is only one Jewish state, to oppose its policies endangers Jews and is therefore anti-Semitic.[38] That logic suggests that Jews critical of Israeli policy are also anti-Semites.

December 2006 brought that paradox more clearly into focus as several anti-Zionist rabbis appeared in Tehran alongside Iranian President Mahmoud Ahmadinejad who urged that Zionism be erased from history. In agreement, the few thousand Jews of the ultra-Orthodox Neturei Karta community reminded those who would listen that the Iranian President is not an anti-Semite but an anti-Zionist. While applauding the contribution that Jews have long made to Iran, Ahmadinejad asked why Palestinians should suffer for an atrocity in which they played no part and why people not alive during the Holocaust should bear its cost.

Founded in the 1930s to counter the Zionist movement, members of Neturei Karta ("guardians of the city") routinely burn the Israeli flag and attend Manhattan's annual Salute to Israel parade holding signs that read "Israel is a cancer for Jews." Rabbi Yisroel Dovid Weiss explained that Ahmadinejad "understands the difference between the Zionists and the Jews who do not embrace the state of Israel."[39]

Asked if the Iranian President is an enemy, Rabbi Weiss replied, "We don't look at him as an enemy. But is he a potential enemy? Well, every person who continues to be excited is one, but even when we're dealing with an enemy we're supposed to approach them with dialogue and try to placate them. Aggression is not going to be successful." To describe the source of their concerns about the Zionist state, members of Neturei Karta explain in wall posters:

> It is known to everyone that the hand of the Zionists was in the murder of millions of Jews in the days of holocaust and rage, both by provoking the fury of the despotic Germans, and by interfering with all manner of rescues…The Holocaust

> happened because of the Zionists. They wanted it… Zionists are able to convince the world that they represent Jews and Judaism, and everybody who speaks against it is anti-Semitic.[40]

The New Anti-Semitism failed as a strategy for discrediting rabbis who were neither anti-Semites nor Jew-haters. Rather than Holocaust deniers, they blamed the Holocaust on those who corrupted Judaism with Zionism, nationalism and its Palestinian progeny: apartheid. Rather than interview dissenting rabbis on CNN's *Situation Room*, former *Jerusalem Post* reporter Wolf Blitzer featured David Duke, a former head of the Ku Klux Klan. Instead of associating the Iranian president with anti-Zionism, his interview of Duke associated him with racism and anti-Semitism.

Anti-Semitism by Association

In January 2008 the U.N. marked its second international day to remember the victims of the Holocaust. Secretary General Ban Ki-moon used the occasion to describe Holocaust deniers as "misguided individuals."[41] With the Iranian President branded globally for Holocaust denial, anyone doing business with Iran became guilty by association. Three months later ADL published ads condemning the Swiss government as misguided for signing an energy contract with Iran.[42] The Holocaust did not need to be mentioned.

Similarly, *Haaretz* interviewed Polish Prime Minister Donald Tusk just prior to his April 2008 arrival in Israel on the first visit by a Polish leader in nearly a decade. The interview featured his grandfather's forced service in Hitler's army during World War II. By the time Tusk arrived in Tel Aviv (after publication of that guilt-by-association article), he was prepared to issue a strong rebuke of Tehran, announcing, "Iran's words toward Israel cancel its right to a place in the international community."[43]

In another paradox facing purveyors of the New Anti-Semitism, a group of progressive Jews called "J Street PAC" emerged in Washington in April 2008.[44] Their goal: to counter AIPAC and the rightward march of Israeli politics. With "anti-Semite" repackaged to disparage anyone critical of Israel, J Street members cannot credibly be cast as anti-Semites. Because many of them are prominent in the Jewish community, "self-hating Jew" will need to be re-defined to include any Jew critical of Israeli policies. That strategy appears to be underway.

Harvard undergraduate Paul Katz was a target of this tactic when, in April 2008, he organized an exhibit exploring the effect on Israelis of their military service enforcing the occupation in the West Bank and Gaza. Morton Klein, president of the Zionist Organization of America, accused Katz of "inciting hatred of Israel." Katz questions how a pro-Zionist Jewish college student became a self-hating Jew "playing into the hands of Israel's enemies"[45] by mounting what *The Jerusalem Post* portrayed as "a ferociously anti-Israel exhibition."

Online Identification and Intimidation

In June 2004, after including the singular noun "Jew" in an Internet search, Google sent the author a warning from its automated search engine featuring this text:

> "If you use Google to search for 'Judaism,' 'Jewish' or 'Jewish people,' the results are informative and relevant. So why is a search for 'Jew' different? One reason is that the word 'Jew' is often used in an anti-Semitic context. Jewish organizations are more likely to use the word 'Jewish' when talking about members of their faith... Someone searching for information on Jewish people would be more likely to enter terms like 'Judaism,' 'Jewish people,' or 'Jews' than the single word 'Jew.' In fact, prior to this incident, the word 'Jew' only appeared about once in every 10 million search queries.... Sincerely, The Google Team
>
> ...p.s. You may be interested in some additional information the Anti-Defamation League has posted about this issue at http://www.adl.org/rumors/google_search _rumors .asp. In addition, we call your attention to the Jewish Internet Association, an organization that addresses online anti-Semitism, at http://www.jewishinternet association.org/."

In fact, an Internet search using ADL-approved words (Jewish, Judaism and Jews) failed to identify materials that were either informative or relevant. No automated warning was generated by searches that used other faith-related nouns such as Buddhist,

Muslim, Methodist, Hindu and Catholic. Contemporary news accounts suggest the automated ADL response was aimed at defusing charges that Google was anti-Semitic even though co-founders Sergey Brin and Larry Page are Jewish.[46]

Google explained that ADL and other Google users were concerned that *Jew Watch* emerged as the first-listed website whenever a search included the word "Jew." Google has since reconfigured its search algorithms so that listings by *Wikipedia* (the online encyclopedia) appear second and third while the first is titled "Offensive Search Results" where the ADL warning now appears on-screen rather than being sent, at ADL's direction, to the web-searcher's personal computer. ADL's Abe Foxman reports: "we are extremely pleased" that users will be "alerted when they are about to enter into a hate zone."

In January 2008 Shimon Peres, Israel's 84-year old president, proposed an extension of the ADL's anti-Semite identification strategy, "You can fight anti-Semitism using social networks, like Facebook."[47] Peres then met with Facebook founder Mark Zuckerberg (age 23) at the World Economic Forum in Davos, Switzerland where they discussed implementation. With today's sophisticated search engines, all 66 million active Facebook users could be monitored 24-7 for any ADL-designated evidence of anti-Semitism. For instance, anyone detected using the singular noun "Jew" for any purpose could automatically be portrayed as an anti-Semite and that behavior posted online as evidencing hateful and socially aberrant conduct (one in 10 million).[48]

> For an indication of Israeli domination of security systems in information technology, see Appendix A ("Canadian & Israeli Security Companies"). Note, for instance, the prevalence of Israeli firms providing security for email.[49]

The Commissars

In December 2004, the author sent an inquiry to Noam Chomsky at the Massachusetts Institute of Technology when Professor Chomsky was described in *The New York Times* as a "self-hating Jew" after he published a critique of Israeli policy. The inquiry read, in part:[50]

> Due to the factual nature of this account, I assume that personal credibility will be the issue that is raised as a way to misdirect attention from the confirmed facts. As I'm not Jewish, the self-hating charge won't work. As I was a partner in the South's largest Jewish law firm and on the board of *Tikkun* (regular contributor, etc.), I don't expect the anti-Semitic schtick will stick though I anticipate a strong run in that direction. Based on your experience, what other types of mud are likely to be slung?

Professor Chomsky's response (in part):

> You'll get the same thing: anti-Semite, Holocaust denier, want to kill all the Jews, etc. It doesn't matter what the facts are. Bear in mind that you are dealing with intellectuals, that is, what we call "commissars" and "apparatchiks" in enemy states.

Chomsky went on to explain how the Six-Day War marked a turning point in the use of anti-Semitism as a means to deflect attention from Israeli policy.

> After 67, any deviation from the Party Line was met with a hysterical flood of vituperation, slanders, lies, mostly from intellectuals, with the left often in the lead. As usual. Where did you find the most vocal Stalinists? The difference is that in this case they were taking a stand very close to US government policy, therefore the media, so were "respectable."

The challenge faced by critics of Israeli policy poses a quandary: how does one prove a negative? How does a "self-hating Jew" prove he or she is not? How does someone portrayed as "anti-Semitic" prove otherwise? Are the accused required to demonstrate their support for Israel regardless of its policies?[51] Once that charge is associated with someone, how can they *dissociate* from the guilt that charge is meant to imply? Is there a rehabilitation process once that slur attaches to its target? How do you prove you are *not* something that you never were?

Separate on the Inside

A true anti-Semite thinks Jewish people are somehow different and should be treated differently—a notion repugnant to democracy's equal protection under the law. Yet Orthodox Jews often are firm believers in separating Jews from their fellow citizens in order to perpetuate the group. Deputy National Security Adviser Elliott Abrams, a prominent neoconservative, argues in his 1997 book *Faith or Fear* that steps should be taken to prevent "prolonged and intimate exposure to non-Jewish culture."

According to Abrams, President Bush's senior adviser for "global democracy strategy," Jewish law "does indeed separate Jews from their fellow citizens and bind them to each other." His concerns with secular government trace their origins to the idea that Jews "are in a permanent covenant with God and with the land of Israel and its people," he explains. "Their commitment will not weaken if the Israeli government pursues unpopular policies."[52]

Much as an anti-Semite should be scorned, Abrams argued, so should any Jew who breaks with that "covenantal community with obligations to God." There lies the faith-based *duty* that binds a nationwide corps of *sayanim* willing to sacrifice U.S. national security on the altar of *their* covenant. As Abrams explains:

> Outside the land of Israel, there can be no doubt that Jews, faithful to the covenant between God and Abraham, are to stand apart from the nation in which they live. It is the very nature of being Jewish to be apart—except in Israel—from the rest of the population.

What Abrams describes is not *dual* loyalty. That covenant mandates a *singular* loyalty—resulting in a propensity to treason by any Jew living *outside* the "land of Israel" who shares his belief in a covenant with the Jewish state. As Israel Shahak explains in *Jewish History, Jewish Religion*:

> The main danger which Israel, as a "Jewish state" poses to its own people, to other Jews and to its neighbors, is its ideologically motivated pursuit of territorial expansion and the

> inevitable series of wars resulting from this aim. The more Israel becomes Jewish or, as one says in Hebrew, the more it "returns to Judaism" (a process that has been under way in Israel at least since 1967), the more its actual policies are guided by Jewish ideological considerations and less by rational ones. My use of the term "rational" does not refer here to a moral evaluation of Israeli policies, or to the supposed defense of security needs of Israel—even less so to the supposed needs of "Israeli survival." I am referring here to Israeli imperial policies based on its presumed interests....
>
> My own early conversion from admirer of Ben-Gurion to his dedicated opponent began exactly with such an issue. In 1956 I eagerly swallowed all of Ben-Gurion's political and military reasons for Israel initiating the Suez War, until he...pronounced in the Knesset on the third day of that war, that the real reason for it is "the restoration of the kingdom of David and Solomon" to its Biblical borders. At this point in his speech, almost every Knesset member spontaneously rose and sang the Israeli national anthem.[53]

The mindset of those who subscribe to such a "Jewish ideology" displaces the singular focus required to defend U.S. national security. As Shahak observes, that worldview also makes Israeli policies "incomprehensible to foreign observers who usually know nothing about Judaism excerpt crude apologetics."[54] Such a belief is not just inconsistent with secular governance, that faith-based allegiance also ensures that anyone sharing that viewpoint will always be obliged to put Israeli interests ahead of American ones.

Abrams' explanation of Judaism's "covenant with God" eloquently captures the "passionate attachment" that George Washington cautioned Americans to avoid in its foreign alliances. In his farewell address, the nation's first president urged an avoidance of "entangling alliances" such as now imperil the U.S. due to its "special relationship" with a theocratic and racist enclave whose leaders induced Truman to *believe* that Zionism was a legitimate basis for sovereignty and democracy.

This "covenant" differs from the U.S. commitment to protect

those who choose to retain and celebrate their cultural, ethnic, racial or national origins. That pride brings to civil society the diversity and vitality on which America's melting pot culture historically has thrived. That pride is very different from those whose primary allegiance lies with another nation state whose exclusivist policies and expansionist goals conflict with American values and jeopardize U.S. national security.

Faith-Based Treason

Abrams' allegiance to the Land of Israel without regard to its policies ("my country, right or wrong") is the belief-based mindset from which treasonous conduct can be evoked by *the people in between.* That mindset provides the fertile ground from which *sayanim* can be recruited as operatives to support Israel's "cause."

Nor is such faith-based treason limited to U.S. residents. The risks of such a covenant endanger the security of *any* nation—be it Russia, Malaysia, Libya, Iran, etc.—where this covenant is found. That risk, moreover, is intuitively well understood. In a 2002 survey of attitudes toward Jews commissioned by ADL, 51% of respondents in 10 European countries agreed with the statement, "Jews are more loyal to Israel than to this country."[55] ADL portrayed this response as an "anti-Semitic stereotype." Yet Abrams' concession confirms a rational basis for those concerns.

Anyone who believes that his "covenant with God" includes "restoration of the kingdom of David and Solomon" is a Colonial Zionist unable to faithfully serve America's interests first. Nor can such a *believer* reliably serve any nation other than the Land of Israel and its expansionist policies for Greater Israel. Such people need not be Jewish Zionists, of course; they can also be Christian Zionists.

In April 2008, American evangelist John Hagee, a fundamentalist Christian Zionist, joined Likud Party stalwart Benjamin Netanyahu at a rally in Israel to support the entirety of Jerusalem remaining under control of the Jewish state.[56] Daniel Kurtzer,[57] former U.S. ambassador to Israel and an adviser to Barack Obama, agrees with Hagee that Jerusalem, as the "cultural capital of the Jewish people," must be central to the peace process.[58]

Fundamentalist Christian support for Israel's retention of

Jerusalem and all of the West Bank endears Christian Zionists to Israeli hardliners such as Netanyahu. An outspoken McCain supporter, Hagee announced that his group, Christians United for Israel, donated $6 million to Israeli causes during the April 2008 pilgrimage that he led to Jerusalem following a visit by McCain and Lieberman. Hagee claims he has given $30 million to Jewish fundamentalist causes.[59] Touting a perspective sharply at odds with U.S. foreign policy, he argues: "Turning part or all of Jerusalem over to the Palestinians would be tantamount to turning it over to the Taliban."[60] Such faith-based policy influences lie at the core of this fact-displacing *modus operandi.*

After dismissing Christian conservatives as "agents of intolerance" during his 2000 presidential campaign, McCain actively courted Hagee's endorsement due to Hagee's support for Israel and because he leads a mega-church with a congregation in the tens of thousands, with an even wider television audience.[61] In a July 2007 speech to Christians United for Israel, Joe Lieberman had this to say about Hagee:

> I would describe Pastor Hagee with the words the Torah uses to describe Moses, he is an *Eesh Elo Kim*, a man of God because those words fit him; and, like Moses he has become the leader of a mighty multitude in pursuit of and defense of Israel.[62]

In mid-May 2008, McCain rejected Hagee's months-old endorsement after an audio recording surfaced in which the televangelist argued, "God sent Adolph Hitler to help Jews reach the promised land." In late-May, Lieberman agreed to address a Christians United for Israel summit held in Washington in July 2008. Lieberman, chairman of the Senate Committee on Homeland Security, called Hagee's group "a vital force in supporting the war against terrorism and defending our ally, Israel."[63]

The New Segregationists

According to the New Anti-Semitism, an "anti-Semite" is anyone who challenges Israeli policy. Confirming how freedom can be turned against those determined to defend it, anyone who challenges Abrams' qualifications to advise on U.S. national security *because of his beliefs* is likely to be portrayed as an anti-Semite—even though those beliefs are irreconcilable with his constitutional oath of office. Similarly, any Jew must necessarily be "self-hating" if he criticizes Israeli policy or the impact on national security of devotees, such as Abrams, committed to expand the Land of Israel in order restore the kingdom of David and Solomon.

In a 1937 article titled, "How The Jews Can Combat Persecution," Winston Churchill argued that Jews are partly to blame for anti-Semitism.[64] The British wartime leader disapproved of their treatment yet noted: "They have been partly responsible for the antagonism from which they suffer." Uncovered in 2007 by Cambridge University lecturer Richard Toye, the unpublished article argued that "the wickedness of the persecutors" was not the only reason for the poor treatment of Jews down the ages.

Churchill laid part of the blame on what he called "the separateness of the Jew." He criticized the "aloofness" of Jewish people and urged an effort to integrate. Yet integration is forbidden to those who believe in the "distinct identity that their covenant imposes on them as an article of faith" according to the senior presidential adviser on global democracy strategy.[65] As Abrams sees it, whether American Jewry survives "depends on whether they still *believe they are above all else members of a religious community*."[66]

The Polish-born Israel Shahak cautions that such "Jewish chauvinism" can be a causal factor in anti-Semitism and urges that both be fought simultaneously. In *Jewish History, Jewish Religion*,[67] he points to the "apartheid character of Israeli behavior in the Occupied Territories" as evidence of the dangers that accompany "fundamentalist Judaism." He reminds readers: "the State of Israel is not a democracy due to the application of Jewish ideology directed against all non-Jews and those who oppose this ideology."

A veteran of the Nazis' Bergen-Belsen concentration camp, Shahak cites historic evidence of "the rabbinical class, in alliance with the Jewish rich, oppressing the Jewish poor in its own interest as well as in the interest of the state—that is, the crown and the nobility." A resident of Israel at his death in 2001, Shahak charged that Israeli oppression of Palestinians in the West Bank is motivated by "Jewish religious fanaticism."

"Colonial Zionism" is a natural offshoot of "totalitarian" Talmudic Judaism, he charges, and the attempt to create a closed Jewish community centered on "exclusivism." As he cautions, "close relations have always existed between zionists and antisemites."[68] As an example, he cites Rabbi Joachim Prinz who in 1934 published *Wir Juden* (*We Jews*) welcoming Hitler's rise to power because the fascists shared the Zionists' belief in the primacy of "race" and Nazi hostility to the assimilation of Jews.[69] In 1999, the AIPAC-allied Committee for Accuracy in Middle East Reporting in America (CAMERA) portrayed Shahak as "one of the world's leading anti-Semites."

The charge of anti-Semitism was originally meant to protect innocent Jews from bigotry and injustice. By contrast, the New Anti-Semitism obscures a common source not only of bigotry and injustice but also transnational criminality and treason wed to an anti-democratic worldview. No one with Abrams' depth of commitment to a foreign state should be expected to perform in a way that is reliably loyal to the country of his birth. Just as the Jewish covenant with the Land of Israel forbids such loyalty, U.S. national security should not expect it.

If America is unable to identify those with a faith-based allegiance to Israel, it cannot protect its national security from those obliged—by their belief in a "covenant with God"—to put the interests of the Land of Israel above all else. That interest includes the steady expansion of the Land of Israel to include the entirety of Greater Israel so that Jews can occupy what the Talmud considers rightfully theirs because they are "chosen" by God. Or so they *believe.*

This nontransparent aspect of Israel's *sayanim* operation makes it essential that U.S. national security be insulated from the incapacity of government personnel to adhere to their constitutional oath to defend the United States. To portray as anti-Semites those seeking to address this *systemic* challenge can only serve to obstruct the investigation required to identify those who fixed the intelligence that induced the U.S. to wage war in the Middle East on behalf of Greater Israel.

In 1991 Abrams was convicted of unlawfully withholding information from Congress in its investigation of the Iran-Contra affair.

In 1992 President G.H.W. Bush pardoned him. In 2007 he helped implement "Iran-Contra 2.0," a covert initiative meant to oust the democratically elected Hamas-led government by provoking a Palestinian civil war with help from operatives in Fatah, the opposition party formerly led by Yassar Arafat. After Hamas's strong showing at the polls, the plan was to collapse the Hamas government with $1.27 billion in U.S. funding, largely for arms shipments to Fatah from Egypt approved by Israel and paid for largely by the United Arab Emirates.

When the plan leaked, Hamas struck first, capturing most of Fatah's arms and ammunition, leaving Hamas stronger than ever and ensuring that a peace settlement became even more unlikely between Israel and the Palestinians.[70] For both the U.S. and Hamas, the situation went from bad to worse as the U.S. was portrayed as attempting to destroy political choice while Palestinians in Gaza, where Hamas rules, became even more dependent on Iran. With 70 percent of Gazans living on less than $2 per day, the U.S. was again made to appear guilty by its association with the only winner in this failed strategy: Israel.

America First?

Much as those subjected to the toxic charge of anti-Semitism cannot defend themselves, so America cannot defend itself from those inside government who *believe* they are obliged to defend the Land of Israel at the expense of U.S. national security. That passionate attachment took political form in May 1948 as an entangled alliance between America and "the chosen people of Eretz Yisrael" (the Land of Israel), the term chosen by President Bush to describe Israel in May 2008.[71]

With the formation of a U.S.-Israeli alliance, treason became inevitable, invisible and systemic. Because the potential of such betrayal lies imbedded in the mind of the believer—and protected by freedom of religion—traitors can operate hidden in plain sight and, thus far, with impunity.

In April 2008, an Israeli think tank published a study that concluded "Muslim anti-Semitism" is a "strategic danger for Israel." Referring to the "hate industry," the study concluded that Iranian anti-Semitism poses a threat "unprecedented since Nazi Germany."[72] The "appeasement" of Iranian "Holocaust Denier" Mahmoud Ahmadinejad remained unstated but implied as yet another mental thread was laid to justify an attack on Iran.

The study was published by a research institute that commemorates the fallen of Israel's intelligence service, the Mossad. In mid-May, on the 60th anniversary of the founding of Israel, former Secretary of State Henry Kissinger, speaking in Jerusalem, added urgency to Tel Aviv's Iranian psy-ops strategy by claiming that Tehran poses not just a threat to the Land of Israel but "an existential threat to the world."[73]

Chapter 8

Would Obama Be Better?

Leadership is a potent combination of strategy and character. But if you must be without one, be without the strategy.
—General H. Norman Schwarzkopf

In April 2007, Senator Barack Obama released the names of his top three campaign contributors. The top two hail from prominent Chicago families (Crown and Pritzker) associated since the 1920s with syndicate operations,[1] an evidentiary trail that will be chronicled in the *Criminal State* series. The third, Hungarian-American George Soros, represents a more modern *modus operandi*, having pocketed $2.9 billion in 2007 alone from a financial hedging operation.[2]

The suspect history of Obama's financial sponsors does not mean he would be a bad president. However, the facts suggest that he would not *be* a candidate if syndicate operatives were not confident of his behavior as a pliable and reliable asset. He may defy expectations, of course. Yet when Congressman Tom Lantos introduced legislation in May 2007 encouraging U.S. companies to divest in Iran, the Illinois Senator dutifully sponsored a Senate version of the Lantos bill.

Seeking to win pro-Israeli votes in the April 2008 Pennsylvania primary, he launched a blog in Israel written in Hebrew. Its purpose: "to help strengthen his ties with the Israeli public."[3] Lest anyone doubt the depth of his sentiments, he also posted online his March 2007 speech to AIPAC.[4] Then in a debate with Hillary Clinton he cited his "stalwart" support for Israel, his deep ties to American Jews and his view of Israel as one of our "most important allies in the region."[5] That was just the beginning.

Upping the political ante, he then described Israel's security as "sacrosanct" (i.e., holy, sacred and not to be tampered with).[6] Not to be outdone, Hillary Clinton announced (one day before the Pennsylvania primary) that she would "obliterate" Iran if it launched a nuclear strike against Israel.[7] In this strongly Jewish state, Clinton's willingness to outbid Obama in her commitment to Tel Aviv paid off with a must-win victory for her flagging campaign.

Hillary Clinton has long supported America's designation of Jerusalem as the capital of Israel,[8] a policy certain to fuel future conflicts. Everyone in the region knows that Israel declared its sovereignty over all of Jerusalem after its 1967 land grab was rebranded the "defensive" Six-Day War. She also praised Israel's massive separation fence—what Palestinians call the Apartheid Wall. The Berlin Wall ran for 95 miles and rose to an average height of 11.8 feet, Israel's barrier, built on Palestinian land, will cover 403 miles at a height of 20 feet.[9]

As an uncritical supporter of Tel Aviv, the New York Senator presented a formidable obstacle to the Illinois Senator's attempt to attract funding from the pro-Israeli campaign-finance network enabled by McCain-Feingold reform. Thus, for instance, the former First Lady insisted that Ariel Sharon's provocative September 2000 march to Jerusalem's Temple Mount was a "legitimate visit to a holy site," a repackaging of reality meant to obscure a successful *agent provocateur* strategy that catalyzed the Second Intifada.[10]

Provoking the Second Uprising

In what Sharon conceded was a political demonstration meant to reinforce the Jewish state's claim of sovereignty since 1967 over a site considered holy to Muslims, Christians and Jews alike,[11] a Likud party delegation accompanied by hundreds of Israeli riot police provided precisely the provocation required to outrage Muslims worldwide and ignite the Second Intifada—one year before the September 2001 terrorist attacks on Israel's chief ally and arms supplier.

Ten days prior to Sharon's march, Palestinians had observed their annual memorial day for the massacre of Palestinians in the Sabra and Shatila refugee camps conducted by Christian Phalangist militia with the assistance and encouragement of General Ariel Sharon who was then Israel Defense Minister. Estimates of those slaughtered range from a low of 700 (confirmed) to a high of 3,500 Palestinians and Lebanese. In addition to slitting throats, axing, shooting and raping their victims, the killings also involved mutilations, including reports of castrations. Sharon-directed troops fired illuminating flares to facilitate a terrifying scene of mayhem and murder that continued uninterrupted for two days and nights. Israeli troops under Sharon's command surrounded the camps, ensuring that no one escaped the carnage.

After the largest protest in Israel's history, a Kahan Commission report found that Sharon "bears personal responsibility" for ignoring the danger of bloodshed and revenge in what the Commission described as a "slaughter" and a "massacre." The Commission recommended his removal as Defense Minister (he later resigned).[12] Yet there was the disgraced general and serial *agent provocateur* leading a heavily armed Likud party contingent to the Muslim world's third most holy site while proclaiming Israeli control as part of what Hillary Clinton described as a "legitimate visit to a holy site."

Likud spokesman Ofir Akounis explained Tel Aviv's rationale for the Sharon-led demonstration at that time and place and under those circumstances: "We are visiting the Temple Mount to show that under a Likud government it will remain under Israeli sovereignty... They are not sovereign on the Temple Mount and they ought to lower their tone. Every Jew has a right to visit there."[13] Riots commenced the next day, resulting in seven Palestinians dead and 300 wounded along with 70 Israeli policemen.

The outcome of that march was perfectly predictable by any competent game theorist —*within an acceptable range of probabilities.* A riot at that site in 1990 resulted in the death of 19 Palestinians and wounding 140. In 1996, Palestinians rioted in the West Bank and Gaza after Israel opened an ancient tunnel near the site. In exchanges of gunfire, 58 Palestinians were killed along with 15 Israeli soldiers. The death toll for the 2000-2007 period of the Second Intifada exceeded 4,300 Palestinians and more than 1,000 Israelis.

Whose Candidacy?

To put the Obama candidacy in perspective, recall that he is the junior Senator from Illinois. Chicago has long served as a major node in the node-and-network system of international organized crime.[14] The Illinois Congressional delegation's senior Senator is Richard Durbin, a lawyer recruited by AIPAC in 1982 to oppose 11-term Congressman Paul Findley. Durbin was elected to the Senate in 1996 and again in 2002. Up for reelection in 2008 against token opposition, he serves as Assistant Majority Leader, the Senate's second most senior position.[15]

Durbin shares a house in Washington with Charles Schumer, the senior Senator from New York and third ranking in the Senate leadership.[16] Both men are junior to Senate Majority Leader Harry Reid of Nevada who is a Mormon (also known as the Lost Tribe of Israel). Reid's assessment of AIPAC: "I can't think of a policy organization in the country as well-organized and respected."[17]

Even if Barack Obama were elected and did *not* behave as an asset, he faces odds that were long ago stacked against anyone running on a platform of change, particularly when it comes to the U.S.-Israeli relationship. The *possibility* of change poses an anxiety-inducing variable for Tel Aviv. Malcolm Hoenlein, head of the Conference of Presidents of Major American Jewish Organizations, sought to ensure that Obama envisioned no change in the U.S.-Israel "special relationship." While making it clear he had no concerns about the candidate, Hoenlein cited a worrisome "zeitgeist" in the Obama campaign: "All the talk about change, but without defining what that change should be is an opening for all kind of mischief."[18]

Concerned about the popularity on college campuses of Mearsheimer and Walt's *The Israel Lobby* (chronicling AIPAC's devastating impact on U.S. foreign policy), Hoenlein conceded that "most Americans see Israel as a dark and militaristic place." Citing "a steady poisoning of the elites," Hoenlein worried that the candidate preferred by many young people is Texas Congressman Ron Paul who is "openly anti-Israel." As Paul's campaign faltered, many of those favoring change in U.S.-Israeli relations gravitated to Obama.

From a game theory perspective, to achieve a desired outcome operatives must identify and manage potential variables. With change an unknown variable, Hoenlein signaled the need for a renewed Obama commitment to Israel. The candidate of change lost no time in reassuring Hoenlein's campaign finance network. Two weeks later, he again voiced unqualified support for Israel, repeating his unchanged commitment to Israel's "special relationship" with the U.S. and again describing Israel's security as sacrosanct.[19]

Six weeks later, Obama launched his Israeli blog with an announcement again describing Israel's security as sacrosanct. Five days later, he joined those who attacked former President Jimmy Carter for meeting with Hamas, the elected Palestinian government in Gaza. Republican McCain called on his opponent to repudiate the former Democratic president and Nobel peace laureate. Obama quickly obliged.[20]

Noting that Israeli leaders had rebuffed Carter during his peace mission, Obama repeated the same objection voiced by McCain: "We must not negotiate with a terrorist group intent on Israel's destruction." One day later, after first ensuring that both candidates were on record criticizing the former president, Israel's U.N. Ambassador Dan Gillerman launched an attack on Carter, calling him a "bigot."[21]

Ensuring Hamas could not meet conditions required to confer with any American leader, Obama recited the same terms cited by Tel Aviv: "We should only sit down with Hamas if they renounce terrorism, recognize Israel's right to exist and abide by past agreements."[22] Lacking was any sense of reciprocity. When did international law repeal the right of an occupied people to resist an occupying power? Israel itself has yet to renounce violence; Tel Aviv regularly deploys deadly force in a disproportionate fashion, routinely killing civilians, including women and children. How could Hamas recognize an entity (the *Land* of Israel) that has yet to define its borders? How can Hamas abide by past agreements that were neither negotiated nor agreed to by a democratically elected government?

The steady increase in the frequency and intensity of Obama's pandering to the Israel lobby initially came in response to the negative publicity given statements by his pastor, Reverend Jeremiah Wright. In a September 2002 sermon, Wright criticized Israel's apartheid policies toward the Palestinians and urged that his congregation consider the connection between 9/11 and Israel's treatment of its neighbors.[23] As mainstream media became awash in snippets from Wright's sermons critical of Israeli policies, Obama increased his outreach to the Jewish community. He also promised to diminish tensions between Black and Jewish communities, noting that "both groups suffer discrimination," a power-of-association framing to which we return below.

Candidate as National Healer

Though branded a fresh face in politics, Obama announced early on in his campaign (February 2007) that our "special relationship" with Israel obliges Americans to defend Israel. Despite abundant evidence to the contrary, this Harvard-trained lawyer argued that, "Israelis want more than anything to live in peace with their neighbors." Peace, of course, would preclude the possibility of Tel Aviv continuing its expansionist policies for Greater Israel. Since early fundraising is critical to the public's perception of a credible candidacy, Obama's early pledge of allegiance to Tel Aviv garnered early syndicate support as shown by the generosity of his top campaign contributors.

A candidate right out of central casting, the first-term Illinois Senator was immediately portrayed as a Democratic successor to the state's Honest Abe Lincoln, the incorruptible Springfield Republican who freed the slaves and healed a divided nation during the fractious Civil War. In the early branding of the candidate, one can see the National Healer working its way into his political packaging.

Featuring a resume that pushes the outer limits of coincidence, his ancestors included not just slaves but also reportedly a genetic lineage to Jefferson Davis, president of the Confederacy.[24] The son of a Kenyan father and a Kansas mother, he emerged as the first Black president of *Harvard Law Review*. Touting his pro-Israeli credentials and endorsed by scions of Chicago's Jewish community, he quickly became the politician-of-choice favored by the in-crowd of New York's financial elite.

By March 2007, a Wall Street round of campaign fundraising netted $2 million as supporters depicted him as the answer to the latest Great Divide. Consistent with this syndicate's long-term agenda for the oil-rich Middle East, Obama also proposed a date-certain withdrawal of U.S. forces from Iraq. Withdrawal would leave in place the fractious dynamics of a sectarian insurgency destined to unite the Shias of Iraq and Iran, a dynamic allegedly not foreseen by the Pentagon's pro-Israeli war-planners—yet an outcome *perfectly predictable* by competent game theorists with even a rudimentary knowledge of Iraqi culture.

Whereas pre-war oil was priced by OPEC in the mid-$20 per barrel range, oil topped $140 per barrel as this account neared completion in July 2008—including a record one-day surge of $11 per barrel after Israeli Deputy Prime Minister Shaul Mofaz, a former Israel Defense Forces chief of staff, announced Tel Aviv's intention to attack Iran. While conspiracy theorists charged that "Big Oil" and "Bush Oil" are the real reasons for this war, the facts point to a simpler, more ominous agenda. If the U.S. proceeds with a date-certain withdrawal, those who induced this invasion (and now seek to induce our speedy withdrawal) will benefit as long-simmering sectarian strife destabilizes the region, sending oil prices higher.

As in other venues, *the people in between* successfully pitted two sides against the middle in a conflict-of-opposites while profiting off the misery of both. At that level of manipulation, markets themselves are the "mark." At that level of geopolitical game theory, oil is not an end but a means. Over the time span chronicled in this account, a change in administrations presents an opportunity, regardless of party.

The Next Clash

Consistent with game theory, withdrawal could enable the Shias of Iraq and Iran to form an oil-rich coalition that could pose a danger not only to the region but also to the global community where moderate Sunnis are far more numerous (Shias account for approximately 150 million of the 1.4 billion Muslims). That conflict-of-opposites within Islam (a clash within *The Clash*) could provide the rationale (with support from the broader Muslim community) to take control of the natural resources of Iraq and Iran, with Israel a "natural ally" in an effort to counter Shia radicalism.

The next *Clash* may well be a battle over resources in which an energy-hungry China protects its national interests in that resource-rich region. Tel Aviv has long nurtured a special relationship with Beijing, an alliance that, among other things, involved Israel (and pro-Israeli Americans) providing China with U.S. technology suitable for adaptation to military purposes.[25]

The U.S. invasion of Iraq led the Chinese to view America as a threat. If the U.S. is seen as the barrier to China achieving an American standard of living, the next conflict-of-opposites may be East vs. West. With a population exceeding 1.3 billion, the People's Liberation Army (PLA) could match current U.S. troop strength in the region by mobilizing one-hundredth of one percent of China's population. The PLA presently has a uniformed ground force of 1.6 million.

As this account neared completion, John McCain attacked Obama's "reckless judgment" for proposing that the U.S. talk with Iran rather than isolate it.[26] Based on evidence confirming the orchestration of serial conflicts-of-opposites, talking to our latest present danger is the most sensible course for avoiding yet another conflict.[27] Iran was an ally until 1979 when radical Shia clergy replaced the U.S.-backed Shah of Iran who defrauded that oil-rich nation of tens of billions of dollars. With that takeover began the rhetoric of "those who hate our values" as the mental threads were laid for what would morph into the plausibility of a global war against "Islamo-fascists."[28]

It has not gone unnoticed that the ongoing pre-staging of war with Iran is identical to the pre-staging of war with Iraq. Most notable among those common ingredients is the advocacy of John McCain and Joe Lieberman. Without McCain operating as a non-Jewish "front" for Tel Aviv, Americans long ago would have identified who orchestrated this debacle and who backed what could soon become an expanded debacle should McCain become president and Joe Lieberman join his administration.

Declaring himself "pro-Israel," Obama called Iran a "genuine threat" *to the U.S.* (he did not explain *how*), suggesting that Tehran, not the nuclear-armed Tel Aviv, is the cause of "a nuclear arms race in the Middle East."[29] It was precisely then that the junior Senator from Illinois sponsored the Lantos legislation urging that U.S. companies divest from Iran—a form of economic warfare. Congress last embraced such legislation to oppose the racist apartheid regime that ruled South Africa. The African-American candidate made no mention of Israel's apartheid policies.

Obama-branding also included publication of *The Audacity of Hope*, echoing Bill Clinton's autobiographical *Between Hope and History*.[30] By March 2007, 20 months before the 2008 election, Obama's book topped *The New York Times* best-seller list. Five months earlier, Obama's face found its way onto the cover of *Time* magazine in October 2006 as the Unifier and Conciliator while Time.com lauded his candidacy in partnership with CNN, a Time Warner subsidiary.[31]

With 2007 book royalties of almost $4 million,[32] Obama emerged as both media star and political phenomenon—an essential pairing for a presidential campaign in the television age. He followed a path pioneered by this syndicate for television host Ronald Reagan a half-century earlier by Chicagoan Jules Stein, founder of the Music Corporation of America,[33] and MCA President Lew Wasserman, a Cleveland native.

The Israeli Alliance

Commencing with his early pro-Israeli contributors, Obama secured the funding required to evolve from a first-term U.S. Senator to a top-tier presidential candidate with a robust online fundraising operation. He shored up his pro-Israeli contributor base with a March 2007 speech to an AIPAC audience in Chicago where he promised: "we must preserve our total commitment to our unique defense relationship with Israel."

Undermining an attempt by Secretary of State Condoleezza Rice to end six decades of Israeli insistence on Palestinian dispossession, including four decades of occupation, domination, intimidation and segregation, the man who would be commander-in-chief assured his audience: "No Israeli Prime Minister should ever feel dragged to or blocked from the negotiating table by the United States."

Four days later, *New York Times* columnist Nicholas Kristof rewarded Obama with the first installment on his media industry payback. An ardent Zionist, Kristof published a glowing endorsement lauding the young candidate's "wisdom"—after two years in the

Senate.[34] Two days later, George Soros praised the first-term Senator, calling him a "transformational figure" with a "fresh voice" able to help America move beyond a period of bitter partisanship—reinforcing his branding as the Lincoln-esque Healer and Conciliator.[35]

Again, this does not mean Barack Obama could not become a fine president. Just because he is an asset does not mean he must remain one. With Obama, that possibility of change at least exists. Hillary Clinton was compromised long ago. The McCain campaign even has a donation button on the website of *Haaretz*, a widely read newspaper published in Tel Aviv.

Obama is clearly compromised. Yet that is to be expected given the systemic nature of this trans-generational corruption. Illinois, New York and Arizona have long been key nodes in this syndicate's nationwide network. The relevant question in 2008 is whether or not he is more compromised than John McCain. Given the 2008 presidential field, the best a voter can do is choose the least problematic candidate. From a game theory perspective, which candidate offers the better *probability* of marginalizing the influence of this systemic criminality?

Obama's background in the Black Liberation movement has much to commend it. Dr. Jeremiah Wright, his pastor at Trinity United Church of Christ, preached the truth as he saw it on the South Side of Chicago. To motivate his congregation to action, he often spoke in blunt terms. If his most famous parishioner follows in that tradition, he may yet become a transformational president.

Hillary Clinton, on the other hand, announced the need for a Cabinet Secretary for poverty on the same day that news reports confirmed that she and Bill Clinton have earned $109 million since leaving the White House in 2001, including $92 million from speaking and publishing.[36] That puts the former First Couple in the top one-hundredth of one percent of all taxpayers. That figure fails to include donations to the Clinton Library in Little Rock, Arkansas. Neither the names of the donors nor the amounts donated have yet been divulged. In time, that information will provide essential clues to identify the full extent of the Clinton-era corruption, including those who persuaded a Democratic president to endorse the North American Free Trade Agreement (NAFTA) over the protests of those in the political party that nominated him for the presidency.

A Liberation Presidency

After serial Democratic and Republican presidencies routinely neglected the aspirations of Blacks, people in South Chicago and New York's South Bronx are bringing to politics a common sense perspective. Majora Carter, Executive Director of South Bronx Sustainable, shows how race and class are reliable indicators of where to find goods as well as "bads." Blacks are more than twice as likely to live in a neighborhood with poor air quality. They are five times more likely to live within walking distance of a power plant or a chemical facility.

Such environmentally hostile conditions create a downward spiral that fuels other social ills such as widespread asthma among children. With fewer parks and outdoor amenities, people living in those communities exercise less, aggravating obesity and diabetes. By focusing on improvements in the physical and social environment (parks, bike paths, landscaping, wetlands restoration, and such), Carter trains residents to create healthy communities from the bottom-up.[37]

To restore a community, steps often must first be taken to create one. People must be reminded of their common interests and know that problems are solvable—as in South Chicago and the South Bronx. The outspoken ministry of Reverend Wright was driven by that need and motivated by riots in Newark and Detroit that began in July 1967—one month after the Six-Day War. The Newark riots left 26 dead and 725 injured and led to 1,500 arrests. Riots in Detroit left 43 dead, 467 injured, 7,231 arrests and 2,509 stores looted or burned. Commentators described the riots as rebellions.

Dr. Wright explained: "I have to have a theology that speaks to the hurt in my community. I want a theology that would empower people to be more creative. To be just as aggressive as they are in the riots, but more constructive."[38] Absent that aggressive attitude, the deeply imbedded criminality described in this account cannot and will not be displaced. Liberation theology addresses the "dispossessed" regardless of race. In the same way that a gifted Chicago pastor created a mega-church with 8,000 members, a gifted presidency is required to remedy today's hurts, both here and abroad.

Racial politics turned a nation on itself in a race-based conflict-of-opposites. That conflict did little to improve the conditions of many of America's 36 million Blacks while its 5 million Jews surged ahead claiming the same discrimination.[39] A Kenyan-Kansan president has the potential to heal that rift and identify those who used that conflict to their advantage while also undermining national security. Yet Obama has pledged his presidency to advance the interests of Israel with relatively scant mention of the ongoing hurt endured by minority communities in the U.S. where Blacks account for 12.9% of all Americans (vs. 1.7% Jewish).

Racism and Anti-Semitism

When America was founded, the vote was limited to white male property owners. Many of the nation's white male Founders included enslaved Blacks among their property. In 1905, four decades after the end of the Civil War, a group of 32 prominent Americans "of color" met on the Canadian side of Niagara Falls where hotels admitted "coloreds." A year later, three whites joined the "Niagara Movement" including Henry Moskowitz, a Jewish social worker. In a solicitation to 60 prominent Americans, an organizational meeting was set for February 12, 1909 to coincide with the 100th anniversary of the birth of Abraham Lincoln.

In August 1908, six months before the scheduled meeting, the Springfield Race Riot in Lincoln's hometown led to seven deaths. That incident is often cited as the spark that ignited the founding of the National Association for the Advancement of Colored People. The NAACP dedicated itself "to promote the equality of rights and to eradicate caste or race prejudice." From the outset, the leadership was heavily Jewish, with only one Black (founder W.E.B. Du Bois) on its founding executive board.

In 1914, Columbia University Professor Joel Spingarn became chairman of the NAACP "and recruited for its board such Jewish leaders as Jacob Schiff, Jacob Billikopf and Rabbi Stephen Wise."[40] Not until 1975 did the NAACP have a black president when W. Montague Cobb took over from Kivie Kaplan, a Boston businessman.

> The career of Rabbi Wise suggests how so few could wield so much influence provided those few are in the right place at the right time and under the right circumstances. Born in Budapest as the son and grandson of rabbis, his father was

sent to New York when he sought to unionize a porcelain plant belonging to Wise's maternal grandfather. His father became rabbi of a conservative uptown Manhattan congregation of German Jews, founding members of B'nai B'rith and the Anti-Defamation League.

Wise became a rabbi in New York in 1893 and soon led the formation of the Federation of American Zionists in collaboration with Theodor Herzl, the Austro-Hungarian founder of modern political Zionism. In 1898 Wise was a U.S. delegate to the Second Zionist Conference in Basel, Switzerland. In 1918 he attended the first American Jewish Congress. The concluding session was held at Independence Hall in Philadelphia where the Declaration of Independence was signed. The meeting ended with the singing of *America* and *Hatikvah*, the Jewish anthem.

He was also a member in 1918 of an elite Jewish delegation that attended the Paris Peace Conference to press for the inclusion of a "bill of rights" for all Jews of the world as a condition for the creation of any new states or the expansion of existing states.[41] Along with Leo Motzkin, Wise encouraged creation of the Bronfman-led World Jewish Congress to oppose Nazism. An adviser on Zionist affairs to Franklin Roosevelt, Wise joined Vice President Harry Truman at an April 1943 rally in Chicago Stadium to urge help for the Jews of Europe. Then head of the American Jewish Congress, Wise was the keynote speaker. Critics later charged that he hindered Holocaust rescue efforts.[42]

In April 1945, eight days after Roosevelt's death, Truman welcomed Rabbi Wise to the Oval Office as chairman of the American Zionist Emergency Council to discuss the resettlement of Jewish refugees in Palestine.[43] Wise remained a political activist for the Zionist state until his death in 1949.

Capturing the Black Community

In evaluating the role played in the civil rights movement by prominent Jews, including numerous high-profile rabbis, anti-Zionist analyst Israel Shahak urges a note of caution when allocating credit.

He reminds us: "Stalin and his supporters never tired of condemning the discrimination against the American or the South African Blacks, especially in the midst of the worst crimes committed within the USSR."[44] That cautionary comment suggests a need to evaluate whether fundamentalist Jews used racism in the U.S. as a means to obscure their own racism while advancing Israel's expansionist agenda behind a protective veil of "anti-Semitism" whenever Israeli policies were challenged.

Shahak urges that we recall how many Jewish supporters of civil rights for American Blacks dissociated themselves from that movement after the Six-Day War when it came time to support Palestinian rights against Israeli occupation and segregation. Warning against the resurgence of "totalitarian Judaism"[45] as evidenced by the Zionists state's treatment of Palestinians, Shahak notes:

> Any support of human rights in general by a Jew which does not include the support of human rights of non-Jews whose rights are being violated by the "Jewish state," is as deceitful as the support of human rights by a Stalinist. The apparent enthusiasm displayed by American rabbis or by the Jewish organizations in the USA during the 1950s and the 1960s in support of the Blacks in the South, was motivated only by considerations of Jewish self-interest, just as was the communist support for the same Blacks. Its purpose in both cases was to try to capture the Black community politically, in the Jewish case to an unthinking support of Israeli policies in the Middle East.[46]

Shahak's candor brings us back to Barack Obama and his reliable support for Israeli policies with little concern for the plight of the Palestinians. Nor has he voiced concern for the impact on U.S. national security of U.S.-Israel relations. Though branded in this presidential field as an early opponent of war in Iraq, only he knows for sure *who* persuaded him to oppose.

Was that advice offered by the same pro-Israeli network that emerged as his top fundraisers? Was his candidacy pre-staged to play the role of charismatic opposition candidate in this latest conflict-of-opposites? Is the junior Senator from Illinois the game theory candidate who will leave in Iraq the dynamics required to catalyze the next crisis?[47] Or does the latent racism in America make it impossible for him to prevail in any case, ensuring a McCain presidency?[48]

Though a fine public speaker, his campaign record suggests he may lack the strength of character required to oppose the elites and extremists identified in this account. In early 2008, mainstream media attacked his pastor for preaching, in the wake of 9/11: "America's chickens are coming home to roost." By making an association between that mass murder and U.S. support for Israeli policies, Reverend Wright's rhetoric became a media flash point with the candidate caught in the middle.

Rather than defend his pastor, Obama tossed him overboard. Rather than put his minister's remarks in the context of liberation theology, he put distance between himself and his friend and mentor of 20 years who officiated at his wedding and baptized his two daughters. Rather than redirect those attacks to draw media attention to decades of abusive Israeli treatment of the Palestinians, the candidate issued yet another statement portraying Israel's security as "sacrosanct."

When it came time to announce a running mate, he chose Delaware Senator Joe Biden, chairman of the Senate Foreign Relations Committee. In a 2007 interview with the American Jewish affairs program Shalom TV, Biden described Israel as "the single greatest strength America has in the Middle East." Biden then conceded "I am a Zionist. You don't have to be a Jew to be a Zionist." Asked about Jonathan Pollard, he argued the Israeli spy should be given "leniency."[49]

Anti-War or Anti-Peace?

Rather than use that negative media coverage as a means to highlight the need for a comprehensive Arab-Israel peace settlement, Obama let pro-Israeli media critics drive his minister into retirement after 36 years as head pastor of his church. Playing the race card, Republican candidates in Mississippi and North Carolina aired ads featuring video clips of Reverend Wright as a way to attack Democratic candidates who endorsed Obama, portraying them as guilty by association.[50]

Nation of Islam leader Louis Farrakhan also featured prominently in guilt-by-association politics, particularly after his February 2008 endorsement forced Obama to issue a "denunciation of Minister Farrakhan's anti-Semitic comments." *Chicago Sun-Times* columnist Mary Mitchell kept the political/media charade in perspective, observing "most black people understand the game":

> The point here, of course, is that these men—one the pastor of an 8,000-member congregation where the church roll reads like a Who's Who of the Chicago black elite, and the other the leader of an organization that has historically saved young men from crime and drugs—are unfit even to speak of Obama.[51]

At every turn, Obama endorsed AIPAC-approved policies. In the wake of an onslaught of negative publicity about Wright and Farrakhan, he used every opportunity to curry AIPAC's favor, including meeting with 100 Jewish leaders in Cleveland before the Ohio primary. The same media outlets airing attacks on Wright and Farrakhan aired every Obama comment in support of Israel, ensuring that his commitment to change would exclude any change in U.S.-Israeli policies.

In an echo of Israel Shahak's warning about those who make charges of racism to obscure even greater abuses, Obama noted, "both groups [Blacks and Jews] share the experience of suffering discrimination." The plight of the Palestinians again went unmentioned. Nor was a word of concern directed at Israel's exclusivist ideology or its ongoing oppression of those whose lands they occupy. Had he been true to his own faith tradition, the candidate could have reminded Americans how, according to the Talmud, Jesus was executed for his contempt of just the sort of exclusivist rabbinical authority reflected in the apartheid policies of the Zionist state.[52]

> *The Power of Association?* On July 29, 2008, more than 140 years after slavery was abolished, the House of Representatives apologized to Black Americans for the "fundamental injustice, cruelty, brutality and inhumanity of slavery and Jim Crow" segregation. Passed by a voice vote, the resolution was

> sponsored by Congressman Steve Cohen, a Jewish Democrat from Tennessee who tried unsuccessfully in 2007 to join the Congressional Black Caucus.[53]

Much as his pastor expressed sympathy for the Palestinians, Obama could have expressed sympathy for Jimmy Carter's attempt to broker peace by meeting with the elected Palestinian leadership of Hamas, an essential party to any peace agreement. At a minimum, he could have reminded the public that Tel Aviv tried to assassinate Khaled Meshal, a key Palestinian leader with whom Carter met (Meshal survived a Mossad attempt to poison him in Jordan in 1997, setting off a diplomatic furor). Instead, Obama attacked Carter not once but twice.[54]

Were he not so beholden to Tel Aviv's interests, Obama could have pointed out how, in the aftermath of that assassination attempt, a defiant Israeli Likud Prime Minister Benjamin Netanyahu announced that the battle with terrorism would be waged "everywhere."[55] America was not excluded. As an opponent of the war in Iraq, Obama could have used media critiques of Reverend Wright to point out how, after 9/11, the "Netanyahu Doctrine" became the Bush Doctrine of preemptive warfare as the U.S. was induced—with fixed intelligence—to wage war everywhere as part of a "global war on terrorism."[56]

> Consistent with game theory, Hamas arose in response to Israeli provocations that destroyed essential Palestinian infrastructure, including schools, power generation facilities and even police stations. That Israeli conduct conflicts with the Geneva Conventions that set standards of international law to address essential humanitarian concerns. In game theory terms, the radicalization of those oppressed and humiliated is a perfectly predictable response—*within an acceptable range of probabilities.*
>
> Though Tel Aviv alleged that its July 2006 invasion of Lebanon was in response to the kidnapping of two Israeli soldiers, that invasion followed a plan finalized more than a year beforehand.[57] With that invasion, avowedly in pursuit of

Hezbollah terrorists, did Tel Aviv seek to further radicalize Hezbollah? Was that invasion a pre-planned provocation meant to make it appear plausible that any response—including a terrorist attack in the U.S.—could be blamed on Iran as Hezbollah's sponsor?

Was that invasion pre-staging for a broader initiative again meant to expand the borders of the Land of Israel? As a former Israel Defense Forces chief of staff said on May 5, 2008: "If an armed conflict erupts it will be simpler to strike Lebanon when Hezbollah is the legitimate ruler."[58] Ten days later, Hezbollah gained the upper hand in a power struggle within the Lebanese government.[59]

Not a Profile in Courage

Obama's campaign conduct has been anything but a profile in courage.[60] By abandoning his friend while catering to pro-Israeli interests, his behavior mirrors other presidents who sacrificed America's interests. Reverend Wright was correct: Israel *is* racist. Jimmy Carter was correct: Israel is an apartheid society. Israel Shahak was correct: the Jewish state is *not* a democracy. Reverend Wright spoke the obvious: six decades of conflict between Israel and its neighbors contributed to the 9/11 terrorist attacks on Israel's closest ally. To suggest otherwise is contrary to known facts.[61]

Israeli policy toward the Palestinians has remained unchanged for six decades—from the ethnic cleansing by Irgun terrorists in 1948 that routed 750,000 Palestinians to the building in 2008 of the Apartheid Wall.[62] The racist mindset fueling this conduct is captured in Irgun leader Menachem Begin's assessment that "Palestinians are beasts walking on two legs," while former Israeli Defense Forces Chief of Staff Rafael Eitan described them as "drugged roaches in a bottle."[63]

As a longtime resident of Israel, Shahak earned the right to endorse the phrase "Judeo-Nazi" to describe policies deployed by Tel Aviv to harass, oppress, intimidate and humiliate Palestinians and others in the region.[64] That decades-long occupation must end in order to have peace, security and stability in the Middle East. Yet to resolve that perennial conflict would deprive Israeli game theorists of a key crisis-on-cue venue and a key rationale for American military and financial support.

Rather than applaud the good intentions of an elder in his own party seeking peace, Obama joined John McCain and other pro-Israelis in their attacks on Jimmy Carter. Rather than words of encouragement in support of a former president seeking to forge a settlement, the candidate signaled Tel Aviv that their delay tactics would continue to succeed in an Obama administration.

As the Democratic primary campaigns reached a fevered pitch in the candidates' Spring 2008 pursuit of Tel Aviv's approval, Obama pledged yet another allegiance to Israel. In Florida, where Jews make up approximately 5% of voters, Israeli influence is magnified by a combination of campaign fundraising, political activism, bloc voting and a large voter turnout. In a two-hour session at a synagogue in Boca Raton orchestrated by Florida Congressman Robert Wexler, he promised in May 2008 that he would show an "unshakable commitment"—not to America but to Israel.[65]

Cautioning his audience, "we've got to be careful about guilt by association," Obama sought to dispel Jeremiah Wright-related concerns that he is not an Israeli loyalist.[66] *The New York Times* reported how the candidate "has committed more fully to showing off his inner Jew."[67] By late May, that approach was gaining political traction. Rabbi Ethan Tucker, stepson of Senator Joe Lieberman, reported that he had contributed to Obama's campaign and would vote for him in the fall.[68]

Rather than risk guilt by his association with Reverend Wright, Obama had by then ditched his friend at the first sign of adverse publicity. Rather then defending a former head of the Democratic Party when Israel's Ambassador to the U.N. called Carter a "bigot" and an "enemy of Israel," Obama joined the chorus of criticism.[69]

That behavior is not leadership; that conduct shows a weakness of character similar to John McCain and Hillary Clinton. More is required of a candidate for commander-in-chief than to allow himself to be "captured" politically so that he embraces, as Israel Shahak warned, "unthinking support of Israeli policies in the Middle East." The good news is that Obama grasps the underlying dynamics at play in the region. He sees that the removal of Saddam Hussein also removed Baghdad as a counterweight to Tehran, granting a strategic advantage to Shia extremists in both countries—a dynamic foreseeable by any game theory-savvy war-planner.[70] He also speaks of the need to look at the "root cause of problems and dangers," though he has yet to acknowledge Israel's ongoing catalytic role.[71] If he realizes the game theory strategy behind *why* those loyal to Tel Aviv fixed U.S. intelligence to create Tehran's strategic advantage, he may yet become a president able to protect this nation's security.

It is also good news that those pro-Israelis closest to President G.W. Bush view Obama as a potential threat to the Zionist state's designs for the region. President Bush attacked Senator Obama in a May 2008 speech to the Knesset commemorating the 60th anniversary of the founding of Israel. It was seen as unprecedented for a U.S. head of state, when speaking to a foreign government body, to launch a political attack targeted at a domestic audience while also, in effect, threatening another nation (Iran) with war.

Why Appease Tel Aviv?

In his speech pledging America's allegiance to Israel, President Bush portrayed as "appeasement" any meeting with the Hamas leadership, as Obama has suggested, even though that leadership came to office in elections sought by the U.S. and certified as fair by the U.S. Much as pro-Israeli presidential speechwriter David Frum, a prominent neoconservative, crafted an "Axis of Evil" phrase for Bush's January 2002 State of the Union Address, neoconservative Elliott Abrams shaped this bellicose speech to the Knesset with its guilt-by-association linkage of Obama to British appeaser Neville Chamberlain from the World War II era.[72]

While pro-Israelis inside the U.S. government were urging that an American president dismiss as an appeaser anyone who proposes to meet with those Tel Aviv deems terrorists, the Israelis were negotiating with Syria through the Turks, and with Hamas through the Egyptians. Only after George Bush delivered that May 15th speech did Tel Aviv publicly concede ongoing negotiations on a peace deal with Syria, deemed by Washington a state sponsor of terrorism.[73]

Nowhere was it mentioned that the U.S. made diplomatic progress only after engaging Libya and North Korea while both nations were classified as terrorist states. Nor was it mentioned that U.S. diplomats were meeting with representatives of Iran or that former Iraqi insurgents were on the U.S. payroll conducting citizen patrols under a violence-suppression initiative known as Sunni Awakening.

If Barack Obama grasps that the provoking of serial conflicts-of-opposites is the *modus operandi* used by *the people in between* to wage unconventional warfare, he will identify those in his networks who are complicit in this syndicate. An ideology shared by those who consider themselves "chosen" lies at the root of the dangers that imperil national security. If he grasps *how* this corruption works by displacing facts with beliefs, this Illinois heir to Abe Lincoln may escape the influence of those who anticipated he would *remain* a pliable asset.

He will be waging an uphill battle. As a law professor at the University of Chicago for a decade, he was imbedded in the "Chicago" mindset. On a par with Harvard in its influence over the "economics" component of the mental environment, the University of Chicago nurtured market fundamentalist icons such as Milton Friedman. It also spawned the "law and economics" movement that imbedded its "consensus" prescriptions in legal systems worldwide.[74]

Those worried about Obama's obedience to Israel have good reason to worry. Anyone doubting who controls the Democratic Party had only to watch the party's August 2008 nominating convention in Denver and witness the party's shunting aside of former president Jimmy Carter. Since his publication in 2006 of *Peace Not Apartheid* chronicling Israel's treatment of the Palestinians, "the Carter problem" had haunted those planning this high-profile venue. By confining his appearance to a videotape, convention organizers protected a pro-Israeli image.[75]

Denied an opportunity to take the podium, even his brief appearance on stage catalyzed walkouts by party regulars concerned at conveying the impression that Democrats are anything other than enthusiastic—and uncritical—supporters of Israel.[76] With that display of control, Tel Aviv confirmed that it not only manages presidents and presidential candidates but also what former presidents can say.

Barack Obama's primary appeal as a presidential candidate is two-fold: he is neither John McCain nor Hillary Clinton. Like them, however, his comments and his conduct reflect a zeal for putting

Israel's agenda ahead of America's interests. For that reason alone, an Obama presidency may prove perilous to national security. But at least with him, there's a *possibility* of change that is clearly lacking in the others.

Chapter 9

The Way Forward

Some frauds succeed from the apparent candor, the open confidence, and the full blaze of ingenuousness that is thrown around them. The slightest mystery would excite suspicion, and ruin all. Such strategems may be compared to the stars, they are discoverable by darkness, and hidden by light.

—C.C. Colton (1780-1832)

Just as the displacement of facts with beliefs induced the U.S. to wage war in Iraq on behalf of Greater Israel, so the barrier to change is also belief. Despite the facts, people find it difficult to *believe* that what was done to America was done by an ally. Nor can they *believe* that this systemic corruption remains ongoing. Despite facts confirming that this criminality is poised to worsen, people have difficulty *believing* that such a failed future awaits them. Yet absent broad-based citizen engagement, that future is *perfectly predictable* as a shared belief in consensus "economics" expands to global scale.

Overcoming denial is the first step on the way forward. Acceptance of today's harsh reality requires an acknowledgment of lengthy premeditation by those who share what the law calls an "evil mind." The definition of psychopath in Chapter 2 highlighted the key personality traits accompanying that mindset: superficial charm, pathological lying, egocentricity, lack of remorse, and callousness.

Those who share that mental state view themselves as *entitled* to operate above the law, even while residing in a nation dedicated to governance based on the rule of law. Those complicit view themselves as a globally dispersed community subject only to the law of "the chosen people of Eretz Yisrael" as President Bush described them in his May 2008 speech to the Israeli parliament. They answer only to God and, by their covenant with God, are loyal first and foremost to the Land of Israel.

As noted above, in 1796 President George Washington cautioned a fledgling America to avoid entangling alliances, citing "the illusion of an imaginary common interest."[1] For a government based on consent of the governed, an alliance with Eretz Yisrael offers only the illusion of shared values between a secular United States and a theocratic Jewish state. The way forward requires that those elected to federal office engage this inconvenient truth in order to restore the rule of law.

This chapter suggests several small steps to identify the source of problems that Washington has thus far proven reluctant to face. Only with transparency can facts displace the manipulated *beliefs* by which the informed choice required for self-governance was corrupted *by the people in between*. Prudence suggests that the perils known to accompany our entangled alliance with Israel henceforth be prevented—rather than, as now, addressed retroactively at far greater cost.

U.S. intelligence agencies are fully apprised of how Israel wages war by way of deception. Game theory suggests the Zionist state will continue to manipulate America to gain strategic advantage until Washington learns to view Tel Aviv with engaged skepticism. National security requires a rejection of the self-deceit that Israel operates as a trustworthy ally in an unstable region while ignoring its multi-decade role in provoking and sustaining that instability.

Based on the six-decade record of U.S.-Israeli relations and the known manipulation of U.S. elections by the Israel lobby, why would any moderate Muslim leader have confidence in America's leadership—by either party? Knowing the virtual control exerted over U.S. foreign policy by the transnational syndicate identified in this account, how can any nation know with whom it is dealing when they negotiate with personnel within the U.S. government?

How can they know an elected U.S. official (such as Illinois Senator Richard Durbin) was not placed in office by the Israel lobby—as Durbin was? How can they know with confidence that a political appointee (such as Elliot Abrams) faithfully represents the interests of the United States rather than the Land of Israel—as Abrams does? In a nation ostensibly governed by informed consent, what remains of America's credibility after having invaded a Middle East nation under the influence of an ally infamous for waging war "by way of deception"?

As this account was being completed, a crisis emerged in Georgia in August 2008 that bore the hallmarks of a well-timed Israeli operation. The "Rose Revolution" that brought Georgian president Mikheil Saakashvili to power in late 2003 enjoyed support from 1992 onward from George Soros' Open Society Institute and its adjuncts.[2] The defense minister lived in Israel for years before returning to Georgia to see its military trained by Israeli advisors and armed with Israel-provided hardware.

The Robert Gates faction in the Bush Administration (vs. the Cheney faction) may have coordinated with Russia to ensure the conflict preempted the use of Georgia as a platform for Tel Aviv to launch an attack on Tehran. The entropic effect of that crisis deflected attention away from settlement of the Israeli occupation while appearing to heighten U.S.-Russian tensions just as John McCain began touting his national security credentials as the candidate best qualified to serve as commander-in-chief.[3] If this was an Israeli operation, it was also staged to make the U.S. look plausibly guilty—by association.[4]

The Reform Candidate

Though branded a reformer for his campaign finance initiative, John McCain's top-tier advisers and fundraisers are Washington lobbyists outnumbered only by those in financial services.[5] Instead of "Pioneers" who raised $100,000 and "Rangers" who raised $250,000 for the Bush campaigns, McCain has "Innovators" ($250,000) and "Trailblazers." By mid-April 2008, 73 Trailblazers had raised $100,000 each.

While serving twice as chairman of the Senate Commerce Committee, McCain wielded great influence over telecommunications policy. He remains a senior member of that committee. Yet

Wayne Berman, his deputy finance chairman, lobbies for Verizon. The head of his campaign's young professional group is a named partner (and Innovator) in the law firm of Isakowitz and Blalock whose clients include Sprint, Nextel and Viacom. Only after securing the Republican nomination did his campaign propose effective limits on lobbying by campaign staff.[6]

Though he touts foreign policy as his primary qualification for office, his conduct as a U.S. Senator suggests complicity in the purposefully deceitful decision-making that led us to war. Iraqi Ahmad Chalabi served as a key source of the fixed intelligence on which the U.S. relied.[7] As mentioned in Chapter 1, Secretary of State Colin Powell, the Bush administration's most credible member, was humiliated when, in February 2003, he relied on Chalabi-sourced intelligence to document Iraqi WMD to the U.N. Security Council as America's justification for its March invasion.

By assuring the global community that Iraq had mobile biological laboratories, Powell discredited the U.S. and damaged the standing of the U.N. By then, John McCain had been for a dozen years Chalabi's "stalwart friend."[8] Portraying Chalabi as "a patriot with Iraq's best interests at heart," McCain served as a key advocate for the $45 million-plus that Chalabi's London-based Iraqi National Congress was paid to deceive us. When McCain first embraced the Iraqi liar in 1991, the Arizonan was recovering from a Senate ethics investigation for his support of Charles Keating, a key funder of his first political campaign. How much more bad judgment can the U.S. afford?

Before moving to Arizona, Keating had served as general counsel for Carl Lindner's American Financial Group in Cincinnati.[9] By the late 1990s, McCain again was back in the thick of syndicate operations when he promoted a land deal in Arizona's Tonto National Forest involving property part-owned by Great American Insurance, a firm led by multi-billionaire Lindner, who touts his role as a major contributor to Jewish causes.[10] At Provident Bank, Keating and his mentor, Lindner, engaged in what the Securities and Exchange Commission found to be fraud and insider abuse. They signed consent decrees admitting no guilt and promising not to do it again.[11]

McCain brings to his candidacy a notorious history in arranging federal land swaps for suspect friends and deep-pocket political operatives such as Lindner. Typically the deals involved an exchange of less desirable land for federal land in prime real estate development areas in a state long notorious for land fraud. Donald Diamond, a wealthy Arizona developer and campaign contributor, received McCain's help on a deal to buy land on Fort Ord, California for $250,000. Less than two years later he sold the parcel for nearly $30 million.[12] He remains a loyal campaign contributor.

Like Keating and McCain's father-in-law James Hensley, Diamond contributed to McCain's first Congressional race in 1982. Diamond met the Vietnam veteran when McCain moved to Arizona to cash in his war hero chits for a Congressional seat.[13] Though McCain now brands himself a Washington outsider and a maverick, he marketed his initial candidacy for Congress as an insider, touting his service as a U.S. Navy liaison with the U.S. Senate.

Soon after he visited Israel in 1979 as Senate liaison, McCain met Cindy Hensley, divorced his wife who had been severely injured in an automobile accident, married Hensley and moved to Arizona where his wealthy mob-related wife, 18 year his junior, lent him funds to mount his first campaign at a time when everyone in the state knew that Barry Goldwater would soon retire from the Senate. Congressman McCain stationed his chief of staff not in Washington but in Tempe, home of Arizona State University, where he championed local issues.[14]

Commander-in-Chief McCain

Had John McCain's father not covered up Israel's murder of 34 Americans aboard the *USS Liberty* during the 1967 Six-Day War, Israel would not have been viewed with such sympathy when Tel Aviv's long-planned expansion of the Land of Israel was marketed as a "defensive" war. As a graduate of the U.S. Naval Academy and a U.S. Navy aviator, one would expect that Captain John S. McCain III (retired), the son and grandson of four-star admirals, would defer to eyewitness accounts of those aboard that ship.

Or that he would at least grant credence to Admiral Thomas Moorer, Chief of Naval Operations, who was appalled at the cover-up and described the Israeli behavior as murder. Or perhaps defer to

Secretary of State Dean Rusk who was on the scene when these events unfolded and was not deceived by Israeli accounts of the incident, calling the attack "outrageous." Or to Captain Ward Boston, retired U.S. Navy lawyer and counsel to the U.S. Navy Court of Inquiry appointed by Admiral McCain. Breaking a decades-long silence, Boston described the Israelis as "murderous bastards."

As an aspiring commander-in-chief, McCain should question why his father forbade Boston to travel to Israel or to contact any potential Israeli witnesses. He should also question why written affidavits of 60 hospitalized eyewitnesses were excluded from consideration. How can he credibly claim that, "the matter was thoroughly reviewed"? Instead, he compounded his father's complicity in the cover-up when he endorsed a book on the incident written by an author with a known pro-Israeli bias who was nowhere near the incident.

Had the "Fall of the Wall" resulted in a post-Soviet reform effort that broadly "owner-ized" the Russian people, Washington might not find itself again at odds with Moscow. The nationwide fraud inflicted on Russia by the Ashkenazi network identified in Chapter 5 was the greatest crime of the 20th century. Rather than acknowledge that the U.S. made a catastrophic mistake in funding the advice offered by complicit academics (largely from Harvard University), John McCain defended the worst of the oligarchs who "piratized" Russia, leaving tens of millions of Russians disenchanted not only with markets and democracy, but also with the United States.

Yet rather than criticize Boris Berezovsky ("the godfather of the Kremlin"), John McCain defended this Ashkenazi mobster. Associated with gangland-style murders both as a businessman and a policymaker,[15] Berezovsky even took Boris Yeltsin to Jerusalem after successfully organizing the media corruption that rigged Yeltsin's 1996 re-election. A dozen years later, that electoral fraud continues to shield the "private" property of Russia's mega-thieves—who, in turn, continue to pretend their "piratized" public property deserves legal protection rather than forceful prosecution..

Rather than criticize this systemic corruption, John McCain portrays the thieves as the aggrieved party while the Russian people suffer the consequences of that U.S.-enabled crime. Any Russian not outraged is ill-informed about the identify of the parties who facilitated that massive fraud.

Widening the Economic Divide

A promise to revive supply-side economics suggests either economic incompetence or a passion for the rich-get-richer legacy of those in this syndicate who positioned Ronald Reagan for the White House. Any presidential candidate who fails to grasp the fundamental flaws in the consensus model will both endanger and further discredit the U.S. by continuing to globalize the oligarch-creating "Washington" consensus.

Unfettered free trade was only the first step in oligarchization. Consensus advocates now propose that a World Investment Organization operate parallel to the World Trade Organization to ensure that national security is the only reason for limiting the cross-border flow of capital.[16] They also propose that the U.N. Security Council and the G-8 (the group of highly industrialized states) be "reconstituted" to insist on the globalization of this money-myopic mindset.

In this "consensus" environment, economic ignorance offers an attractive feature in a presidential candidate. McCain's alliance with Boris Berezovsky suggests that he endorses the Russian oligarch's conviction that wealth should dictate to government. As the Ashkenazi godfather sums up his governing philosophy: "I think that if something is advantageous to capital, it goes without saying that it is advantageous to the nation"[17] That statement captures the essence of the Washington consensus, including the international "code of conduct" advocated by former Treasury Secretary Lawrence Summers, a key operative in enabling the oligarchization of Russia.

Absent any indication of political philosophy—other than proclaiming himself both a maverick and a "true conservative"—should Americans under a McCain presidency expect to be governed by the values peculiar to capital markets? That unknown factor may also explain his support for the Climate Security Act of 2007, introduced by Joe Lieberman. Lieberman proposes to aid the environment by creating a "cap-and-trade" system for carbon emissions. Yet the bill also creates pollution permits worth over $5 trillion with no indication whether this new "currency" will accelerate the rich-get-richer legislative legacy common to both political parties. Though carbon credits could help, they can also make a bad situation far worse—by accelerating oligarchization.

As Americans enter the worst financial crisis since the 1930s, both candidates have allied their campaigns with the financial services elite who pocketed vast fortunes, often profiting off the misery of others and typically with the aid of taxpayer-secured debt—*our* full faith and credit. Anyone aspiring to the presidency for the right reasons would engage the best financial minds to correct trends that are certain to continue to divide America against itself. Instead, John McCain promises to resurrect the rich-get-richer "economics" of the Reagan era.

As a harbinger of policies he may propose, Harvard Professor Martin Feldstein has again emerged as a presidential adviser. Chair of Reagan's Council of Economic Advisers, Feldstein's disdain for workable patterns of ownership and income matches McCain's confessed economic ineptitude. Should a McCain/Feldstein team endorse a "true conservative" agenda, including George Bush's proposed repeal of the inheritance tax, the U.S. will soon have a permanent aristocracy whose wealth was financed in large part by leveraging *our* full faith and credit.

The Israeli-American Presidency

The most perilous aspect of a McCain presidency, however, is his unquestioning support for Israel and for policies sought by pro-Israelis. From his senior position on the Commerce Committee, for example, he could have opposed Ashkenazi-ation of the public's airwaves.[18] Instead, he embraced it. Or perhaps, like economics, he did not understand it. In Russia, the airwaves were taken over by an Ashkenazi-syndicate elite (Boris Berezovsky and Vladimir Gusinsky), while those with opposing views were routinely murdered.

Here the takeover was less obvious though no less effective in denying the public access to the unbiased information required for informed choice, including fact-based decisions about going to war in Iraq. With mainstream media largely in the hands of those with an undisclosed pro-Israeli bias, Americans can rely on one certainty: no matter when or where the next terrorist attack occurs, Iran will be portrayed as the Evil Doer and Israel the vulnerable victim of the Holocaust-denying anti-Semites of Tehran.

As this account neared completion, President Bush was celebrating the 60th anniversary of Israel's founding with enthusiastic support from all the major networks. Though a reappraisal of America's special relationship with Israel is long overdue, that remains unlikely regardless which candidate wins the White House at a time when the mental environment remains awash in pro-Israeli impressions.

The pop culture domain has long been inundated with sympathetic portrayals, commencing no later than the publication in 1958 of *Exodus* by Leon Uris and the sale of 20 million books (1958-1980) depicting Israelis as smart, honest and courageous and Palestinians as stupid, conniving and cowardly.[19] The 1960 blockbuster film by that title was directed by Otto Preminger and starred Paul Newman. Setting an early Evil Doer tone, the fiancée of Newman's character was tortured and murdered by Arabs.

The late Congressman Tom Lantos never tired of massaging public perceptions with high-profile productions that advanced the geopolitical agenda for Greater Israel. To build support for the Persian Gulf War of 1991, he convened the Congressional Human Rights Caucus in October 1990 to hear from "Nurse Nayirah," who testified how she witnessed Iraqi troops dumping Kuwaiti babies out of their incubators and leaving them to die. The "nurse" was later identified as the daughter of the Kuwaiti ambassador. Lantos claimed ignorance of the contrived account. In the 2002 lead-up to war in Iraq, Home Box Office aired *Live from Baghdad*, featuring scenes with the incubator allegations.

Holocaust-themed books have become a virtual industry. In 2006 Elie Wiesel's Holocaust memoir, *Night*, was featured on *The New York Times* best-seller list, where it remained for 80 weeks. Though first translated into English in 1960, Wiesel's survivor account was included in the *Times* list 46 years later when pop culture icon Oprah Winfrey chose it for her book club in January 2006.[20] After remaining atop the nation's premier best-seller list for 19 months, *The Times* removed it (after it sold three million additional copies for a total of ten million) when it was decided that Wiesel's memoir was not a best-seller after all but a classic like *Animal Farm* or *To Kill a Mockingbird*.[21]

Ten weeks later, *The New York Times* announced that the Pulitzer Prize for general nonfiction had been awarded to Saul Friedlander for *The Years of Extermination: Nazi Germany and the Jews, 1939-1945*.[22] Drawing attention to the creation of such impressions is certain to fuel charges of "conspiracy theory." Yet Holocaust awareness has long been a theme deployed with success to draft Jews overseas into serving as *sayanim*.

As AIPAC ensured there was no daylight between U.S and Israeli policy in the Middle East, the results became ever more calamitous. Only now has it become apparent that a state based on fundamentalist Judaism is neither a democracy nor a hapless victim but an apartheid state, an aggressor and a serial *agent provocateur*. Israel's expansionist goals could only be achieved by way of deception. Thus the strategic role of media and pop culture in shaping the mental environment.

Mindset Manipulation

From April to June 2008, Barack Obama reshaped his campaign to address Tel Aviv's interests, initially in response to his pastor's candid remarks about Israeli policy. Though the candidate's speaking skills are well honed, the ease and speed with which he dumped his minister and deferred to the Israel lobby suggests that integrity and courage are personal traits he has yet to master—or that he chose to put aside in deference to the political practicalities of presidential campaigns.

That situation could change once the candidate realizes how the pro-Israeli community used racism in the U.S. as a means to obscure its own segregationist policies, and as a means to provoke serial conflicts-of-opposites. Yet Obama's June 2008 commitment to AIPAC conventioneers saw the candidate of change parroting the language of rightwing Israeli political leaders Ariel Sharon and Benjamin Netanyahu when he promised the U.S. will stand "shoulder to shoulder" with Israel (Sharon's signature phrase) because we share the same values.

Among America's allies, Israel is the only state that routinely demands restatements of our commitment. After reassuring Tel Aviv of his "unshakeable commitment" in a half-dozen speeches in the space of a few weeks, Obama again felt obliged to massage his key funders in May 2008: "we will keep Israel's security a priority...the bond between the United States and Israel is unbreakable."[23] One can only wonder why, if Israel has been loyal *to us*, Tel Aviv would require constant reassurances *from us*?

Similarly, in mid-May, *Haaretz* published a lengthy article claiming that "Jews bend over backward to stay neutral in U.S. vote."[24] Why is Israel the only nation that feels obliged to offer assurances of political neutrality—unless the Israel lobby is intimately involved in U.S. elections? When Tel Aviv feels obliged to deny partisanship and restates "the official policy is not taking sides," does that mean pro-Israeli operatives have thoroughly infiltrated both sides?

Both McCain and Obama endorse the notion of a "Jewish state." Yet neither candidate has acknowledged that a theocratic and blood-line-based nation is anathema to the secular values of democracy, its rejection of royalty and its abhorrence of bloodline-derived political status. That rejection includes those who consider themselves "chosen" because they share a common lineage traceable to King David.[25]

In the final days before deciding whether the U.S. should recognize Israel, Harry Truman "was preoccupied with the fear that Zionist aspirations would lead to a racial or a theocratic state."[26] Those concerns led Zionist leader Chaim Weizmann to write Truman a series of letters including a seven-page, single-spaced missive reassuring him that Zionists envisioned a thoroughly secular state similar to the Americans and the British. Truman reinforced that understanding in his May 14, 1948 recognition of the provisional government not of "the Jewish state" (a description he crossed out) but of the State of Israel.

Despite those assurances, Truman's worst fears have since been realized, as have the concerns of the Arab community, the Palestinians and Secretary of State George Marshall. The former WWII general anticipated the troublesome dynamics that have since jeopardized national security due to America's entangling alliance with a nuclear-armed theocratic state with an apartheid domestic policy and an expansionist foreign policy. Is six decades enough? Is it time to revisit the legitimacy of Zionism as a basis for sovereignty and its compatibility with American values? The "state" that a U.S. president agreed to recognize under extraordinary circumstances bears little resemblance either to what was promised or what Israel has become.

For instance, the language of the Balfour Declaration issued by the British Foreign Office November 2, 1917 clearly stated what was envisioned for the non-Jewish communities in Palestine:

> His Majesty's Government view with favour the establishment in Palestine of a national home for the Jewish people, and will use their best endeavours to facilitate the achievement of this object, it being clearly understood that nothing shall be done which may prejudice the civil and religious rights of existing non-Jewish communities in Palestine, or the rights and political status enjoyed by Jews in any other country.

This Government has been informed that a Jewish state has been proclaimed in Palestine, and recognition has been requested by the provisional Government thereof.

The United States recognizes the provisional government as the de facto authority of the new ~~Jewish~~ State of ~~state~~ Israel.

Harry Truman

Approved,
May 14, 1948.

The Way Forward

The systemic criminality and ongoing treason described in this account works through agents, assets and *sayanim* (volunteers). To indict those complicit, law enforcement must identify and depose the volunteers. To access active lists of *sayanim* may require suspension of the diplomatic immunity that the Zionist state has thus far enjoyed even while dispatching its spies to the detriment of U.S. national security.

With those lists, FBI personnel can interview the *sayanim* corps to clarify the scope, scale, duration and long-term goals of this trans-generational operation. With interviewees on notice that this matter involves capital crimes (including treason while this nation is at war), that process may uncover cooperative witnesses able to shed light on the pre-staging of September 11, 2001. With that goal in mind:

- U.S. Attorneys should be allowed to grant limited immunity for those willing to testify.
- Amnesty should be considered for those who identify operative *sayanim* networks.
- Testimony should be sought from those who declined to be recruited as *sayanim*.
- The FBI should offer cash rewards for evidence of Israeli espionage and the disclosure of active *sayanim* networks.

Should that investigation uncover complicity by Israeli officials, Israel's embassy and its consular offices should be closed, its diplomatic corps expelled and its staff (Israeli and American alike) detained for questioning. U.S. diplomats should be withdrawn from Israel and the embassy closed and replaced with a modest interest section. Should an investigation identify evidence of complicity within community centers or places of worship, federal investigators should search there for evidence of *sayanim* support systems.

Former U.S. military officers who were dispatched by the Pentagon to offer expert commentary on the Iraq war should be interviewed to identify all those who conceived, organized and directed that program. In addition to identifying conflicts of interest (such as consulting for defense contractors while offering commentary as independent military analysts), those commentators should identify all those with whom they collaborated in acting for the Pentagon as "message-force multipliers."[27] With this Defense Department program, America discredited itself at considerable cost—from within.

To determine personal responsibility for the media component of this opinion-shaping operation, television and radio producers as well as print media editors should be interviewed and profiles prepared of all participants and collaborators in this Pentagon-directed program. Federal notice should be posted that print media operations as well as the broadcast licenses and facilities of those firms identified as complicit in this propaganda program are subject to seizure under the Trading with the Enemy Act.[28]

The State Department should convene an international conference with the goal of designating Jerusalem an international city under the protection of the United Nations and available to followers of all three monotheistic traditions that consider the site significant—Islam, Christianity and Judaism. The U.S. delegate to the U.N. should introduce a 60th Anniversary resolution urging reconsideration of the legitimacy of the Zionist state's status as a sovereign nation entitled to U.N. membership. A similar resolution should be introduced in both houses of the Congress and referred to appropriate committees.

Congressional Oversight

The Secretary of Defense should long ago have ordered a war crimes investigation of the *USS Liberty* incident. The Senate Armed Services Committee, chaired by Michigan Democrat Carl Levin, with John McCain its senior Republican member, should convene hearings to identify why those hearings have been delayed for 41 years. Witnesses should include the current Secretary of Defense as well as all previous secretaries still living. Any interested current or former member of the Joint Chiefs of Staff should be allowed to testify. All evidence related to the incident should be released to the public, including transcripts of communications between Israeli Air Force pilots and ground control during the attack.

The Armed Services Committee should also hold hearings on the practicality of moving ahead with a 2001 report by the Army School of Advanced Military Studies calling for 20,000 troops to enforce an Israeli-Palestinian peace accord. The plan, reported in *The Washington Times* of September 10, 2001,[29] described Israel's armed forces as "known to disregard international law to accomplish mission," and the Mossad as "ruthless and cunning. Has capability to target U.S. forces and make it look like a Palestinian/Arab act." The committee should determine: (a) why this plan has not yet been implemented, and (b) what barriers remain to implementation as a means to enforce the two-state solution agreed-to as the primary component of the road map.

The Senate Permanent Subcommittee on Investigations should convene hearings on the implications of the *sayanim* system for Homeland Security. Senator Levin chairs the subcommittee, on which Norman Coleman of Minnesota, originally a Democrat from Brooklyn, serves as the senior Republican. That hearing should be convened jointly with the Senate Committee on Foreign Relations, chaired by Democrat Joe Biden of Delaware, with Republican Dick Lugar of Indiana the senior Republican. Witnesses should include the Attorney General, the Secretary of Homeland Security, the Director of the Federal Bureau of Investigation, the Director of Central Intelligence and the Director of the Defense Intelligence Agency.

Parallel hearings should be convened by the Committee on Homeland Security and Government Affairs, chaired by Independent Joe Lieberman. In addition to executive branch witnesses, House members who should testify include:

- California Congressman Howard Berman, Chairman of the House Committee on Foreign Affairs, and his Republican counterpart, Ileana Ros-Lehtinen of Florida.
- New York Congressman Gary Ackerman, chairman of the Subcommittee on the Middle East and South Asia.
- New York Congresswoman Nita Lowey, chairman of the Appropriations Subcommittee on State, Foreign Operations and Related Programs.
- New York Congressman Jerrold Nadler, chairman of the Subcommittee on the Constitution, Civil Rights and Civil Liberties and a member of the Subcommittee on Crime, Terrorism and Homeland Security.
- Intelligence community invitees should include Rita Hauser, a former member of the President's Foreign Intelligence Advisory Board during the war-planning period (2001-2004).[30]
- Pentagon advisory personnel who should testify include Richard Perle, chairman of the Defense Policy Advisory Board, former Deputy Secretary of Defense Paul Wolfowitz

and former Under Secretary of Defense Douglas Feith in charge of the Office of Special Plans.

- Former executive branch officials should be included, including Lewis Libby, former chief of staff to Vice President Dick Cheney.

The Committee on Foreign Relations should convene hearings to determine the extent to which Russian oligarchs have been granted preferential treatment in the U.S., who sponsored them, and why. The Russian ambassador should be invited to testify on the extent to which: (a) U.S. advisory teams facilitated the oligarchization of Russia, and (b) the granting of asylum to Russian emigrés by U.S. allies impeded Russia in enforcing the rule of law. Former Treasury Secretaries Robert Rubin and Lawrence Summers should testify.

The Committee should also determine to what extent the granting of asylum to Israelis would improve U.S national security, including weapons specialists such as Mordechai Vanunu, whose photographs confirmed Israel's nuclear weapons program. Vanunu spent 18 years in prison, including more than 11 years in solitary confinement. Since his release in 2004, Israel has restricted the whistleblower's speech and movement.

The Committee on Finance should convene hearings to consider the tax-exempt status of the American Israel Public Affairs Committee, as well as the status of the Conference of Presidents of Major American Jewish Organizations and its 51 member organizations. The Committee should direct the FBI to interview the 10,000 largest AIPAC contributors over the past decade to identify the extent to which, in collaboration with AIPAC, AIPAC members played a role in financing federal or state elections.

The investigation should also identify to what extent AIPAC influenced McCain-Feingold campaign finance reform to enable the creation of "527" organizations such as the Carl Lindner-supported Swift Boat Veterans for Truth. The committee should consider a referral to the Foreign Relations and Intelligence Committees to advise if AIPAC should be required to register as an agent of a foreign government. Should AIPAC personnel be found complicit in the criminality described in this account, its tax-exempt status should be revoked retroactively and all AIPAC contributors for the past four decades so notified by the Internal Revenue Service (i.e., since the 1967 Six-Day War). A list of those contributors should be posted online.

The tax-exempt status of Harvard University also should be re-examined in light of the advisory role played by the Harvard Institute for International Development in the oligarchization of Russia. A parallel investigation should examine the Harvard Management Company and the role played by Harvard's endowment in that Ashkenazi-ation process.

The tax-exempt status of the nation's 100 largest think tanks should be examined to identify those that advocated war in Iraq based on intelligence now known to have been fixed around a predetermined agenda. Donor lists should be examined and compared with donors to pro-Israeli tax-exempt organizations such as AIPAC and the Conference of Presidents of Major American Jewish Organizations and its 51 member organizations. Where there is overlap, donors should be interviewed by the FBI to determine the extent of coordination around a political agenda for Greater Israel.[31]

The committee should consider, in conjunction with the Committee on the Judiciary, enforcement action to seize the properties of those found complicit in the criminality chronicled in this account. The Senate Committee on the Judiciary, chaired by Patrick Leahy of Vermont, with Arlen Specter of Pennsylvania the senior Republican, should convene hearings to consider whether revised and updated standards are required for an effective Trading with the Enemy Act based on what is now known about the waging of unconventional warfare by "the people in between." The hearings should determine whether current legislation is sufficient for seizing the assets of those complicit in the transnational organized crime network identified in this account.[32]

Members of the Committee who should be asked to testify include Diane Feinstein of California, Charles Schumer of New York, Richard Durbin of Illinois, Russell Feingold of Wisconsin, Jon Kyl of Arizona, (ranking Republican on the Subcommittee on Terrorism, Technology and Homeland Security), and Ron Wyden of Oregon, who also serves on the Intelligence Committee. The Committee should consider how those convicted of espionage or treason can be made ineligible for parole, pardon, clemency or commutation.

The Senate Committee on the Judiciary should convene hearings to assess AIPAC's status as an agent of a foreign government. The committee should examine whether AIPAC has operated outside the registration requirements of the Foreign Agents Registration Act (enacted in 1938) by promoting foreign-influenced lobbying. To the extent that AIPAC has shaped policy, legislation and lawmaking, it should be required to detail that influence and criminal sanctions should be sought for AIPAC personnel complicit in wielding that influence.

The Senate Committee on Appropriations, chaired by Robert Byrd of West Virginia, should convene hearings on the extent to which funding now provided to Israel should be shifted to the education and care of military personnel returning from wars in Iraq and Afghanistan. The Committee should request recommendations from the Committee on Armed Services on the extent to which the Israeli government should participate in the Joint Strike Force Fighter program, have access to the Lockheed F-35 fighter and otherwise continue to be the beneficiary of technologies developed for defense of the U.S.

The Senate Committees on Finance and Appropriations should convene joint hearings to determine the extent to which complementary forms of monetization and exchange could relieve emerging fiscal pressures. As the U.S. cannot tax its way out of today's consensus-model predicament, new thinking should be engaged to mobilize resources without relying exclusively on a unitary national currency created with debt. The Foreign Relations Committee should examine how U.S. foreign assistance could be improved by enabling such complementary systems of market exchange as a means to offset the *perfectly predictable* effects of the "Washington" consensus.[33]

The Senate Banking Committee should convene hearings on the relationship between use of the public's credit capacity and the accumulation of private fortunes since 1980. The relationship between tax policy, appropriations policy and banking should be examined from the perspective of how financing techniques can play a role in broadening the distribution of wealth and income. As U.S. debt cannot easily be disavowed, the Committee should consider to what extent private wealth financed through public debt (as with deficit-financed supply-side economics) should be appropriated for public purposes.[34]

Both logic and experience suggest that the U.S. Senate emerged as a priority target for game theorists to imbed systemic corruption in the legislative branch. Members of the House stand for reelection every two years and Presidents every four. With six-year terms, fewer members (100 vs. 435) and a history of serving multiple terms, "the world's greatest deliberative body" has long been the focus of astute game theorists. Thus the need for a sustained Senate effort to restore the informed choice required for representative government.

House Committees should convene parallel hearings. The bicameral Joint Economic Committee, chaired by New York Senator Charles Schumer, should examine the "closed system of finance" (described in Chapter 6) to determine if there is any set of policies that would not concentrate wealth and income so long as finance relies on that system. Witnesses should include the chairman and ranking minority member of the tax-writing committees (Finance and Ways and Means), the Secretary of the Treasury, the chairman of the Federal Reserve and the current (and past) president(s) of the World Bank.

The General Accountability Office should undertake a full cost study to identify and quantify the overall costs of America's 60-year alliance with Israel. That study should include not just direct outlays, loans and military assistance, but also an analysis of indirect costs that would not have been incurred but for the recognition of Zionism as a legitimate sovereign state. Those costs should include a projection of future costs due to Israeli conduct, including the transfer of U.S. technology to foreign governments (such as China) by Israel and its supporters.[35] The facts suggest that the cost of the war in Iraq should also be included as a separate item.

Securing the Nation

To identify the scope of the systemic criminality during the Clinton administration, the FBI should offer a cash reward for a complete list of donors to the Clinton Library, including the amount and timing of the donations. The Department of Justice should summarize the relationship of donors to the administration and publish a profile of each donor, including all known civic affiliations and their home addresses.

The systemic nature of this criminality suggests that Americans alone can no longer secure their country—the corruption is too imbedded and elected officials are too intimidated by the Israel lobby. To solve this transnational criminality requires multilateral engagement to remedy the perils that this syndicate now poses to world peace.

On the same day in mid-May 2008 that President G.W. Bush reassured the Knesset that America is proud to be Israel's "closest ally and best friend in the world," Speaker of the House Nancy Pelosi said that the establishment of Israel was "one of the bright spots in the Twentieth Century." Three days later, Speaker Pelosi announced she is confident that all three presidential candidates support Israel.[36]

Within 48 hours of Pelosi's statement, Israeli Foreign Minister Tzipi Livni announced that, consistent with Tom Lantos' prediction (and with John McCain's support), Israel is unlikely to reach agreement with the Palestinians on core issues for a two-state solution during 2008.[37] Three days after Livni's announcement, Prime Minister Ehud Olmert proposed to Pelosi that the U.S. impose a naval blockade on Iran, an act of war also pursued through a House resolution pursued by New York Congressman Gary Ackerman.[38] Meanwhile, Prime Minister Olmert's office directed attention away from the peace process by annoucing Israel's talks with Syria, mediated through Turkey.[39]

> A leading contender for Prime Minister to replace Ehud Olmert, Livni was a Paris agent for Mossad in the 1980s when it ran a series of missions to murder Palestinians in European capitals. "Tzipi was not an office girl," said an acquaintance. Her closest female partner now heads her ministerial office. Her mother, Sarah, who died recently at age 85, was a leader of Irgun who was arrested for terrorist crimes, including train robbery.[40]

With a changeover in U.S. administrations, a new team will arrive to fill positions corrupted by pro-Israelis such as Richard Perle, Paul Wolfowitz, Lewis Libby, Douglas Feith and so forth.[41] Regardless which political party wins the White House in November 2008, eminently qualified people with remarkably similar mindsets will be available to staff the next administration—and, despite their constitutional oath of office, to perform with a pro-Israeli bias consistent with their "covenant with God."

As the Bush administration draws to a close, Homeland Security chief Michael Chertoff announced that he will adopt Israeli airport security methods such as behavior-detection technologies designed to spot sinister intentions among travelers.[42] The model will be Ben-Gurion International Airport, which relies heavily on behavioral science and biometric sensors to detect suspicious behavior, enabling security to identify, arrest and detain on a preemptive basis.

Historians may cite President George W. Bush's May 2008 speech before the Israeli Knesset as the precise moment when it became clear that an American president refused to take responsibility for his role in inflicting untold damage on U.S. national security. "Israel's population may be just over 7 million," the commander-in-chief assured the Knesset, "but when you confront terror and evil, you are 307 million strong, because America stands with you."

To determine if that assertion has a basis in fact, a national referendum should gauge the depth of Americans' support for the Zionist state as the largest recipient since WWII of U.S. economic and military assistance.

- Do Americans agree that Israel should remain first-ranked as a recipient of U.S. foreign aid?
- Do Americans agree that Tel Aviv should continue to receive $8.5 million per day in U.S. military assistance?
- Do Americans agree that the U.S. military should be deployed to wage war in Iran on Israel's behalf?
- Do Americans want to continue U.S. support of Israel's armed occupation of Palestinian land?

Rather than defend the interests of the U.S., this president committed America to wage *perpetual war* in the Middle East at a long-term overall fiscal cost now on track to exceed $3 trillion—all of it borrowed. As this account neared completion, the U.S. sent 7,000 more troops to Afghanistan from a military already stretched thin by maintaining 140,000 troops in Iraq.[43] The strategy deployed to date reflects a profound misunderstanding of the game theory dynamics that deceived the U.S. to wage war in the Middle East for Greater Israel.

The global community is mistrustful of our words, extremists have been emboldened, and our allies feel less secure.[44] It is not Iran but Israel that must be restrained to protect U.S. national security and to repair the worldwide damage done by the "Washington" consensus. Based on John McCain's unwavering support for Israeli policies and his unquestioning espousal of an "economics" that he concedes he does not understand, American voters must question not just his loyalty but also his judgment.

By naming as his running mate Alaska Governor Sarah Palin, McCain put a heartbeat from the presidency a candidate steeped in Pentecostal Christianity. As a firm believer that Israel represents God's chosen people, Palin was on message in her first television interview when she agreed with the neocons that Israel has the right to take military action against Iran, and the U.S. should not "second-guess the measures that Israel has to take to defend themselves." While you cannot fault someone for their beliefs, you can fault an elected official for displacing the will of the majority with the beliefs of a minority. America was founded to escape just that sort of faith-based decision-making in order to protect personal freedom.

Though Barack Obama may appear marginally better qualified, his pro-Israeli bias confirms that neither candidate can be relied upon to restore our national security. Nor can we reasonably expect from either candidate anything other than more of the same "consensus" prescriptions. The facts suggest that an informed and politically engaged public is now America's best hope for ensuring that, never again, will such systemic criminality be allowed to wield control over American democracy.

Sixty years ago, we legitimized this phenomenon when President Harry Truman agreed to associate our hard-earned credibility with an enclave of elites and extremists. In a democracy, responsibility for a nation's actions resides not with our leaders but with informed and engaged citizens. With access to accurate and unbiased information, American democracy can be restored and freedom protected from those described in this account. Our national will resides dispersed in the personal resolve of each of us. The challenge lies in how best to ally with others to ensure this extremism is no longer associated with America's true values.

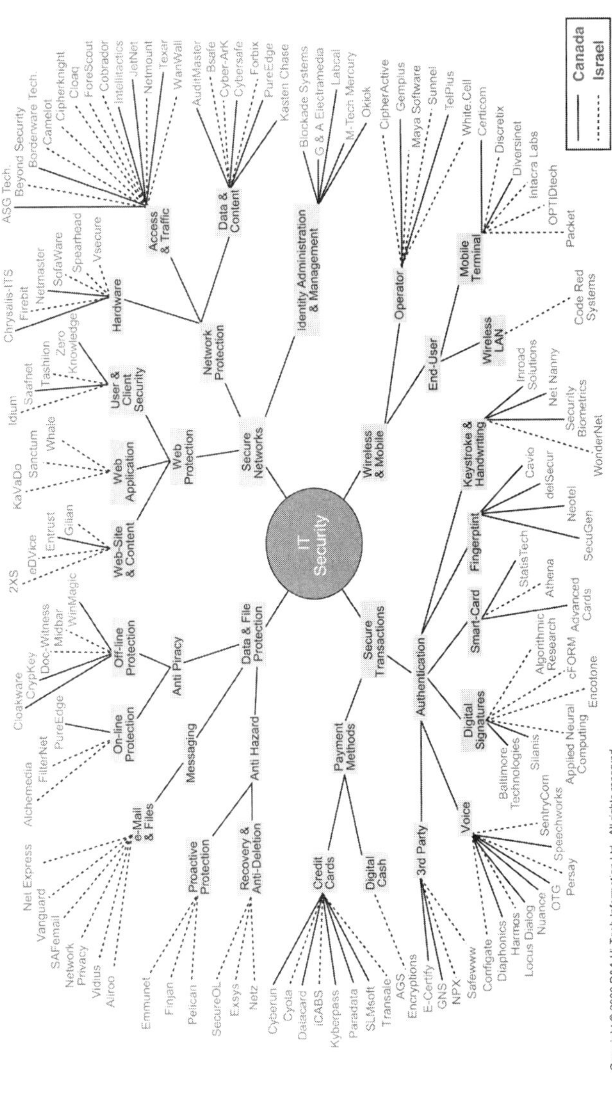
D&A maps: Canadian & Israeli Security Companies
IT Security
Secure Networks
Network Protection
Hardware
Chrysalis-ITS
Firebit
Netmaster
SofaWare
Spearhead
Vsecure
Access & Traffic
ASG Tech.
Beyond Security
Borderware Tech.
Camelot
Cipherknight
Cloaq
ForeScout
Cobrador
Intellitactics
JetNet
Netmount
Texar
WanWall
Data & Content
AuditMaster
Bsafe
Cyber-ArK
Cybersafe
Forbix
PureEdge
Kasten Chase
Identity Administration & Management
Blockade Systems
G & A Electramedia
Labcal
M-Tech Mercury
Okiok
Web Protection
User & Client Security
Idium
Saafnet
Tashilon
Zero Knowledge
Web Application
KaVaDo
Sanctum
Whale
Web-Site & Content
2XS
eDVice
Entrust
Gilian
Wireless & Mobile
Operator
CipherActive
Gemplus
Maya Software
Sunnel
TelPlus
End-User
Mobile Terminal
White.Cell
Certicom
Discretix
Diversinet
Intacra Labs
OPTIDtech
Packet
Wireless LAN
Code Red Systems
Data & File Protection
Anti Piracy
Off-line Protection
Cloakware
CrypKey
Doc-Witness
Midbar
WinMagic
On-line Protection
Alchemedia
FilterNet
PureEdge
Messaging
e-Mail & Files
Net Express
Vanguard
SAFemail
Network Privacy
Vidius
Alroo
Anti Hazard
Proactive Protection
Emmunet
Finjan
Pelican
Recovery & Anti-Deletion
SecureOL
Exsys
Netz
Secure Transactions
Authentication
Keystroke & Handwriting
Inroad Solutions
Net Nanny
Security Biometrics
WonderNet
Fingerprint
Cavio
delSecur
Neotel
SecuGen
Smart-Card
StatisTech
Athena
Advanced Cards
Digital Signatures
Algorithmic Research
cFORM
Encotone
Applied Neural Computing
Silanis
Baltimore Technologies
Voice
SentryCom
Speechworks
Persay
OTG
Nuance
Locus Dialog
Harmos
Diaphonics
Configate
3rd Party
AGS Encryptions
E-Certify
GNS
NPX
Safewww
Payment Methods
Credit Cards
Cyberun
Cyota
Datacard
iCABS
Kyberpass
Paradata
SLMsoft
Transale
Digital Cash
Canada
Israel

Endnotes

Introduction

1 "A definition of Zionism," Jewish Virtual Library, http://www.Jewishvirtuallibrary.org/source/Zionism/zionism.html.

2 "I think there is a strain within the pro-Israel community that says unless you adopt an unwavering pro-Likud approach to Israel that you're anti-Israel...that can't be the measure of our friendship with Israel." Remarks of Barack Obama to Jewish leaders in a February 25, 2008 meeting in Cleveland.

3 "The third reason to fear Keating was that not a penny of his purchase of Lincoln Savings came from his pocket. Michael Milken and the junk bond operations he controlled at Drexel Burnham Lambert provided all the cash for the deal. Milken had a standard operating procedure in such cases. Drexel greatly overfunded the buyer. Keating needed $51 million to purchase Lincoln Savings, but Drexel issued over $125 million in junk bonds out of American Continental Corp. (ACC), the holding

company that Keating used to acquire Lincoln Savings. ACC was a failing real estate development company even before it had this crushing debt dumped on it... Milken wanted companies like ACC to be in desperate circumstances; that maximized his leverage over Keating." William Black, *The Best Way to Rob a Bank Is to Own One* (Austin: University of Texas Press, 2005), p. 65. Preliminary research suggests that ACC emerged from restructuring an American Financial Corporation subsidiary, American Continental Homes.

4 The organized crime origins of Ronald Reagan's political ascendancy will be chronicled in the *Criminal State* series.

5 See John J. Mearsheimer and Stephen M. Walt, *The Israel Lobby and U.S. Foreign Policy* (New York: Farrar, Strauss and Giroux, 2007).

6 Bundling operations may involve a corporate executive directing his/her executive corps (and their spouses) to maximize ("max out") the permissible campaign contributions to a candidate, with each executive's compensation adjusted to reflect the contribution (though without any direct *quid pro quo*).

7 "According to political analyst Rhodes Cook, the number of competitive races for House seats has dwindled in recent years from a high of 111 competitive races in 1992 to a low of 32 in 2004." The number of competitive races was 37 in 1988 and 57 in 1990. Andrew Kohut, "Midterm Match-Up: Partisan Tide vs. Safe Seats," Pew Research Center for the People & the Press, February 13, 2006. http://pewresearch.org/pubs/2/midterm-match-up-partisan-tide-vs-safe-seats.

8 See "The Measure of Their Achievement," http:www.jewishachievement.com/about/about.html.

9 Comment by Michael Steinhardt during an interview on *The Charlie Rose Show*, March 9, 2005.

10 Jeffrey H. Birnbaum, "For Campaign Contributions by the Wheelbarrow, the Back Door is Open," *The Washington Post*, May 30, 2008, p. A11.

11 Tom Harkin, Democrat of Iowa, is the second-ranking career recipient of pro-Israel political action committee funds, with a total of $541,950. Janet McMahon, "Pro-Israel PACs: Disguises and Permutations," *Washington Report on Middle East Affairs*, August 2008, p. 26.

12 In May 1999, Senators McCain and Feingold shared the 10th annual John F. Kennedy Profile in Courage Award, associating their reform with the Kennedy legacy. See http://www.jfklibrary.org.

13 See Kalle Lasn, "Why Won't Anyone Say They're Jewish?," *Adbusters*, March/April 2004.

14 Key intellectuals in the neoconservative movement include Leo Strauss (1988-1973), Max Schachtman and author Ben Wattenberg whose 1970 bestseller, *The Real Majority*, popularized the neocon perspective.

15 In June 2008, the Senate Intelligence Committee "Phase 2" report was especially critical of statements by the president and the vice president linking Iraq to Al Qaeda and raising the possibility that Saddam Hussein might supply the terrorist group with weapons of mass destruction. Chairman John D. Rockefeller IV wrote: "Representing to the American people that the two had an operational partnership and posed a single, indistinguishable threat was fundamentally misleading and led the nation to war on false premises." The first phase of the inquiry, begun in the summer of 2003 and completed in July 2004, identified grave faults in the CIA's analysis of the threat posed by Saddam Hussein. Mark Mazzetti and Schott Shane, "Bush Overstated Evidence on Iraq, Senators Report," *The New York Times*, June 6, 2008, p. A11.

16 See The Center for Public Integrity, Progress for America Voter Fund. http://wwww.progressforamerica.com/pfa.

17 In 1995, Great American Insurance paid for Corsi, John Doe and others to travel to Poland to found a mutual fund similar to B'nai B'rith mutual funds that Corsi established in Israel.

18 Luisa Kroll, "World's Billionaires," *Forbes,* March 5, 2008.

19 David Barboza, "Little-Known Entrepreneurs Putting China Near Top of Billionaires' List," *The New York Times*, November 7, 2007.

20 "China has 146 billionaires," *China Daily*, January 1, 2008. *Forbes* reported 66 billionaires in China.

21 Nathan Ausubel, *Pictorial History of the Jewish People* (New York: Crown Publishers, 1953).

22 See Landon Thomas Jr., "A Growing Trophy Case," *The New York Times*, July 10, 2008, p. C1.

23 Barak Ravid, "Obama pledges to coordinate Iran policy with Israel," *Haaretz,* July 24, 2008.

24 David Leonhardt and Majorie Connelly, "81% in Poll Say Nation Is Headed On Wrong Track," *The New York Times*, April 4, 2008, p. 1

25 Quoted in Jeremy Grant, "Learn From the Fall of Rome, US Warned," *Financial Times*, August 14, 2007.

26 The announced deficit does not reflect the full cost of military operations in Iraq and Afghanistan, the potential $50 billion cost of an economic stimulus package, or the possibility of lower tax revenues if personal income or corporate profits decline. Robert Pear and David M. Herszenhorn, "White House Predicts Bush Will Leave $482 Billion Deficit," *The New York Times*, July 29, 2008, p. C1.

27 Ruth Marcus, "Billing the Grandkids," *The Washington Post*, June 11, 2008, p. A19. By September 30, 2008, the wars in Iraq and Afghanistan will have cost the U.S. an estimated $845 billion. That cost estimate includes not only military operations but also embassy costs, post-war reconstruction and other war-related expenses. See Joseph Stiglitz and Linda Bilmes, *The Three Trillion Dollar War* (New York: W.W. Norton, 2008).

28 Ibid.

29 See Israel Shahak, *Jewish History, Jewish Religion* (London: Pluto Press, 1994).

30 "The State of Israel decided this week to compensate Jonathan Pollard, now serving the seventeenth year of imprisonment out of a life sentence in a United States federal penitentiary, with a one-time grant of $1 million to 'correct an injustice that has been done to him for many years.' The grant does not apparently signal any progress in the diplomatic realm to achieve Pollard's release from prison." Ellis Shuman, "Pollards reject $1M Israeli compensation offer," *Haaretz*, August 31, 2001.

31 Quoted in Mitchell Bard, "Israeli Lobby Power," *Midstream* 33, no. 1 (January 1987), p. 8. Cited in John J. Mearsheimer and Stephen M. Walt, *The Israel Lobby* (New York: Farrar, Strauss and Giroux, 2007), p. 153.

32 "In London alone, there are about 2,000 who are active, and another 5,000 on the list." Victor Ostrovsky and Claire Hoy, *By Way of Deception* (New York, St. Martin's, 1990), p. 86. Independent verification of Ostrovsky's claims has not been possible.

33 Ostrovsky's comment about "100% Jewish" suggests a racial qualification. Independent verification of this claim has not been

possible. Israel Shahak cautions against "the totalitarian Jewish community and its power, and by attempts to reimpose it, of which Zionism is the most important." Yet he also cautions against "the myth of the 'Jewish race' comparing it to the myth of the Aryan race. Israel Shahak, *Jewish History, Jewish Religion* (London: Pluto Books, 1994), pp. 51, 66-71.

34 Victor Ostrovsky and Claire Hoy, *By Way of Deception* (New York, St. Martin's, 1990), pp. 86-89.

35 Andy Newman, "Ex-Engineer for Army Charged With Leaks to Israel in '80s," *The New York Times*, April 23, 2008, p. A21.

36 Yossi Melman, Shahar Ilan and Barak Ravid, "Ezra: New spy case won't harm U.S.-Israel ties," *Haaretz*. April 23, 2008.

37 Ibid.

38 Larry Neumeister, "Army engineer charged with passing secrets to Israel in '80s," Foxnews.com, April 22, 2008.

39 Yossi Melman, Shahar Ilan and Barak Ravid, "Ezra: New spy case won't harm U.S.-Israel ties," *Haaretz*. April 23, 2008.

40 As U.S. attorney for the District of Columbia, Joseph E. di Genova oversaw the spy scandal that ensnared Pollard. He reports that the Israelis undermined his investigation when at least four individuals were flown out of the country despite Israeli assurances they would remain in the U.S. during the investigation. "The Israelis, of course, lied to us. They said there were no other spies and they had destroyed all the documents they got at the time," he said. "It was obvious they had other people supply the information so they could target the finds." Associated Press, "Ex-prosecutor: Israel lied about extent of anti-U.S. spying in the 80s," *Haaretz*, April 24, 2008.

Chapter 1: Game Theory and the Mass Murder of 9/11

1 Reportedly announced in an Israeli Cabinet session and later described on *Kol Yisrael* radio, the Israeli Broadcasting Authority.

2 Louis Uchitelle, "American and Israeli Share Nobel Prize in Economics," *The New York Times*, October 11, 2005. Aumann is a specialist in non-cooperative game theory. An article written by Thomas C. Schelling, co-recipient of the prize with Aumann, prompted film director Stanley Kubrick to make the 1964 movie *Dr. Strangelove or: How I Learned to Stop Worrying and Love the Bomb*.

3 Seymour M. Hersch, "Plan B," *The New Yorker*, June 28, 2004.

4 In a Pentagon study based on more than 600,000 documents recovered after the invasion, the U.S. military acknowledged in March 2008 that Saddam Hussein had no direct operational link to Al Qaeda. Elana Schor, "Saddam Hussein had no direct ties to al-Qaida, says Pentagon Study," Guardian.co.uk, March 13, 2008.

5 In July 2008, *The Wall Street Journal*, citing the Kurdistan regional government's representative in the U.S., confirmed that the envoy had been approached by neoconservative war-planner Richard Perle about oil concessions in the Iraqi Kurdistan region of northern Iraq. Susan Schmidt and Glenn R. Simpson, "Perle Linked to Kurdish Oil Plan," *The Wall Street Journal*, July 29, 2008, p. A4.

6 The Trojan was a communication device planted by Israeli Navy commandos in Tripoli. The device received prerecorded digital transmissions from an Israeli Navy ship and rebroadcast the transmission on another frequency, enabling the misleading broadcast to be picked up by U.S. and other intelligence agencies. Due to triangulation methods used to verify the source, the Trojan had to be planted near Libya's known broadcasting center. That need was fulfilled when an Israeli operative rented an apartment and prepaid the rent for six months. [See the introduction re Israel's worldwide system of volunteers (*sayanim*).] When the content of the misleading message was intercepted by U.S. intelligence and confirmed by trusted sources (i.e., Tel Aviv), the Mossad's deception was complete. French and Spanish intelligence were highly skeptical that the careful Libyans would suddenly begin to broadcast their intentions, particularly when the wording was similar to Mossad reports on Libya. That suspicion was confirmed with the interception of an after-incident report. Familiar with Israeli duplicity and staffed by personnel less plagued than U.S. intelligence agencies by conflicting allegiances, Paris and Madrid viewed that report as further proof the transmissions were Israeli disinformation intended to provoke a reaction.

7 Cited in Victor Ostrovsky, *The Other Side of Deception* (New York: HarperCollins, 1994), pp. 113-117.

8 By March 2001, the Taliban were known in the region for their Islamic fundamentalism and their oppression of women but they had not yet been branded globally as Evil Doers. That

portrayal emerged with their destruction of Afghanistan's ancient Buddhas at Bamiyan (one of them 53 meters tall) built during the third and fifth centuries AD at a crucial node on the Silk Road. That widely publicized "cultural holocaust" created a consensus of Taliban evil doing at a time when the mass murder of 9/11 was still six months in the future.

9 Michael Slackman, "Israeli Bomblets Plague Lebanon," *The New York Times*, October 6, 2006, p. 1.

10 Associated Press, "John McCain Jokes About Bombing Iran at U.S. Campaign Stop," *International Herald Tribune*, April 19, 2007.

11 The first intifada began in 1986 and ended in 1993 when peace negotiations offered hopes of justice. To suppress this rebellion against people armed largely with stones, Israeli Defense Minister Yitzhak Rabin adopted the "break the bones" policy whereby those throwing stones—largely children—were held down and their bones broken. During the first five days of the policy, Gaza's Shifa Hospital treated 200 people, mostly for broken elbows and knees though three had fractured skulls. David McDowall, *Palestine and Israel: The Uprising and Beyond* (Berkeley: University of California Press, 1989), p. 7.

12 Why would Israel weaken its benefactor? See Chapter 5 chronicling the emergence of a predominantly Ashkenazi oligarchy in resource-rich Russia while the fast-globalizing, consensus model-driven free trade in goods and capital pits the U.S. against China with ownership concentrating in both countries at an accelerating pace. *Entropy* traces its root to the combination of *energy* and *turning*. With beliefs and emotions uniting people during crisis (as with 9/11), the strategic entropy would be the fictions (versus facts) deployed when people were at their most vulnerable in order to shape outcomes that otherwise could never be achieved absent the crisis.

13 Cited in Emad Mekay, "Iraq was Invaded 'to Protect Israel'—US Official," *Asia Times Online*, March 31, 2004.

14 On April 12, 2004, the author hand-delivered three copies of a 152-page research compilation to the offices of the 9/11 Commission. The copies signed for there were addressed to Mr. Zelikow, chairman Thomas Kean and Vice Chairman Lee Hamilton. That compilation chronicled John Doe's lengthy firsthand experience

with the criminal syndicate chronicled in this account. That compilation described his meeting in Baghdad in early 1997 with Dr. Nidhal Al Hamdani, head of Iraq's nuclear weapons program (mothballed since 1991), and the fact that Mr. Doe could not persuade U.S. State Department personnel to confer with him on his return. The account also chronicled evidence confirming that, shortly after his return, FBI agents in the Minneapolis office sought to frame John Doe for a fraud orchestrated in Poland in 1995 with the participation of Dr. Jerome Corsi, co-author of *Unfit for Command* and *Minuteman* and author of *Atomic Iran*. Though the 9/11 Commission took testimony from more than 1,200 witnesses, Mr. Doe was not contacted.

15 Senator Ernst F. Hollings, "Bush's Failed Mideast Policy Is Creating More Terrorism," *Charleston Post and Courier* (online), May 6, 2004.

16 Cited in Akiva Eldar, "Sharp Pen, Cruel Tongue, *Haaretz*, April 13, 2007.

17 Michael Kinsley, "What Bush Isn't Saying About Iraq," Slate.com, October 24, 2002.

18 Dean's wife is Jewish and his children were raised Jewish. An outspoken supporter of Israel, the co-chair of his presidential campaign was Steven Grossman, a former president of AIPAC.

19 The anthrax mailings killed five, including two postal workers, and sickened 17 others, spreading fear on Capitol Hill and nationwide. In June 2008, the Justice Department agreed to pay biological weapons expert Steven J. Hatfill a $4.6 million settlement to withdraw a lawsuit he filed after he was named a "person of interest" in the investigation. Scott Shane and Eric Lichtblau, *The New York Times*, June 29, 2008, p. 1. On July 29, 2008, government microbiologist Bruce E. Ivins committed suicide, reportedly shortly after being informed that he would be indicted. On August 6, 2008, FBI officials presented a circumstantial case alleging that Ivins acted alone in mailing the anthrax letters. Scott Shane and Eric Lichtblau, "F.B.I. Presents Anthrax Case, Saying Scientist Acted Alone," *The Washington Post*, August 7, 2008, p.1. See Eric Lichtblau and Davd Johnson, "Doubts grow on FBI's anthrax evidence," *International Herald Tribune*, August 16, 2008. On August 8, 2008, federal prosecutors excluded Hatfill from involvement in the anthrax mailings. Carrie Johnson and

Joby Warrick, "Prosecutors Clear Hatfill in Anthrax Case," *The Washington Post,* August 9, 2008, p, A3.

20 Online reports suggested that FBI investigations following 9-11 uncovered an Israeli-directed operation that dispatched Israeli "art students" to the U.S., including many who had served in military intelligence and electronic signal intercept units. According to those investigations, cells of four to six Israelis each rented apartments in close proximity to Islamic terrorist cells in Phoenix, Arizona and in Miami and Hollywood, Florida. Two other Israelis in the ring settled in Fort Lauderdale, Florida where eight hijackers lived just north of town. Independent verification of this account has not been confirmed.

21 Reportedly announced in an Israeli Cabinet session, reported on Kol Yisrael radio.

22 James Bennett, "Sharon Invokes Munich in Warning U.S. on 'Appeasement,'" *The New York Times*, October 5, 2001.

23 Alan Sipress and Lee Hockstader, "Sharon Speech Riles U.S.," *The Washington Post*, October 6, 2001.

24 "Chalabi had known Richard Perle since 1985, and he had known Paul Wolfowitz for years as well." Chalabi's early sponsors also included Douglas Feith and David and Meyrav Wurmser, co-authors with Perle of *A Clean Break* (1996) written for Israeli Prime Minister Benjamin Netanyahu and urging the removal of Saddam Hussein as part of a strategy to expand the Land of Israel and "secure the realm." Aram Roston, *The Man Who Pushed America to War* (New York: Nation Books, 2008), pp. 134-36.

25 Miller's reporting helped take the U.S. to war in Iraq with a series of stories that relied largely on Ahmad Chalabi and Douglas Feith in articles that were routinely featured on page one of *The New York Times.* A September 8, 2002 story published six months before the invasion reported that the Bush administration worried that "the first sign of a 'smoking gun'...may be a mushroom cloud." Secretary of State Condoleezza Rice then repeated that provocative language on CNN's *Late Edition* with Wolf Blitzer. In the lead-up to war, "the *Times* placed more credence in defectors, expressed less confidence in inspectors, and paid less attention to dissenters." Michael Massing, "Now They Tell Us," *The New York Review of Books*, February 26, 2004. Secretary of

Defense Rumsfeld granted Miller a unique "embedding agreement" with the U.S. military unit charged with scouring Iraq for weapons of mass destruction. In effect, Rumsfeld gave Miller the "exclusive" story—had there been any WMD. Franklin Foer, "The Source of the Trouble," *New York Magazine*, May 31, 2004.

26 John McCain first befriended Ahmad Chalabi in 1991 soon after the Keating 5 scandal subsided and a decade before the 9/11 attack provoked the 2003 invasion of Iraq. Aram Roston, *The Man Who Pushed America to War* (New York: Nation Books, 2008), pp. 174-75, 231.

27 Those publications included *The New York Times*, *The Washington Post*, *Vanity Fair*, *Atlantic Monthly*, the *Times of London*, the *Sunday Times of London*, several newspapers in Australia and several Knight Ridder papers.

28 "Pentagon stops payments to Iraq's Chalabi," MSNBC News Services, May 18, 2004. http://www. msnbc.msn.com/id/5003 986/.

29 The forthcoming *Criminal State* series chronicles numerous instances in which dysfunctional personalities are catalyzed to act out profiled needs in ways that prove strategically advantageous based on the time, place and circumstances of their behavior. It may prove useful for specialists in psychological operations to examine the circumstances surrounding the timing of these sniper attacks.

30 Quoted in James Bennett, "DeLay says Palestinians Bear Burden for Achieving Peace," *The New York Times*, July 30,2003.

31 Quoted in Jake Tapper, "Questions for Dick Armey: Retiring, Not Shy," *The New York Times Magazine*, September 1, 2002.

32 See press release of April 12, 2002 from New York Congressman Eliot Engel from the Bronx, a borough of New York City.

33 The Oval Office visit was widely portrayed by observers as a way for Ariel Sharon to boost his prestige. The attack reinforced Sharon's opposition to substantive peace negotiations.

34 John R. Burns, "At Least 143 Die in Attacks At Two Sacred Sites in Iraq," *The New York Times*, March 3, 2004, p. 1.

35 Philip Shenon, "Criticism From Many Quarters Greets Plan to Split C.I.A.," *The New York Times*, August 24, 2004, p. A12.

36 Senator Carl Levin has received more funds from pro-Israeli political action committees (PACs) than any other member of

the Congress. Levin ranks first among the "Top Ten Career Recipients of Pro-Israel PAC Funds" with $727,737. Tom Harkin of Iowa is a distant second at $541,950. Janet McMahon, "Pro-Israel PACs: Disguises and Permutations," *Washington Report on Middle East Affairs*, August 2008, p. 26.

37 Israeli TV reported that the shipment was sent by a firm called Piad, headed by Avichai Weinstein. On March 30, 2004, New York jeweler Yehuda Abraham pleaded guilty to operating a money-transfer scheme that provided terrorists with shoulder-fired missiles (typical of *sayanim*, prosecutors conceded the suspect did not know the criminal objective of the transaction he facilitated). Ronald Smothers, "Jeweler Admits Transferring Money for Missiles," *The New York Times*, March 31, 2004, p. A21.

Chapter 2: Organized Crime in Arizona

1 William Hale ("Big Bill") Thompson was the sole speaker at the inaugural of Louisiana Governor Huey Long, elected in 1928. Thompson served as Mayor of Chicago from 1915 to 1923 and again from 1927 to 1931 when Chicago mob boss Al Capone backed Thompson's return to the mayor's office. On Thompson's death, two safe deposit boxes in his name were discovered with nearly $1.5 million in cash ($12.8 million in 2007 dollars). Franklin Delano Roosevelt was also sworn in as Governor of New York in 1928 with Herbert Lehman his Lieutenant Governor.

2 "Chicago businessman and underworld associate Moses Annenberg was not originally invited to the conference, but after running into Capone, the well known Annenberg was most likely invited to confer with the leaders on business matters concerning the national race wire." Jay Robert Nash, *World Encyclopedia of Organized Crime* (New York: Perseus Books, 1993).

3 The "hit men" in Murder, Inc. were predominantly Ashkenazi. The most infamous of this nationwide corps of contract killers included Abraham "Kid Twist" Reles, Abraham "Pretty" Levine, Irving "Knadles" Nitzberg, Harry "Pittsburg Phil" Strauss, Jacob "Gurrah" Shapiro, Buggsy Goldstein and Allie "Tick Tock" Tannenbaum, plus the notorious Mendy Weiss and Charlie "The Bug" Workman who, on October 23, 1935, entered the Palace Chop House and Tavern in Newark, New Jersey and murdered

Dutch Schultz along with three members of his gang: Lulu Rosenkrantz, Abe Landau and Abbadabba Berman. Schultz was then threatening to kill Tom Dewey, New York City's special prosecutor on organized crime. That murder would have generated just the sort of attention that the national syndicate was created to avoid. In November 1948, New York Governor Dewey lost his Republican presidential bid in a surprise upset by the widely unpopular Truman from Kansas City in a vote decided by an electoral margin provided by Illinois and the Chicago Outfit. Albert Fried, *The Rise and Fall of the Jewish Gangster in America* (New York: Columbia University Press, 1963), pp. 204-205.

4 A history of Harry Truman's political genealogy will appear in the *Criminal State* series.

5 The pejorative nickname—the "Mickey Mouse Mafia"—was used in a biography of mobster Mickey Cohen, an early fundraiser for Richard Nixon, to distinguish the Italian-branded Mafia from the Jewish core of organized crime. Brad Lewis, *Hollywood's Celebrity Gangster—The Incredible Life and Times of Mickey Cohen* (New York: Enigma Books, 2007), p. 312.

6 In addition to Lansky and Siegel, attendees included Morris "Moe" Dalitz, Louis "Lepke" Buchalter, Joseph "Doc" Stacher, Jacob "Gurrah" Shapiro, Herman "Curly" Holtz, Louis "Shadows" Kravits, Harry Teitlebaum, Philip "Little Farvel" Kovalick, and Harry "Big Greenie" Greenberg.

7 http://www.thehistorychannel.co.uk/site/tv_guide/full_details/Crime/programme_2299.php

8 Amy Silverman and John Dougherty, "Haunted by Spirits," *Phoenix New Times*, February 17, 2000.

9 Sharon Theimer, "Beer Executive Could Be Next First Lady," Associated Press, April 3, 2008.

10 Ibid. at p. 13.

11 David M. Halbfinger, "For McCains, a Public Path but Private Wealth," *The New York Times*, August 23, 2008, p. 1.

12 Amy Silverman and John Dougherty, "Haunted by Spirits," *Phoenix New Times*, February 17, 2000.

13 A member of that same law firm induced John Doe into several business transactions that were pre-staged frauds.

14 See Goldwater/Miller 2008: http://goldwatermiller08.com

15 Jon Kyl has long been a key recipient of campaign contributions

coordinated by the Israel lobby that supported his election both as a four-term Congressman and as a three-term U.S. Senator first elected in 1994.

16 Son Daniel Pipes is director of the Middle East Forum and a professor at Pepperdine University in Malibu, California. Invited by Chairman Gary Ackerman of New York to testify in February 2007 before the House Foreign Affairs Subcommittee on the Middle East on the subject "Next Steps in Israeli-Palestinian Peace Process," Pipes observed: "Israel's success in crushing the Palestinians' will to fight would actually be the best thing that ever happened to them…Palestinians need to experience the certitude of defeat to become a normal people." Pipes' web site offers a *Boston Globe* comment: "If Pipes' admonitions had been heeded, there might never have been a 9/11." A Harvard graduate, Pipes also taught at the University of Chicago and the U.S. Naval War College. His Middle East Forum sponsors Campus Watch, an organization that dispatches personnel to influence debate by disrupting and heckling lecturers on campuses who are either supportive of Palestine or critical of Israeli policies. On July 5, 2004, Pipes appeared on CNN urging that Sheik Moqtada al-Sadr be granted immunity (after his Mahdi rebels killed dozens of Americans) in order to bring him into the Iraqi government, a stance also supported by Ahmad Chalabi whose activities have enjoyed the support of John McCain since 1991. Harvard University recognizes Professor Pipes as one of its 100 most influential living graduates. His organization qualifies for tax-exempt status under U.S. law. In September 2007, Pipes became an adviser to the presidential campaign of former New York mayor Rudy Giuliani who thereafter recommended that the U.S. attack Iran in order to protect Israel ("we will prevent them or we will set them back five or 10 years"). Giuliani quoted in Toby Harnden, "We must bomb Iran, says US Republican guru," *Telegraph*, January 11, 2007.

17 General Tommy Franks called Feith "the [expletive] stupidest guy on the face of the earth." Al Kamen, "In The Loop," *The Washington Post*, June 20, 2008, p. A17.

18 Spending on intelligence has nearly doubled since 1997. The 2007 intelligence budget totaled $43.5 billion. The overall cost for fiscal 2007 exceeded $50 billion when the cost of intelligence

by the military services is added. Walter Pincus, "Intelligence Budget Disclosure Is Hailed," *The Washington Post,* October 31, 2007, p. A4.

19 Based on the rhetoric posted on its web site, CPD III is the likely source of the conflict-of-opposites characterization ("Islamo-fascism") that worked its way into the commander-in-chief's rhetoric after he ordered the invasion of Iraq. See www.fightingterrror.org.

20 "Eric Lipton and Scott Shane, "Anthrax Case Renews Questions On Bioterror Effort and Safety," *The New York Times,* August 3, 2008, p. 1.

21 In July 2008, Dr. Bruce E Ivins, an anthrax specialist at Fort Detrick's Army medical lab, committed suicide. As this account was being completed, commentators were still speculating on what, if any, conclusions to draw from his death. Scott Shane, "Evidence in Anthrax Case Is Said to Be Primarily Circumstantial," *The New York Times,* August 4, 2008, p. A13.

22 James Risen, "Use of Contractors in Iraq Costs Billions, Report Says," *The Washington Post,* August 12, 2008, p. A 13.

23 Brad Lewis, *Hollywood's Celebrity Gangster—The Incredible Life and Times of Mickey Cohen,*" (New York: Enigma Books, 2007), p 148-149.

24 Ibid.

25 Julius Stulman, president of B'nai B'rith, sponsored the publication of a series of books that helped explain how this phenomenon operates through overlapping fields of relationships that stretch across time and distance. Showcasing pioneers in psychology such as Abraham Maslow and Ervin Laszlo, Stulman served as editor and publisher. Similar to a "Venn Diagram" of overlapping circles, this fields-within-fields framing offers a means to visualize how this field-based phenomenon is sustained. *Fields Within Fields…Within Fields* (New York: The World Institute Council, 1968-1972). Stulman's New York Lumber Exchange reportedly imported large amounts of Russian lumber during the corrupt Yeltsin era. Stulman presented this multi-volume set of materials to Dr. Glenn Olds who was then U.N. Ambassador (1969-1971). Dr. Olds gave the materials to John Doe from whom the author received them.

26 See William K. Black, *The Best Way to Rob a Bank is to Own One* (Austin: University of Texas Press, 2005), pp. 64-65.

27 Great American Insurance Company, a division of Lindner's American Financial Group, funded a delegation to Poland in 1995 to establish a mutual fund based on Corsi's experience in creating two mutual funds in Israel for B'nai B'rith (both funds reportedly failed). E.J. Kessler, "Campaign Confidential," *The Jewish Daily Forward*, September 10, 2004. The strategic import of that Lindner-financed, Corsi-assisted effort will be described in the *Criminal State* series.

28 Sasha Issenberg, "McCain's identity formed as first term Congressman," *Boston Globe*, May 30, 2008.

29 Leon Black is founder and head of New York-based Apollo Management, L.P., a private equity firm, specialists in leveraged buyouts (Black was head of leveraged buyouts at Drexel). In one three-day period in December 2006, Apollo Group struck $37 billion worth of deals when it closed a new $12 billion LBO fund, acquired Realogy (owner of Coldwell Banker, Century 21 and Sotheby's International Realty) and bought Harrah's Entertainment, the world's largest casino company, in conjunction with David Bonderman of Texas Pacific Group. Harrah's operates 39 casinos in the U.S., including Caesars Palace in Las Vegas and the Showboat in Atlantic City. The complicity of Black's father in a Chiquita-related Honduran bribery scandal was the reported reason for his suicide. Andrew Ross Sorkin and Michael J. de la Merced, "Deal Maker's 3-Day Tally: $37 Billion," *The New York Times*, December 20, 2006. By 2007, Black was 82nd on the *Forbes 400* list with personal wealth of $4 billion.

30 Steinberg used the cash flow from Reliance to fund numerous acquisitions, including Flying Tiger, Days Inn, Pargas and others. He sold his 34-room triplex apartment at 740 Park Avenue in Manhattan for $37 million to Stephen Schwarzman of Blackstone Group. John D. Rockefeller, Jr. was the resident's former owner. Schwarzman sold his previous duplex residence to Tyco executive Dennis Kozlowski for $18 million. Deborah Schoennman, "Schwarzman Redux: Manufacturing Exec Signs $18 Million Deal," *The New York Observer*, April 16, 2000. In September 2005, Kozlowski was sentenced to 25 years in prison for his part in stealing hundreds of millions of dollars from the manufacturing conglomerate. Grace Wong, "Kozlowski gets up to 25 years," CNNMoney.com, September 19, 2005. In April 2008, firms led by Schwarzman, Bonderman and Black

purchased from Citigroup $12.5 billion in distressed leveraged loans. That portfolio reportedly included loans extended to them by Citigroup to finance leveraged buyouts. Michael J. de la Merced and Eric Dash, "Citi Is Said to Be Near Deal to Sell $12.5 Billion of Loans," *The New York Times*, April 9, 2008.

31 *See* James B. Stewart, *Den of Thieves* (New York: Touchstone, 1991).

32 Riklis and his colleagues reportedly funneled hundreds of thousands of dollars to General Ariel Sharon to use in his legal battle against *Time* magazine when the Nakash brothers, owners of Jordache Enterprises (makers of designer jeans) reportedly paid a retainer to the law firm of Shea & Gould and thereafter paid the bulk of his legal expenses. New York District Attorney Robert Morgenthau appeared as a character witness for Sharon. Riklis was the husband of Hollywood actress Pia Zadora. Robert I. Friedman, "Who's Paying Ariel Sharon's Bills," *Journal of Palestine Studies*, Vol. 14, No. 3 (Spring 1985), pp. 181-184.

33 For more than a half-century, John Doe's step-uncle worked with Donald Stralem in Manhattan where both resided. In response to his step-uncle's request Doe once picked up his step-uncle at the Stralem estate in Palm Springs and drove him to a friend's house in Malibu.

34 "Campaign of 1960" http://www.jfklibrary.org/Historical +Resources/ JFK+in+History/Campaign+of+1960.htm

35 Julie Creswell, "So What if the Chips Are Down?" *The New York Times*, August 3, 2008, p. BU 1.

36 "Greenspun Wins '50 Case Pardon: Nevada Editor Convicted in Israeli Arms Case," *The New York Times*, October 28, 1961.

37 In the 1964 presidential race, Republican nominee Barry Goldwater carried only six states and 36 percent of the popular vote. A 1964 speech delivered on behalf of Goldwater at the presidential nominating convention in San Francisco's Cow Palace brought Ronald Reagan to national prominence. Reagan was then co-chairman of the California Republicans for Goldwater. Contemporaneous news reports claimed that Reagan's speech drew more campaign contributions than any speech in political history. Bart Barnes, "Barry Goldwater, GOP Hero, Dies," *The Washington Post*, May 30, 1998, p. 1. When Senator Russell Long retired in 1987, the author joined him in a law practice with retiring Senator Paul Laxalt.

38 Stephen Lemons, "Goldwater Uncut," *Phoenix New Times*, October 19, 2006.

39 "He was the eldest son of Baron and Josephine Williams Goldwater, and the grandson of 'Big Mike' Goldwasser, a Jewish immigrant from an area of Poland that was then ruled by the Russian czars. Although Jewish on his father's side, Mr. Goldwater was raised in the Episcopalian tradition of his mother." Bart Barnes, "Barry Goldwater, GOP Hero, Dies," *The Washington Post,* May 30, 1998, p. 1. Goldwater's, the family department store chain, would remain in family hands until 1962 when the company was sold to Associated Dry Goods, Corp. of New York for $2.2 million in stock.

40 Dean Smith, "Young Arizona shaped a young Goldwater," AZcentral.com, January 18, 1987.

41 "Goldwater's closest friend, Harry Rosenzweig, would be linked by more than one publication to prostitution in this state." Stephen Lemons, "Goldwater Uncut," *Phoenix New Times*, October 19, 2006.

42 Ira Morton, "Time Capsule—A legend in his time," *Jewish News of Greater Phoenix*, March 25, 2005.

43 The 1964 election marked the beginning of the fracturing of the Democratic Party in the South and a takeover of Arizona by the Republican Party when Goldwater carried the traditionally Democratic states of South Carolina, Georgia, Alabama, Mississippi and Louisiana. The only other state he won was Arizona.

44 During the Reagan Administration, Goldwater served as chairman of the Senate Armed Services Committee (1981-1987) and the Senate Intelligence Committee (1981-85).

Chapter 3: John McCain and Financial Frauds

1 Sasha Issenberg, "McCain's identity formed as first term Congressman," *The Boston Globe*, May 30, 2008. The late Mark Harroff previously served as press secretary for Senator William Cohen (1973) until establishing Smith and Harroff in 1973, a political consulting and public relations firm with experience in more than 100 Republican campaigns.

2 Richard L. Berke, "Four Senators Deny Doing Favors For Keating in Exchange for Cash," *The New York Times*, November 17, 1990.

3 Amy Silverman, "Postmodern John McCain: the presidential

candidate some Arizonans know—and loathe," *Phoenix New Times*, August 7 2008.

4 Head of an economic forecasting firm, Townsend-Greenspan & Company, Greenspan was retained by the New York law firm of Paul Weiss Rifkind Wharton & Garrison to conduct a study of the thrift industry and make a recommendation concerning the scope of direct investments made by Lincoln Savings and Loan. Nathaniel C. Nash, "Greenspan's Lincoln Savings Regret," *The New York Times*, November 29, 1989.

5 Margaret Carlson, "Keating Takes the Fifth," *Time*, December 4, 1989.

6 See "The S&L Crisis: A Chrono-Bibliography," posted online by the Federal Deposit Insurance Corporation at http://www.fdic.gov/bank/historical/s&l/index.html.

7 Questioning how Keating Five Senators could rely on his analysis to justify their intervention, Greenspan asks, "How could anyone use any evaluation I would have made in early 1985 as justification more than two years later?" Nathaniel C. Nash, "Greenspan's Lincoln Savings Regret," *The New York Times*, November 29, 1989. Questioning the depth of journalistic analysis, other commentators note, "We should all be the targets of such investigative reporting." Robert Kuttner, "Alan Greenspan and the Temple of Boom," a book review in *The New York Times*, December 17, 2000.

8 The government then borrowed those tax receipts, enabling higher government spending. By 2000 the Social Security payroll tax was the largest tax paid by 80% of wage earners. Levied at a flat rate regardless of income, that tax remains the nation's most regressive, taxing most those who can afford it least. For 90% of Generation X (born 1965 to 1982), the payroll tax became their largest tax while also raising labor costs and pushing jobs offshore.

9 Keating operated as a directed agent in a 'control fraud' orchestrated by Michael Milken, Carl Lindner and others yet to be identified who reportedly instructed Keating which bonds Lincoln S&L would purchase with its deposits, creating a captive market for Drexel's junk bonds while shifting to taxpayers the risk of default.

10 Greenspan was a colleague and disciple of free market philosopher

Ayn Rand (Alisa Rosenbaum), a Russian émigré novelist and advocate of radical individualism and unfettered laissez-faire capitalism best known for her authorship of *The Fountainhead* (1943) and *Atlas Shrugged* (1957).

11 "Jack Atchison. In 1986 and 1987 Atchison was a managing partner of Arthur Young & Co., the accounting firm that audited Lincoln. Under Atchison's direction, the thrift was given a clean bill of health. Later Atchison took a $930,000-a-year-job as a vice president with Lincoln's parent company, American Continental Corp." Margaret Carlson, "Keating Takes the Fifth," *Time*, December 4, 1989.

12 As University of Texas-Austin Professor James K. Galbraith points out, Greenspan was "not just a run-of-the-mill conservative but a philosophical extremist" in the perfection he ascribed to financial markets. James K. Galbraith, "The Free Ride of Mr. Greenspan," *The Texas Observer*, February 23, 1996.

13 The figures apply to losses incurred between 1986 and 1995. See Timothy Curry and Lynn Shibut, *The Cost of the Savings and Loan Crisis: Truth and Consequences, FDIC Banking Review*, volume 13, no. 2, December 2000.

14 University of Chicago Professor Leo Strauss emerged as the intellectual leader of the predominantly Jewish neoconservatives who advocated war with Iraq. The role of bias ranks in influence with that of belief in displacing facts with fiction. See Kalle Lasn, "Why Won't Anyone Say They're Jewish?" *Adbusters*, March/April 2004.

15 Gore quoted in Michael Weisskopf, "The Kingmaker," *Time*, May 28, 2000. In 1997, through Gary Winnick, a former Milken colleague at Drexel Burnham Lambert, McAuliffe bought a $100,000 stake in Global Crossing prior to its initial public offering. He sold his stake at the market peak in 1999 for $18 million. In February 2001, McAuliffe was elected chairman of the Democratic National Committee. Over the next four years, he raised more than $525 million. He had previously served as finance chairman for the Committee. His ties to Global Crossing compromised McAuliffe's ability to attack Republican ties to the Enron scandal during the 2002 midterm congressional elections where Republicans won a majority in the U.S. Senate. A 1999 suit brought by the U.S. Department of Labor (*Herman vs.*

Moore) alleged that, as part of a pension fund investment in Florida commercial property, McAuliffe received a 50% stake in a partnership in which he invested $100 and $38.7 million was invested by a pension fund for the International Brotherhood of Electrical Workers. Although union officials agreed to pay six-figure penalties for their role and the union was forced to pay $5 million for its lack of prudence, McAuliffe kept the $2.45 million he was paid for his $100 investment made by a company owned by him and his wife, the former Dorothy Swann. The property, acquired from the Resolution Trust Corp at $10 million below the appraised price, was one of the distressed properties held by American Pioneer Savings Bank, a S&L placed in receivership a year earlier at a taxpayer cost of $500 million. American Pioneer was owned by Richard A. Swann, Dorothy's father, who McAuliffe first met as a 22-year old when Swann was finance chair of Florida's Democratic Party. After helping Swann break a fundraising record, he was sent to California where he worked with Lew Wasserman and Walter Shorenstein. In 1995, he acquired a bankrupt home-construction business with the help of Carl Lindner's American Financial Group. From 1991 to 1996, Lindner, along with his family and employees, donated $724,000 to Democrats. Paula Dwyer, "The Heat on Clinton's Moneyman," *Business Week*, December 22, 1997 (published by the Laborers International Union of North America). http://www.laborers .org/BusinessWk_12-22-97.html. In partnership with Lindner, McAuliffe's American Heritage Homes Inc. emerged as the second-biggest homebuilder in Orlando. In 2008, he reemerged as campaign chairman for Hillary Clinton. As *Time* magazine explained in May 2000: "Not since Hollywood mogul Arthur Krim roamed the Lyndon Baines Johnson White House has one fundraiser done so much for one political family. He has raised more than $300 million for Clinton causes, including the presidential library ($75 million), Clinton's legal bills ($8 million), Hillary's Senate campaign ($5 million) and the President's millennium celebration ($17 million)." See also Byron York, "McAuliffe's Shady Business Past," *National Review*, July 16 2002; Jeffrey R. St. Clair, "The Political Business of Terry McAuliffe," *Counterpunch*, October 19, 2004. McAuliffe's offer to purchase the Clintons a house in Chappaqua, New York as part of her Senate campaign was accepted and then rejected after an onslaught of negative media reports. Numerous reports suggest that McAuliffe's personal wealth approaches $100 million. In early 1997, McAuliffe took offices in a Washington, DC building owned by Pacific Capital Group, a Winnick company. After Clinton endorsed Global Crossing in a Los Angeles political event, the company won a $400 million contract from the Pentagon after prodding from the White House. Winnick soon donated $1 million to the Clinton presidential library (the Pentagon later rescinded the contract). Much as Lindner contributed to both Clinton and Dole, Winnick contributed to both Clinton and G.H.W Bush. In 1997, Winnick paid Bush in Global Crossing stock for a one-hour speech in Tokyo for which Bush's fee was $80,000. The value of Bush's shares rose to more than $14 million. With its bankruptcy filing in January 2002, Global Crossing became the seventh largest filing in U.S. history. Between 1998 and 2001, Winnick sold some $600 million in Global Crossing stock while other executives sold an additional $900 million. Winnick also generated another $123 million through a financial "collar." "As Global Crossing Sinks, Gary Winnick Stays Dry," *Business Week*, October 22, 2001. Hours before the end of the first quarter 2001, Winnick engaged in a $375 million "capacity swap" whereby firms sold access to each other's networks and booked the sales as revenues to exceed the consensus estimate of securities analysts. Michael Weisskopf, "Global Crossing: What Did Winnick Know?," *Time*, October 7, 2002. Richard Perle was retained to assist in the sale of Global Crossing's fiber optic network to Hutchinson Whampoa whose controlling shareholder, Li Ka-Shing, has close ties to the Chinese military.

16 See American Politics Journal at http://www. americanpolitics.com/080797ThompsonLindner.html.

17 Mike Gallagher & Cameron McWhirter, "Chiquita vice chairman, on canceling trip of Panamanian foreign minister: Contributions buy influence," *Cincinnati Enquirer*, May 3, 1998, posted online at http://www.mindfully.org/Pesticide/chiquita12.htm

18 Ibid.

19 Average 2006 pay for the top 25 private equity and hedge fund managers was $570 million. Schwarzman was paid a reported

$398.3 million in 2006 ($1,091,000 per day) and $350 million in 2007 ($958,904 per day). Associated Press, "Blackstone's Chief Received $350 Million in Pay in 2007," *The New York Times*, March 13, 2008, p. C2. In a June 2007 initial public offering, Schwarzman retained a stake in Blackstone then valued at approximately $7.7 billion while cashing out an interest valued at ~$450 million that added to his personal wealth of $3.5 billion. Blackstone Group was founded in 1985 with $400,000 in capital.

20 Zell invested $315 million to acquire control of the Tribune Company, including a reported $13 billion in debt financed through an employee stock ownership plan leaving Zell with the right to buy up to 40% of the company in the future.

21 The ability to bundle mortgages into securities was facilitated with tax law changes enacted during the Reagan era.

22 *The Wall Street Journal,* January 23, 2004. The net operating loss carry-forwards from formerly bankrupt firms can shelter profits from tax. When combined with the tax shelter offered by depreciation, investments in distressed properties typically become self-financing provided one has access to acquisition debt, a financial need met by the sale of mortgage-backed securities, many of them acquired by tax-subsidized pension plans.

23 Published interview of January 31, 2000.

24 Enacted December 1982, the Garn-St. Germaine Depository Institutions Act of 1982 gave expanded powers to federally chartered S&Ls and enabled them to diversify their activities to increase their profits. Major provisions included: elimination of deposit interest rate ceilings; elimination of the previous statutory limit on loan to value ratio; and expansion of the asset powers of federal S&Ls by permitting up to 40% of assets in commercial mortgages, up to 30% of assets in consumer loans, up to 10% of assets in commercial loans, and up to 10% in commercial leases. The result divorced thrifts from the communities they were originally created to serve. William Seidman's post as chief White House adviser to Gerald Ford for domestic policy was assumed by Stuart Eizenstat when Jimmy Carter defeated Ford for the presidency in November 1976. Carter's failed domestic policy ("stagflation") helped elect Ronald Reagan whose reform of the thrift industry was championed by Utah Senator Jake Garn, a Mormon (aka "the lost tribe of Israel").

Chairman of the Senate Banking Committee (1981-87), Garn named Danny Wall chairman of the Federal Home Loan Bank Board in July 1987. A principal craftsman of the Garn-sponsored legislation, Wall had served on Garn's staff for 11 years.

25 Rustand, like football player Ford, was a star college athlete. Student body president at the University of Arizona, Rustand became Arizona's first Academic All-American in basketball in 1965. He has since served on nearly fifty boards of directors. He is currently managing director of SC Capital Partners LLC, a Newport Beach, California investment banking firm.

26 John Doe relocated to Tucson with his family in 1977 and was introduced to Warren Rustand, the politically prominent Mormon, who sought Doe out to play tennis and repeatedly inquired about his genealogy. On several occasions, Rustand reportedly sought to introduce Doe to former President Ford. Doe declined.

27 Henry Sender, "Breakfast with the FT: David Bonderman," *Financial Times*, June 21, 2008. The financial leverage available to investors in S&Ls was steadily increased with each decrease in the net worth requirements from 5% to 4% of total deposits in November 1980 to 3% in January 1982 along with a 1981 change allowing troubled S&Ls to issue "income capital certificates" that were included as capital. When combined with the elimination of deposit interest rate ceilings, repeal of the statutory limit on loan to value ratio and the diversification of permissible lending activities, the S&L industry became an invitation to taxpayer fraud by *the people in between.* The "Southwest Plan" introduced by the Federal Home Loan Bank Board in 1988 disposed of 205 S&Ls with assets of $101 billion by consolidating and packaging insolvent Texas S&Ls and selling them to the highest bidder.

28 Peter Smith, "TPG tops buy-out league with $101bn," *Financial Times*, December 27, 2006, p. 1.

29 Henry Sender, "Breakfast with the FT: David Bonderman," *Financial Times*, June 21, 2008.

30 In analyzing the "fields within fields" of relationships through which this phenomenon operates, it became relevant that John Doe first encountered Eli Broad when a former Broad employee became Doe's childhood physician at age six. That relationship commenced after his previous physician, an uncle, died in 1958

at age 42, reportedly of a cerebral hemorrhage. Dr. Robert T. Birndorf was the new physician's good friend and also a former Broad employee. It was not until 1982 that Doe met Birndorf who participated in a sophisticated fraud committed against Doe that included Security Pacific Bank and the comptroller of Hewlett Packard. During the pre-staging of that fraud, Birndorf informed Doe that he and Doe's physician had attended the same high school, college and medical school and that Doe's physician had been the best man at Birndorf's wedding.

31 In 1979, John Doe and his family relocated to Irvine, California where they became active in the Irvine First Ward of the Mormon Church. In 1980, Mormon Doug Skeen and his family moved to Irvine and bought a home nearby. Skeen became active in the First Ward men's group where he took a keen interest in Doe, socialized with his family and became involved in his business. Doe also had an equity position in one of Doe's companies and a financial stake in the Birndorf-Hewlett Packard fraud litigation. The evidence will show that Skeen and his cousin, Mormon Leo Beus, an Arizona attorney, were associated with serial frauds committed against Doe.

32 Author's research from public sources. Founded in Shanghai to sell maritime insurance in the 1920s, in 1992 A.I.G. received the first foreign license to sell financial products in China. In the fourth quarter 2007, A.I.G. announced a $5.3 billion loss followed by a first quarter 2008 loss of $7.8 billion. Jenny Anderson, "A.I.G. says It Is Subject to Inquiries," *The New York Times*, June 7, 2008, p. B3.

33 In May 2007, Howard Marks and Bruce Karsh, co-founders of Oaktree Capital Management, sold 16 percent of their Los Angeles money management firm on a private Goldman Sachs exchange, raising $1 billion. Each now has a net worth of $1.4 billion and both are members of the *Forbes 400*. Marks is a former assistant to Eli Broad at SunAmerica. In 1995, he and Karsh founded Oaktree with 2007 assets under management of $47 billion.

34 James R. Barth, Susanne Trimbath and Glenn Yago, *The Savings and Loan Crisis: Lessons from a Regulatory Failure* (Kluwer Academic Publishers, 2004).

35 William K. Black, *The Best Way to Rob a Bank is to Own One* (Austin: University of Texas Press, 2005).

Chapter 4: McCain Family Secret: The Cover-up

1 See note to President Johnson on White House stationery dated June 8, 1967 from W.W. Rostow that reads, "The *LIBERTY* is listing badly to starboard." Featured in James M. Ennes, Jr., *Assault on the Liberty* (Reintree Press, 1979).

2 Initially 171 Purple Hearts were awarded; three more were awarded later.

3 By not being required to register as a foreign agent, AIPAC has thus far obscured its geopolitical goals. Though AIPAC's Internal Revenue Service filing reports $51.3 million in 2005 revenues, the overall operating budget may be substantially higher

4 Kenen also founded and edited *Near East Report*, AIPAC's monthly in house publication that was later edited by Wolf Blitzer. In 1973, *Jerusalem Post* editor Ari Rath hired Blitzer as Washington correspondent, a role Blitzer retained until he moved to Cable News Network (CNN) in May 1990.

5 See Grant F. Smith, *Foreign Agents: The American Israel Public Affairs Committee from the 1963 Fulbright Hearings to the 2005 Espionage Scandal* (Washington, D.C.: Institute for Research: Middle East Policies, 2007).

6 Ken Ringle, "The Attack on *Liberty*," *The Washington Post*, February 1, 2003, p. C1.

7 The National Security Adviser was then known as special assistant to the President for national security affairs. Born in New York City in October 1916, Walt Whitman Rostow was the son of a Russian Jewish immigrant family. His older brother, Eugene, was dean of Yale Law School, 1955-65. During the Reagan Administration, Eugene Rostow served as director of the Arms Control and Disarmament Agency (1981-83), the most senior Democrat in that Republican Administration. He was succeeded in that position by Kenneth Adelman (1983-87), a member of the Committee on the Present Danger. During WWII, Walt Rostow served as a major in the Office of Strategic Services where he recommended enemy targets to the U.S. Air Force. From 1961 to 1966, he chaired the State Department's policy planning council.

8 When Ronald Reagan left Warner Brothers in 1949, his producer Brian Foy also left. Foy was then appointed executive producer at Eagle-Lion Studios headed by Arthur Krim who acquired United Artists in 1951 with his longtime partner Robert S.

Benjamin. Foy hired Johnny Roselli as an Eagle-Lion producer on Roselli's release from Atlanta Penitentiary. A senior figure in the Chicago Outfit, Roselli was also a member of the Friar's Club, a Los Angeles men's club whose membership included numerous pop-culture and mob-related figures, including Ronald Reagan, Mickey Rooney, Groucho Marx and Sydney Korshak, Hollywood's best-known consigliere, senior labor racketeer and adviser to Lew Wasserman of MCA. Dan E. Moldea, *Dark Victory* (New York: Penguin, 1986), pp. 79, 83. During WWII, Robert S. Benjamin was executive officer of the Army Signal Corps Photographic Center in Astoria, Queens (a borough of New York City). In 1947, Reagan narrated the Signal Corps film *Stilwell Road* about General Joseph "Vinegar Joe" Stilwell who fought against the Japanese in Burma. In 1967, Lyndon Johnson appointed Benjamin a delegate to the United Nations. In 1978, Ambassador Benjamin and Arthur Krim left United Artists following its acquisition by Transamerica Corporation and founded Orion Pictures. See *Robert S. Benjamin: A Citizen's Citizen* published by the United Nations Association where Benjamin served as chairman (Adlai Stevenson II described Benjamin as "a citizen's citizen"). The *Criminal State* series will describe the influence on Ronald Reagan's career by Jules Stein, Lew Wasserman, Sydney Korshak and Walter Annenberg.

9 To forge a more potent connection with Washington, MCA President Lew Wasserman worked closely with Arthur Krim who helped organize a 1962 birthday party for President Kennedy at Madison Square Garden where Marilyn Monroe sang a breathless rendition of *Happy Birthday*, followed by an all-night party at Krim's Upper East Side town house. The success of the event (it brought in more than $1 million) led Krim to create a "President's Club" promising a chance to meet the President for $1,000 per person. Wasserman brought the President's Club to Hollywood with a June 1963 $1,000 per plate dinner at the Beverly Hilton Hotel just when Kennedy was pressuring Tel Aviv for inspections of its nuclear facilities at Dimona. After Kennedy was assassinated in November, Wasserman-led fundraising raised more money for Lyndon Johnson than had ever been raised for a Democrat in California. Connie Bruck, "The Personal Touch," *The New Yorker*, August 13, 2001. "While some

credit Sinatra with making the Monroe connection to the White House—Sinatra introduced Marilyn to JFK at Peter Lawford's Malibu beach house, a popular show biz hangout—there is evidence that it was really Mickey [Cohen]." Brad Lewis, *Hollywood's Celebrity Gangster—The Incredible Life and Times of Mickey Cohen* (New York: Enigma Books, 2007), p. 265.

10 L. Sandy Maisel and Ira N. Forman (eds.), *Jews in American Politics* (New York: Rowman & Littlefield, 2001), p. 308. Judah P. Benjamin, a Senator from Louisiana, was the first acknowledged Jewish Senator. Elected as a Whig in 1852, he was reelected as a Democrat in 1858 and served until February 1861 when he was appointed Attorney General to the provisional Confederate States. In November he was appointed Secretary of War and in February 1862 Secretary of State in the Cabinet of Jefferson Davis where he was an advocate of "cotton diplomacy" (withholding cotton from European countries that would not barter for arms and supplies). He served in that capacity until 1865 when he moved to Great Britain where he practiced law until 1883. He died in Paris in 1884.

11 Commodities trader Bernard Baruch was appointed by Woodrow Wilson to chair the War Industries Board. See James Grant, *Bernard Baruch* (New York: John Wiley & Sons, 1997).

12 Howard M. Sachar, *A History of the Jews in America* (New York: Alfred Knoft, 1991), p. 250.

13 See John Maynard Keynes, *The Economic Consequences of the Peace* (New York: Harcourt, Brace and Howe, 1920).

14 During the 1944 election year, FDR allowed the entry of 900 Jews. During Christmas 1945, with the war over, President Harry Truman allowed those 900 immigrants to remain in the U.S. Post-WWII, Morgenthau chaired a December 1947 fundraising campaign by the United Jewish Appeal (UJA) in support of Israel's 1948 war for the Zionist state. Morgenthau was assisted by Edward M.M. Warburg, a Kuhn, Loeb partner, and Canadian-born Henry Montor (né Goldberg), executive director of the UJA whose 1946 campaign raised $101 million for the Zionist cause ($864 million in 2007 dollars). Golda Meir, a Russian-born Jew, relocated from her home in Milwaukee to Palestine in 1921 where she became a member of the Jewish Agency directorate. Meir traveled the U.S. in 1948 as a UJA spokesperson when she and

Morgenthau raised $178 million ($1.3 billion in 2007 dollars). Had Morgenthau not been appointed at that time and in that circumstance, it's doubtful Israel would now function "as the bedrock of American-Jewish identity." Howard M. Sachar, *A History of the Jews in America* (New York: Alfred Knopf, 1991), p. 618-19. From 1947 to 1950, the UJA raised $465 million under Morgenthau's chairmanship. From 1951 to 1954, he led a $500 million bond campaign for Israel ($3.2 billion in 2007 dollars). Robert M. Morgenthau (Junior's second-born child) was appointed by President Kennedy as U.S. Attorney for the Southern District of New York where he served 8-1/2 years. In 1974, he made the first of eight successful bids for election as District Attorney of New York. New York Mayor Ed Koch recruited Morgenthau to plan a museum and memorial to victims of the Holocaust. On September 17, 2003, Morgenthau oversaw the dedication of a memorial garden in Battery Park, a central feature in the $60 million, four-story, 82,000-square-foot extension of the museum named the Robert W. Morgenthau wing, the first new construction after 9/11. Born July 1919, Morgenthau was elected in 2006 to a new four-year term. During more than four decades in law enforcement, Morgenthau oversaw the non-prosecution of systemic financial frauds that set records not only for their scope, scale and duration but also for their negative impact on national security, as will be chronicled in the *Criminal State* series. As Israeli Prime Minister, Golda Meir (a compromise candidate on the death in 1969 of Levi Eshkol) negotiated with President Nixon a policy of "strategic ambiguity" regarding Israel's development of the nuclear weapons that President Kennedy was determined to halt in June 1963. The Nixon-Meir accord left the Zionist state a U.S.-sponsored non-signatory to the Nuclear Non-Proliferation Treaty. The NPT seeks to prevent the spread of nuclear weapons and weapons technology. The Treaty established a safeguard system under the responsibility of the International Atomic Energy Agency (IAEA) that verifies compliance with the Treaty through IAEA inspections. Opened for signature in 1968, the Treaty entered into force in 1970. See http://www.un. org/depts/dda/WMD/treaty.

15 Grace Halsell, "How LBJ's Vietnam War Paralyzed His Mideast Policymakers," *Washington Report on Middle East Affairs*, June 1993, p. 20.

16 Since antiquity, "ritualized friendships" have been used to create and sustain "fields within fields...with fields" of relationships through which influence can be sustained across generations.

17 Grace Halsell, "How LBJ's Vietnam War Paralyzed His Mideast Policymakers," *Washington Report on Middle East Affairs*, June 1993, p. 20. George Ball offers an overview of U.S. rationalizations for non-interference to prevent an Arab-Israeli conflict. American policymakers felt that Egypt's President Nasser had been ungrateful toward the U.S. after President Eisenhower rescued him during the Suez affair, 1956-57. Knowing of Israel's military preeminence, the conflict would show that the Soviets were ineffective protectors of Arab nations, thereby strengthening America's role in the region. By destroying Soviet-provided equipment, Israel would relax its incessant lobbying for more U.S. weapons, an expensive burden. Others thought the conflict might catalyze regional uprisings to overthrow extremist Arab regimes. Lastly, it was envisioned that an Israeli victory would make possible a solution to the Arab-Israeli conflict once it was realized that, with three victories in 19 years, Israel could not be eliminated. As Ball concedes: "The political parts of this analysis proved lamentably inaccurate...it is now easy to see that the Arabs had more staying power than the administration thought, and that Israel would refuse to return any but a small portion of its captured territory." George W. Ball and Douglas B. Ball, *The Passionate Attachment* (New York: W.W. Norton, 1992), pp. 55-56.

18 Ibid., p. 55.

19 Grace Halsell, "How LBJ's Vietnam War Paralyzed His Mideast Policymakers," *Washington Report on Middle East Affairs*, June 1993, p. 20.

20 John L. Loeb of Loeb, Rhoades investment bank was married to a member of the Lehman banking family. In 1953, Sam Bronfman's elder son, Edgar, married Ann Margaret Loeb, the daughter of John L. Loeb and the granddaughter of the founder of the investment house of C.M. Loeb Rhoades and Company. The marriage did not last. See Stephen Birmingham, *The Rest of Us—The Rise of America's Eastern European Jews* (London: Macdonald & Co., 1984), p. 318. One of Johnson's unofficial advisers was Edwin L. Weisl, a New York attorney who was a senior law partner to Cyrus Vance at Simpson, Thatcher & Bartlett. "Not only was this law firm general counsel to Lehman

Brothers, but Weisl himself was dubbed by *Fortune* magazine as 'Lehman's eighteenth partner.'" Murray N. Rothbard, *Wall Street, Banks and American Foreign Policy* (Burlingame: Rothbard-Rockwell Report, 1995), p.p. 47-48.

21 During the Roosevelt Administration, Fortas served as an assistant to Interior Secretary Harold Ickes until Ickes transferred him to the Securities and Exchange Commission.

22 For a detailed account of Johnson's victory over former Texas Governor Coke Stevenson, see "The Stealing" in Robert A. Caro, *The Years of Lyndon Johnson: Means of Ascent* (New York: Random House, 1990), pp. 303-317.

23 Laura Kalman, *Abe Fortas* (New Haven: Yale University Press, 1990), pp. 200-202.

24 Fortas was previously a partner in the Washington law firm of Arnold, Fortas and Porter. Prior to joining the Robert M. Bass Group in 1983, David Bonderman (a founding principal in Texas Pacific Group, a private equity firm) was a partner specializing in bankruptcy in the Arnold & Porter law firm. See Chapter 3 ("John McCain and Financial Frauds").

25 An Orthodox Jew from Memphis, Tennessee, Fortas moved to Washington in 1933 to work with New Deal legal realist Jerome Frank and then practice law with Thurman Arnold, a former professor at Yale Law School and another noted legal realist, New Dealer and co-founder of Arnold, Fortas and Porter. As a political confidante and close friend to Johnson, Fortas also represented Bobby Baker, Johnson's senior aide when the future President served as Senate Majority Leader. Baker's close ties to Chicago mob boss Sam Giancana, Meyer Lansky associate Ed Levinson and Ben Siegelbaum (an ally of Teamster President Jimmy Hoffa), led to Baker's involvement in Serve-U-Corporation, an organized crime operation that profited from vending machines provided to government contractors. President Kennedy was sufficiently upset by the Bobby Baker scandal that he told his secretary, Evelyn Lincoln, he was planning to replace Johnson with Florida Senator George Smathers as his running mate in 1964. Sally Denton and Roger Morris, *The Money and the Power* (New York: Vintage Books, 2001).

26 *See* Richard Helms, *A Look over My Shoulder* (New York: Random House, 2003), p. 299.

27 According to a law clerk in Fortas' Supreme Court office who

overheard the conversation, Fortas warned Israeli Ambassador to the U.S. Avraham Harman that Secretary of State Rusk was not a strong Israel supporter, suggesting that "Rusk will fiddle while Israel burns." Fortas then reportedly told the Israeli Ambassador who was returning to Tel Aviv to report to the cabinet that Israel could not count for support on any other country, including the U.S. Given his close relationship to Johnson, the biographer concludes, "the Israelis surely would have assumed he was speaking for the President." Laura Kalman, *Abe Fortas* (New Haven: Yale University Press, 1990), pp. 301.

28 Peter Hounam, *Operation Cyanide* (London: Satin Communications, 2003), p. 235.

29 Walworth Barbour was U.S. Ambassador to Israel from 1961 to 1973. The American International School in Even Yehuda, Israel is named after him.

30 Harry McPherson, *A Political Education* (Austin: University of Texas Press, 1972), p. 415.

31 Laura Kalma, *Fortas* (New York: Yale University Press, 1990), pp. 300-302.

32 Richard Helms, *A Look over My Shoulder* (New York: Random House, 2003), p. 300. In his 1968 Senate confirmation hearings as Johnson's nominee to succeed Earl Warren as Chief Justice, Fortas denied continuing as an adviser to Johnson while serving on the Supreme Court in violation of the Constitution's separation of powers between the executive branch and an independent judiciary. The Fortas nomination was withdrawn after a Senate filibuster. Fortas' conduct is typical of *the people in between.*

33 John Loeb of Kuhn, Loeb & Co. was the fourth person in attendance at the Fortas dinner with McNamara and Johnson the night before the Six-Day War commenced.

34 *The Warburgs* (New York: Vintage Books, 1993), pp. 47-48.

35 In 1872, Schiff and former Union Army Major General James H. Wilson (1837-1925) joined forces in an attempt to acquire a share of a Japanese bond issue. Though the venture failed, the relationship blossomed as evidenced in decades of correspondence. A hero of the Civil War, Wilson served under Ulysses S. Grant and trained General William T. Sherman's cavalry for the March to the Sea. In May 1865, men under his command captured Jefferson Davis, president of the Confederacy.

36 Schiff arranged for $200 million in loans for Japan during the Russo-Japanese War of 1904-05, a role for which he was decorated by the Emperor of Japan. In July 1997, Al Gore's daughter Karenna married Andrew Schiff, the great-great-grandson of Jacob Schiff. The groom's father was the managing partner of Kuhn, Loeb & Company (Lehman Brothers Kuhn Loeb, Inc.). Dr. Andrew ("Drew") Schiff works in New York for Perseus-Soros BioPharmaceuticals. "Andrew Schiff, Karenna Gore," *The New York Times*, July 13, 1997.

37 The recurring pattern throughout Israel's attempt to expand their agreed-to borders has been the seizure of land followed by an attempt to claim "facts on the ground" as evidence of *de facto* authority, legality and precedent. Thus, President G.W. Bush's joint statement and exchange of letters with Prime Minister Ariel Sharon on April 14, 2004 was widely characterized as "Balfour II" when Bush cited "the realities on the ground, including already existing major Israeli population centers" to rationalize an agreement ceding Israeli-occupied Palestinian territories to Israel following U.S.-Israel discussions from which Palestinians were excluded. See "President Bush Commends Israeli Prime Minister Sharon's Plan," Office of the Press Secretary, April 14, 2004. British Foreign Secretary Arthur James Balfour, in a November 1917 letter to Walter Rothschild (a.k.a. Lord Rothschild), ceded to a private Zionist organization a "national home" for Zionist Jews in Palestine on land belonging neither to Balfour nor to the World Zionist Federation. President G.W. Bush's *de facto* approach ("realities on the ground") was destined to provoke more resentment in the Arab world while associating U.S. foreign policy with Colonial Zionism, further outraging Muslims and fueling the regional dynamics required to make *The Clash* appear plausible. As a form of psy-ops and global "emotion management," the Bush-Sharon White House photo-op of April 14, 2004 served as a high profile provocation. From a game theory perspective, the response was perfectly predictable when the announcement catalyzed more terrorism, endangered coalition troops in Afghanistan and Iraq and created more instability throughout the Middle East while reinforcing the branding of Israel as an innocent victim surrounded by hostile anti-Semites.

38 Grace Halsell, "How LBJ's Vietnam War Paralyzed His Mideast

Policymakers," *Washington Report on Middle East Affairs*, June 1993, p. 20.

39 James Ennes, officer on deck when the attack began, reports that the *USS Liberty* crew, "were specifically told not to collect Israeli signals." With no Hebrew linguists aboard, the ship's intercept operators and linguists were instructed, when picking up an Israeli signal, to "log it and drop it." Ennes also reports that it is "common knowledge within the intelligence community" that whenever the U.S. military sought funds to train Hebrew linguists, the Israel lobby ensured the funds were not forthcoming. Ennes email correspondence with author of April 18-19, 2008.

40 General Moshe Dayan may have ordered that the *USS Liberty* be sunk in order to preclude the possibility that the Israeli invasion would be halted before Israeli troops could occupy the Golan Heights the following day. In *Jewish History, Jewish Religion* (1995), Israel Shahak, an anti-Zionist Holocaust survivor, describes the "Biblical borders of the Land of Israel, which rabbinical authorities interpret as ideally belonging to the Jewish state" that include "in the south, all of Sinai and a part of northern Egypt up to the environs of Cairo; in the east, all of Jordan and a large chunk of Saudi Arabia, all of Kuwait and a part of Iraq south of the Euphrates; in the north, all of Lebanon and all of Syria together with a huge part of Turkey (up to Lake Van); and in the west, Cyprus."

41 Others suggest the attack was meant to prevent the disclosure of ongoing Israeli war crimes against Egyptian prisoners of war. Researchers point to a July 1967 CIA report quoting an Israeli official who conceded that Tel Aviv knew the *Liberty's* identity and its mission but not who else besides the U.S. may have access to its intercepts, so it put the intelligence-gathering ship out of commission to be sure. Others suggest that Tel Aviv may have sought to blame the attack on the Egyptians, then a Soviet client state.

42 Before U.S. military leaders could assess the attack, the Israeli embassy in Washington phoned New York Senator Jacob Javits (1957-1981) and Illinois Congressman Roman Pucinski (1952-1973) and they announced on the floor of the Senate and the House that the attack was a case of mistaken identity. *Congressional Record—House*, June 8, 1967, p. 15131; *Congressional Record—Senate*, June 8, 1967, p. 15261.

43 Grace Halsell, "How LBJ's Vietnam War Paralyzed His Mideast Policymakers," *Washington Report on Middle East Affairs*, June 1993, p. 20.

44 CIA Director Richard Helms reports: "The day after the attack (on the *USS Liberty*), President Johnson, bristling with irritation, said to me, '*The New York Times* put that attack on the *Liberty* on an inside page. It should have been on the front page!'" Richard Helms, *A Look over my Shoulder: A Life in the Central Intelligence Agency* (New York: Random House, 2003), p. 301.

45 Clifford was also chairman of the President's Foreign Intelligence Advisory Board. Richard Holbrooke co-authored Clifford's memoirs. Atlanta attorney Stuart Eizenstat arranged for Holbrooke to brief Jimmy Carter on foreign policy in 1976. Holbrooke served as author of the first volume of the Pentagon Papers released by Daniel Ellsberg in early 1971, discrediting the Nixon presidency and U.S. foreign policy in general.

46 "In choosing March 31, the President was well aware of the fact that President Truman had chosen March 31, 1952, as the date he announced his withdrawal as a candidate for reelection." W. Marvin Watson and Sherwin Markman, *Chief of Staff* (New York: St. Martin's Press, 2004), p. 283.

47 Clark Clifford with Richard Holbrooke, *Counsel to the President* (New York: Random House, 1961), p. 523.

48 The attack on the *USS Liberty* was the second deadliest assault on a U.S naval vessel since WWII. On May 17, 1987, an Iraqi-fired, French-made Exocet missile struck the *USS Stark* killing 37 seamen. As U.S. interests required that Iraq not lose its ongoing war with Iran, the response from Washington was muted. Iraqi President Saddam Hussein apologized and agreed to pay reparations. The *Stark* incident led to an increase of U.S. naval ships in the Persian Gulf to escort convoys of Kuwaiti tankers that were being attacked by Iran, leading to several hostile exchanges and increased tensions, fueling *The Clash.* After a day-long skirmish between Iranian and U.S. forces in April 1988, the Ayatollah Khomeini and Hashemi Rafsanjani, Speaker of the Iranian Parliament, sought a new course to defuse tensions.

49 "Admiral Kidd and I were given only one week to gather evidence for the Navy's official investigation, though we both

estimated that a proper Court of Inquiry would take at least six months." Ward Boston, Jr., "Forty Years Later, Searching for Truth," *The San Diego Union Tribune*, June 8, 2007.

50 See "Declaration of Ward Boston, Jr., Captain, JAGC, USN (Ret.)" dated January 8, 2004 in which Capt. Boston recollects a conversation with Admiral Issac C. Kidd, president of the court, after Admiral Kidd spoke with Admiral McCain. http://ussliberty.org/report/exhibit%252025.pdf

51 Excerpted from declaration of Ward Boston, counsel to the U.S. Navy court of inquiry.

52 Author's phone discussion with James Ennes of April 9, 2008.

53 See John Crewdson, "New revelations in attack on American spy ship," *Chicago Tribune*, October 2, 2007 (online at www.ussliberty.org/pdf/tribunebooklet.pdf). See also www.ussliberty.org/smoking.htm.

54 Clark Clifford and Richard Holbrooke, *Counsel to the President: A Memoir* (New York: Random House, 1991), p. 224. The *Criminal State* series will include an account of Clifford's role in influencing Truman's recognition of Israel in May 1948, in large part to satisfy pro-Zionist campaign contributors in the 1948 presidential elections. Las Vegas publisher Hank Greenspun and Israeli arms dealer Adolph "Al" Schwimmer are the likely source of funds reportedly then delivered aboard Truman's campaign train. An ardent Zionist and avid gunrunner, compared to what Greenspun did for Israel, *The Jerusalem Post* wrote (in comparing Greenspun to Israel's most damaging spy against America): "Jonathan Pollard's act was pure innocence." Denton & Morris, *The Money and the Power* (New York: Vintage Books, 2001), pp. 59-74. During an arms embargo with Israel, Greenspun set up weapons transit depots in Panama, the Dominican Republic and Nicaragua. The Nicaraguan operation pre-staged the Reagan-discrediting "Iran-Contra" scandal in which Schwimmer was the primary gunrunner when funds from covert arms sales to Iran were used to support anti-Communist guerillas in Nicaragua. As a rule, the first stop was Czechoslovakia where the government placed an airstrip at the Zionists' disposal. Howard M. Sachar, *A History of the Jews in America* (New York: Alfred A Knopf, 1992), p. 615. Fifty-four years later, Czech operatives claimed that 9/11 terrorist leader Mohamed

Atta met with an Iraqi intelligence official in Prague, an account (since dismissed) promoted by former CIA chief James Woolsey, co-chairman of the Committee on the Present Danger. Clifford played a key role in crafting the National Security Act of 1947 that established the CIA and separated foreign from domestic intelligence gathering, an "intelligence gap" exploited in the pre-staging of 9/11. Clifford played a four-decade role as a trans-presidency asset identified early on for his usefulness in enabling, with partner Robert Altman, an international fraud that helped Middle Eastern investors acquire U.S. banks. Operating in 78 countries, the Bank of Credit and Commerce International was accused of committing a $13 billion fraud that involved money laundering, bribery, smuggling, support of terrorism and the sale of nuclear technologies. That fraud catalyzed a candidate-discrediting scandal during the 1992 presidential campaign of G.H.W. Bush, helping elect Bill Clinton and a pro-Israeli administration that pre-staged the war in Iraq. Along with Iran oil-trader Marc Rich, Schwimmer was granted clemency on January 20, 2001 by president Bill Clinton.

55 Richard Helms, *A Look over my Shoulder: A Life in the Central Intelligence Agency* (New York: Random House, 2003), p. 301.

56 Quoted in Bryant Jordan, "Key Investigators Express Belief That Israel Deliberately Attacked U.S. Ship," *Navy Times*, June 26, 2002.

57 Quoted in Associated Press, "Lyndon Johnson ordered cover-up: Former navy lawyer," *Toronto Star*, October 22, 2003. Admiral Moorer believed that Johnson ordered the cover up to maintain ties with Israel.

58 Ibid., p. 302. Contrary to media accounts, the "hot line" was not a telephone line but a dedicated teletype device for the sending and receipt of encrypted messages. Established after the Cuban missile crisis, the U.S. component was then located not in the White House Situation Room but in the Pentagon.

59 That experience informs those who question why U.S. policy-makers, regardless of party, decline to apply the political pressure required to end Israeli aggression against Palestinians. Had Egypt been the genuine aggressor, as Tel Aviv sought to induce others to believe, that aggression could have triggered a U.S. response, not a prospect that Egypt would have sought as a Soviet client state.

60 Associated Press, "Lyndon Johnson ordered cover up: Former navy lawyer," *Toronto Star,* October 22, 2003. See also "Declaration of Ward Boston, Jr., Captain, JAGC, USN (Ret.)" dated January 8, 2004 in which Capt. Boston recollects a conversation with Admiral Issac C. Kidd, president of the court, in which Kidd said that he had been ordered by Johnson and McNamara "to conclude that the attack was a case of 'mistaken identity' despite overwhelming evidence to the contrary."

61 *Liberty's* "satellite dish" bounced a microwave signal off the moon. If the ship and the National Security Agency could see the moon at the same time, they could communicate. Thomas Moorer, "A Fair Probe Would Attack *Liberty* Misinformation," *Stars and Stripes*, January 16, 2004.

62 A. Jay Cristol, *The Liberty Incident: The 1967 Israeli Attack on the U.S. Navy Spy Ship* (Washington, D.C.: Brassey's, Inc., 2002).

63 See A. Jay Cristol, "Why You Shouldn't Pay Attention to the Claims That Israel Attacked the *USS Liberty* Deliberately," June 11, 2007. Online at http://hnn.us/articles/39936.html.

64 Quoted in Associated Press, "Lyndon Johnson ordered cover up: Former navy lawyer," *Toronto Star*, October 22, 2003.

65 Ward Boston, Jr., "Time for Truth About the *Liberty*," *San Diego Union*, June 8, 2007.

66 "Why You Shouldn't Pay Attention to the Claims That Israel Attacked the *USS Liberty* Deliberately," online at http://hnn.us/articles/39936.html. James Ennes confirmed that Cristol is Jewish.

67 John Crewdson, "New revelations in attack on American spy ship," *Chicago Tribune*, October 2, 2007.

68 Thomas Moorer, "A Fair Probe Would Attack *Liberty* Misinformation," *Stars and Stripes*, January 16, 2004.

69 Paul Findley, *The Dare to Speak Out: People and Institutions Confront Israel's Lobby* (Chicago: Lawrence Hill Books, 1985), Chapter 6.

70 Thomas H. Moorer, *Stars and Strips*, "A fair probe would attack *Liberty* misinformation," January 16, 2004.

71 After the cover up, Admiral Kidd served as Commander Cruiser-Destroyer Flotilla 12. Promoted to vice admiral, he then commanded First Fleet, followed by command of Sixth Fleet. He was promoted to admiral in 1971 where, as Chief of Naval

Materiel, he served as the Navy's top Procurement and Logistics Officer with command of a civilian and military workforce of more than 350,000 men and women. He became Supreme Allied Commander in Chief Atlantic and Commander-in-Chief U.S. Atlantic Fleet on May 30, 1975.

72 *Christian Science Monitor*, June 22, 1982. Nor did the award mention which nation attacked the *USS Liberty*, leaving ambiguous the enemy for which McGonagle was decorated for valor under enemy fire. Commentators suggest that such ambiguity is typical for intelligence-related operations.

73 Statement of Ambassador Edward Peck regarding the *USS Liberty*, delivered at the U.S. Navy Memorial, June 8, 2007. http://www.ifamericans knew.org/us_ints/ul-peck.html

74 Conversation of June 15, 2005 with Gary Brummett, then president of the *USS Liberty* Veterans Association who reported his confirming conversation with McGonagle's daughter, Susan.

75 Boston quoting Admiral Kidd in John Crewdson, "New revelations in attack on American spy ship," *Chicago Tribune*, October 2, 2007.

76 Quoted in John B. Quigley, *The Case for Palestine: An International Law Perspective* (Raleigh-Durham: Duke University Press, 2005).

77 Serge Schmemann, "General's Words Shed a New Light on the Golan," *The New York Times*, May 11, 1997.

78 Brummett suggests this amount is greatly inflated. He describes survivors who received checks for $50 to $400 in return for signing a release holding Israel harmless (he signed a release for $200). He also suggests that survivor payments were made not by Israel but by private Jewish groups. Several sources suggest that any Israeli payments were offset by additional funds paid to Israel as U.S. military assistance.

79 *A Report: War Crimes Committed Against U.S. Military Personnel*, June 8, 1967. Submitted to the Secretary of the Army in his capacity as Executive Agent for the Secretary of Defense, June 8, 2005. Online at www.ussliberty.org/report/htm

80 Email to author of February 28, 2008 from Gary Brummett; author email exchange of April 18-19, 2008 with James Ennes.

81 Israel eventually acquired 42 new-build F-4Es, 12 new-build RF-4Es, and 162 ex-U.S. Air Force F-4Es.

82 The *Criminal State* series will document the Israeli theft of U.S.

technology, including the systematic corruption of U.S. technology transfer centers, an effort reportedly advanced with funds promised by A.I.G.

83 See Chapter 7 ("The New Anti-Semitism").

84 From a game theory perspective, Israel's nuclear weapons capability provides an additional means to influence U.S. decision-makers to come to Israel's aide should Tel Aviv claim the Jewish state is endangered and may, in response, deploy its nuclear weaponry as a defensive measure. This strategic use of uncertainty is characterized as "constructive ambiguity" by George Ball in explaining how, "trained in their own school of diplomacy, they insisted on fuzzy language so that they could then start haggling from scratch." *The Passionate Attachment*, p. 62. From a game theory perspective, the privileged mindset of those who view themselves as "chosen" also adds an increment of strategic advantage because, as this *modus operandi* is grasped by an informed global public, Israeli extremists may opt for a modern-day Masada by deploying their nuclear weaponry to destroy themselves and others rather than face the prospect of accountability for trans-generational crimes against humanity. The game theory (expectations-based) component of Israel's nuclear-state status in the Middle East was acknowledged in November 2006 by Israeli Deputy Defense Minister Ephraim Sneh when he explained that "an Iranian nuclear bomb could destroy the Zionist enterprise even if the bomb was never used, since its very existence would lead Jews to emigrate from Israel." Aluf Benn, "A meeting in handcuffs for Ehud Olmert, George Bush," *Haaretz,* November 12, 2006.

85 Perle's impact on U.S. national security provides a case study in *the people in between.* Within months of Perle commencing work with the Senate Foreign Relations Committee in 1969, he became embroiled in an incident involving the leaking of a classified CIA report alleging past Soviet treaty violations. Before CIA Director Stansfield Turner could fire CIA analyst David Sullivan, he was hired by Senator Henry "Scoop" Jackson where Sullivan thereafter worked with Perle, the person to whom Sullivan leaked the material. In 1970, a wiretap on the Israeli Embassy detected Perle discussing classified information supplied to him by National Security Council staff member Helmut Sonnenfeldt who was investigated in 1967 for providing

classified information to an Israeli official concerning the commencement of the Six-Day War. Perle played a key role in the Jackson-Vanik amendment conditioning the shipment of U.S. grain to Russia on the emigration of Jews from Russia. Perle played a critical role in pre-staging and orchestrating the use of Iraqi Ahmad Chalabi as a conduit for fixed intelligence in support of the war in Iraq. He also served as the policy-shaping chairman of the U.S. Defense Policy Advisory Board while enabling what U.K. officials characterized as a "corporate kleptocracy" at Hollinger International, a pro-Zionist publisher and promoter of the war in Iraq. Hollinger was then led by Conrad Black, since imprisoned.

86 Dean Rusk, *As I Saw It* (New York: W.W. Norton & Co., 1990), p. 388.

87 For example, see the U.S. attack on Tripoli (Chapter 1).

88 After Israel bombarded Beirut for a full nine weeks, the U.N. Security Council unanimously demanded an immediate cease-fire on August 1, 1982 and dispatched military observers. When Palestine Liberation Organization leaders refused to comply with General Ariel Sharon's demand that they leave promptly, he canceled the cease-fire, unleashed another heavy bombardment on West Beirut and sent in troops. When President Reagan questioned whether Israel's use of American weaponry and munitions was for "legitimate self defense," Prime Minister Menachem Begin assembled in Jerusalem 190 Jewish-American leaders. After delivering a bitter harangue, the former Irgun terrorist clarified Tel Aviv's assessment of international law (as well as its regard for the U.S.) when he shouted to those assembled: "No one should preach to us. Nobody, nobody is going to bring Israel to her knees. You must have forgotten that the Jews kneel but to God." Quoted in George W. Ball and Douglas B. Ball, *The Passionate Attachment* (New York: W.W. Norton, 1992), p. 125.

89 Israeli Air Force Commander Motti Hod cited in Andrew and Leslie Cockburn, *Dangerous Liaison* (New York: Harper, 1991), p. 150.

90 Ibid., pp. 149-150.

91 George W. Ball and Douglas B. Ball, *The Passionate Attachment*, p. 55.

92 Mathilde Krim, Ph.D., was founding chairman of the American

Foundation for AIDS Research. She allied with pop-culture icon Elizabeth Taylor to form the AIDS Medical Foundation. Taylor was already involved in similar efforts due to her friendship with actor Rock Hudson who died of AIDS in 1985.

Chapter 5: The Presidency and Russian Organized Crime

1 Michael Meacher, *Independent*, October 17, 1988.

2 "It's already clear that a new arms race is being unleashed across the world…It's not our fault, we didn't start it…In effect, we are being forced to retaliate." Vladimir Putin, February 8, 2008. Catherine Belton, "Russia forced into 'new arms race,'" *Financial Times,* February 8, 2008.

3 Grigory Yavlinsky, "Russia's Phony Capitalism," *Foreign Affairs*, May/June 1998. The author suggests that the actual amount may have exceeded $1 billion at a time when candidate campaign spending was limited to $2.9 million. The writer is a Russian economist, political figure, reformer and co-founder of Yabloko, a Russian political party. Yabloko representatives sought to impeach Boris Yeltsin.

4 Catherine Belton, "Nevzlin Faces Murder Charges," *The Moscow Times*, July 27, 2004. "Nevzlin is charged with ordering the killing of several business executives and officials from 1998 to 2004, and this trial is closely linked to that of Alexei Pichugin, the oil firm's former security chief, who was jailed for life last August on charges of involvement in the same murders." Catrina Steward and Matt Siegel, "Nevzlin Goes on Trial in Absentia for Murder," *The Moscow Times*, March 20, 2008, p. 5.

5 Contemporary reports, denied by Yukos spokesman Yury Kotler, claimed that Khodorkovsky had transferred control over Yukos shares to the UK-based Lord Jacob Rothschild. "Yukos share rights 'transferred,'" BBC News, November 11, 2003 (online); Catherine Belton, "Kremlin Tempers Attack on Yukos," *The Moscow Times*, November 3, 203.

6 Elisabeth Bumiller, "McCain Urges New Arms Pact With Moscow," *The New York Times*, May 28, 2008, p. 1.

7 "Menatep" is the acronym for the local chapter of a youth center in Moscow's Frunze district called the Inter-Branch Center for Scientific and Technology Program. Menatep Group emerged from the commercial activities of this center, particularly its

trade in computers. Registered in 1988, Menatep Group's 1991 public offering was the first since the Bolshevik Revolution. Its growth surged after 1991 on the currency speculation triggered by hyperinflation (2,500% in 1992). By 1993 Menatep was the authorized bank for several city and regional governments.

8 Reportedly many of those deals involved exports of state-owned oil, timber and aluminum for Boris Berezovsky. Reports suggest that Marc Rich, the international commodities trader, was an early and active trader in Russian commodities, particularly aluminum. The fact that Berezovsky adopted capital flight strategies pioneered by Rich suggests that Rich was a direct or indirect mentor to Berezovsky and other Russian traders and financiers, including Khodorkovsky. Paul Klebnikov, *Godfather of the Kremlin* (New York: Harcourt, Inc., 2000), pp. 61-65, 204.

9 Of all the international financial institutions with access to Russia's true financial condition, the IMF had the best information. Stanley Fischer served as first deputy managing director of the IMF from September 1994 through August 2001 (the senior IMF official in charge of operations and policy worldwide). In February 2002, he became vice chairman of Citigroup and president of Citigroup International charged with oversight of global risk management (i.e., financial risk), working with CEO Sanford Weill and executive committee chairman Robert Rubin, former treasury secretary in the Clinton Administration. A Menatep company paid just $9 million more than the reserve price of $150 million for 45% of Yukos. That initial stake was increased to 78% for a total purchase payment of $309 million.

10 Alekperov consolidated three oil producers into Lukoil, an acronym taken from the names of three major oil fields. In 1995, after Prime Minister Victor Chernomyrdin agreed to transfer those state-owned oil fields to Lukoil, Alekperov emerged as president and Lukoil modeled itself after vertically integrated firms. Lukoil's proven oil reserves exceeded 20 billion barrels in 2004, second only to Exxon-Mobil. Erin E. Arvedlund, "The Russian Contender for King of the Oil Patch," *The New York Times*, May 21, 2004. State-owned Gazprom has proven reserves of 116 billion barrels, exceeded only by Saudi Arabia with 260 billion barrels and Iran with 128 billion barrels. Lukoil acquired Getty Oil assets in 2000 and began converting its 1,300 gas

stations to Lukoil outlets. In 2004, Lukoil acquired 800 stations from ConocoPhilips. *Forbes* valued Alekperov's 2008 net worth at $13 billion, ranking him 56th among the world's billionaires. Lukoil also owns a controlling interest in Imperial Bank, several television stations, and 19.9% of the Russia newspaper *Isvestia,* enabling Alekperov to mute criticism while also currying favor with the Kremlin. Lukoil leases refineries in the U.S. as it operates worldwide with ~600 affiliated firms and ~160 subsidiaries, including operations in Libya and Iraq according to *Forbes.* Lukoil was the first Russian firm to acquire a publicly traded U.S. corporation. According to oligarch Mikhail Fridman, the market capitalization of Lukoil grew 467% from 2003 to 2008, to $95 billion. Clifford Levy and Sophia Kishkovsky, Russian Strikes Back a BP's Chairman, and Oil Dispute Flares Again, *The New York Times,* June 17, 2008, p. C3.

11 "The banks that collected these huge interest earnings—Onexim, Menatep, Alfa and Stolichny, among others—put almost nothing back into the Russian economy." Paul Klebnikov, *Godfather of the Kremlin* (New York: Harcourt, Inc., 2000), pp. 210, 279-80.

12 In an earlier scenario evidencing intermarriage into a politically powerful Russian family, Svetlana, daughter of Joseph Stalin by his second wife, married Mihail Kaganovich on July 5, 1950. Mihail was the son of Lazar Kaganovich, vice president of the Council of People's Commissars and the only Ashkenazi member of the Politburo, Russia's inner cabinet. Lazar's sister, Rosa Kaganovich, became Stalin's third wife after they met at the opening ceremony for the Moscow subway the construction of which was overseen by her father. Svetlana defected in March 1967 while traveling in India. Her mother's death is variously attributed to suicide and poisoned tea. Known as the "Iron Commissar" and Stalin's trusted trouble-shooter, Lazar Kaganovich became deputy premier of the Soviet Union. Thus, Stalin's Ashkenazi brother-in-law became the second-ranking official in the Soviet hierarchy. Meanwhile, with Svetlana's marriage to Lazar Kaganovich's son, Stalin's daughter became his own sister-in-law. During the 1920s, Kaganovich served as the senior Soviet official overseeing the starvation of eight to 15 million Ukrainian farmers. *See* L.W. Phelps-Owen, "Mme. Stalin

Virtually Unknown," *The Washington Post*, July 10, 1949, p. S9; Reuters, "Stalin's Daughter Reportedly Wed," *The New York Times*, July 16, 1951, p. 2; James Reston, "Stalin's Daughter Apparently Defects And Consults With U.S. Aides in India," *The New York Times*, March 10, 1967, p. 1; Reuters, "Red Ship Returns," *The Washington Post*, April 10, 1956, p. 4.

13 Andrew E. Kramer, "Out of Siberia, A Russian Way to Wealth," *The New York Times*, August 20, 2006, p. BU1.

14 Although the Russian government held a right to repurchase the shares, that option was not exercised. Vladimir Dubov, a member of the Duma's budget committee and a 7% shareholder in Yukos, swayed a December 2002 vote against a tax law that would have allowed foreign oil firms to obtain set tax regimes, thereby reducing their risk of entry into the Russian marketplace. In the spring of 2004, Dubov led a fight to defeat a natural resource tax.

15 Trained as a mathematician and an expert on decision theory, Berezovsky would be intimately familiar with the game theory mathematics that underlie this systemic criminality, including the ability to coordinate its "probabilistic" operations with minimal direct communication among key operatives.

16 In October 2003, the 35-year old Ashkenazi oligarch Oleg Deripaska paid Roman Abramovich $2 billion for an additional 25% of Russian Aluminum (RusAl), raising Deripaska's stake to 75% and giving him control over approximately one-eighth of worldwide aluminum production.

17 Abramovich manages his assets offshore through Millhouse Capital, an investment fund. Abramovich and Deripaska created Russian Aluminum (RusAl) in 2000, an acquisition vehicle for state-owned properties. By 2002, annual revenues topped $4 billion. Abramovich sold his interests in RusAl and Aeroflot, the privatized national airline from which Berezovsky is accused of embezzling $600 million. With a *modus operandi* akin to the casino skim, firms acquired by Berezovsky reportedly would see their capitalization eroded as their cash flow was redirected to his next acquisition.

18 Tai Adelaja, "Deripaska Doubles Wealth to $40Bln," *The Moscow Times*, February 19, 2008, p. 7.

19 Paul Klebnikov, *Godfather of the Kremlin* (New York: Harcourt Brace, 2000), p. 320.

20 According to a Reuters report: "*The Wall Street Journal* has tied the entry ban to what it called concerns that Deripaska may have ties to organized crime in Russia, citing unnamed U.S. law enforcement officials." Lobbying on his behalf has been coordinated by 1996 presidential candidate Bob Dole and his Alston & Bird law partners who were paid $260,000 in 2005 for work on "Department of state and visa policies and procedures" tied to Deripaska. Jim Wolf, "U.S. revoked Deripaska visa—State Dep't official," *Reuters*, May 11, 2007 (online). In May 2007, Canadian auto-parts manufacturer Magna International Inc. announced that a unit of Russia's Basic Element (controlled by Deripaska) would invest $1.54 billion in Magna. That investment provided Deripaska with control of six of the 14 seats on the Magna board of directors and a means for the firms in his conglomerate to capitalize on growth opportunities in Russian and Chinese automotive markets. *Reuters*, "Magna says Russian Machines to invest in firm," May 10, 2007.

21 Jeffrey H. Birnbaum and John Solomon, "Aide Helped Controversial Russian Meet McCain," *The Washington Post*, January 25, 2008, p. A1.

22 "Senator's Supporters Are Invited to Lunch With a Lord," *The Washington Post,* March 15, 2008, p. A6.

23 Landon Thomas, Jr., "The Man Who May Become the Richest Rothschild," *The New York Times*, March 9, 2007.

24 Additional research will be required to determine the relationship, if any, between the interests of Rothschild and Deripaska in the Russian aluminum industry and John McCain's recommendation that a $35 billion U.S. Air Force contract to replace refueling tankers be awarded not to a U.S. manufacturer but to the European Aeronautic Defense and Space Company (EADS) and its Airbus subsidiary. On appeal, the U.S. Government Acountability Office agreed with the Boeing Company that the Air Force unfairly evaluated the merits and overall costs of the Boeing bid. Leslie Wayne, "Audit Says Tanker Deal Is Flawed," *The New York Times*, June 19, 2008, p. C1.

25 http://www.spiegel.de/international/0,1518,462862,00.html

26 "Russian-Jewish billionaire to build U.K.'s priciest mansion," *Haaretz*, April 29, 2008.

27 "Tycoon Abramovich buys world's most expensive house for $500M," *Haaretz,* July 10, 2008.

28 "Roman Abamovich governor of Chukotka again," *Pravda*, November 21, 2005.

29 Michael Schwirtz, "A Billonaire Govenor Resigns in Russia," *The New York Times*, July 4, 2008, p. A4.

30 Marshall Goldman, *The Piratization of Russia* (New York: Routledge, 2003), pp. 128-134.

31 Journalists described Rabbi Lazar as a "representative from an obscure sect of ultra-orthodox Jews." Tom Gross and Guy Chazan, "Gusinsky arrest raises fears for Russia's Jews," Telegraph.co.uk, June 19, 2001. See full-page advertisement of April 29, 2008 in *The New York Times* (p. A13) touting the teachings of "The Lubavitcher Rebbe Rabbi Menachem Schneerson." The ad reads: "The Rebbe, scion of the royal House of David, makes it very clear that Judaism charges us—the most ordinary mortals—with the task of bringing Moshiach." Moshiach is messiah from a Hebrew word meaning "the anointed one" envisioned as a descendant of King David. As 12th in Maimonides' 13 principles of faith, the Moshiach will rebuild the Temple in Jerusalem, gather Jews from all over the world and bring them back to the Land of Israel. U.S. casino mogul Sheldon Adelson is also a Lubavitch supporter, giving large sums for the Hasidic Chabad-Lubavitchers to build a center in Las Vegas. Connie Bruck, "The Brass Ring," *The New Yorker*, June 30, 2008, p. 43.

32 In 1994, Yeltsin gave Luzhkov control over the federal government's inventory of state-owned property, enabling Luzhkov to generate a separate source of revenue to fund projects that drew frequent charges of corruption, favoritism and use of his position for personal gain. In 1997 alone, Moscow reportedly took in $1 billion from privatization.

33 *The Moscow Times* estimates her 2008 wealth at $7 billion. Tai Adelaja, "Deripaska Doubles Wealth to $40Bln," *The Moscow Times*, February 19, 2008, p. 7.

34 Kaganovich (aka "Iron Lazar") and Vyacheslav Molotov are widely credited with orchestrating the widespread terror-famine in Ukraine (known in Ukraine as Holodomor) that starved to death an estimated six to seven million people from 1932 to 1933.

35 Stephen Lee Myers, "A powerhouse remakes Russia's capital," *International Herald Tribune*, June 27, 2005.

36 Jeanne Whalen, "Russia's Health Care Is Crumbling," *The Wall Street Journal*, February 13, 2004, p. A9.

37 Quoted in Jaspar Gerard, "Gorbachev calls for Russian millionaires to repay money," *The Sunday Times* (UK), June 5, 2005.

38 Marshall Goldman, *The Piratization of Russia* (New York: Routledge, 2003), p. 177.

39 Duncan Gardham, "Oil billionaire named in Litvinenko inquiry," *Telegraph* (U.K.), December 28, 2006.

40 Mark Mackinnon, "Fugitive vows to keep fighting for Russia," *The Globe and Mail* (U.K.), April 29, 2005.

41 "Nevzlin Faces Murder Charges," *The Moscow Times*, July 27, 2004.

42 Catrina Stewart and Matt Siegel, "Nevzlin Goes on Trial in Absentia for Murder," *The Moscow Times*, March 20, 2008, p. 5.

43 The *Criminal State* series will chronicle the close working relationship among those ideologically aligned around the Zionist cause. The late Tom Lantos' wife, Annette, and their two daughters are converts to the Church of Jesus Christ of the Latter Day Saints (Mormon). In April 2001, Congressman Lantos was presented a doctorate of humane letters during commencement ceremonies at Brigham Young University, America's primary learning center for Mormons ("the Lost Tribe of Israel"). In June 2008, Mrs. Lantos was presented the Presidential Medal of Freedom from President G.W. Bush on behalf of her husband. During that same ceremony, the Medal of Freedom was presented to Laurence H. Silberman, an federal appeals court judge who co-chaired a commission that investigated the intelligence community's flawed prewar claims about Iraq's weapons programs. William Branigin, "President Presents Medals to Honor the Contributions of Six," *The Washington Post*, June 20, 2008, p. A9.

44 Reuters, "Russian court finds Jewish oligarch living in Israel guilty on four counts of murder," *Haaretz*, August 1, 2008.

45 "Yukos figure 'guilty of murders,'" *BBC News*, August 1, 2008.

46 *The Charlie Rose Show*, March 9, 2006 (available online).

47 Rothstein was widely reputed to be a key participant in fixing the 1919 World Series, also known as the "Black Sox Scandal" when Rothstein agents paid members of the Chicago White Sox to lose. Known as the "Moses of the Jewish mob," Rothstein's other nicknames included Mr. Big, The Fixer, The Man Uptown, The Big Bankroll and The Brain.

48 "Michael Steinhardt's Voyage Around His Father," Forbes.com, November 8, 2001. Since its founding, the DLC has been overseen

by president Al From. The Nevzlin-Steinhardt meeting may be explained by the oft-repeated redeployment of stolen funds to leverage larceny into perceived legitimacy and geopolitical influence. In March 2001, New York University's School of Education was renamed the Steinhardt School of Education after a $10 million donation from Michael and Judith Steinhardt (i.e., 2% of the funds realized from the treasury-note fraud). The Steinhardt School is near NYU's Edgar Bronfman Center for Jewish Student Life. In February 2007 Steinhardt sold his interest in *The New Republic* as did Martin Peretz, its editor since 1974 and Al Gore Junior's tutor and mentor while Gore was a student at Harvard. While working as a *New Republic* correspondent in Italy, CIA station files described Michael Ledeen as an agent of influence of a foreign government (Israel). Ledeen was then hired in 1981 by Paul Wolfowitz, director of policy planning at the State Department. In 1983, he was hired on the recommendation of Richard Perle as a Defense Department consultant on terrorism before becoming a consultant to the National Security Council and later a consultant to the Pentagon's Office of Special Plans under Douglas Feith. The former *New Republic* correspondent now serves on the board of the Jewish Institute of National Security Affairs along with Richard Perle and Stephen Bryen.

49 Michael Steinhardt, *No Bull* (New York: John Wiley, 2001), pp. 273-281.

50 See the introduction for an explanation of the *sayanim* corps of undercover operatives and the need to maintain and expand a cadre of those who can be recruited to volunteer assistance when asked because they *believe* their assistance will advance the cause of the Zionist state.

51 Ruth Schuster, "'We want the non-committed Jews,'" *Haaretz*, May 28, 2008.

52 Connie Bruck, "The Brass Ring," *The New Yorker*, June 30, 2008, p. 43.

53 William Black calls them "financial superpredators." Control frauds "do not simply defeat controls; they suborn them and turn them into allies." As Black points out: "[T]he scariest aspect of control frauds is that they can occur in waves, causing systemic damage." What is described in this account is not

stealing from a public agency; this syndicate steals from the public, often with the public an unwitting accomplice. Here lies the role of consensus beliefs and the capacity of people to do immoral acts while *believing* they are behaving morally. Thus the recurring role of self-deceit. As Black explains, control frauds "are adept at finding the weak link in any institutional chain." Because finance is institutional, the temptation, the opportunity and the payoff are substantial and the expertise is available, particularly among *the people in between.* "The S&L industry was not a major purchaser of junk bonds, but it provided Milken's most important group of 'captives.' They were critical to the overstating of junk bond values..." The credit crisis triggered by the subprime mortgage market used a similar "trash for cash" approach in plundering value from the public, largely through defrauding financial markets where pension assets are dominant. Black cites the political and social results of the national scale control fraud in Russia: "Life expectancy has fallen dramatically, violence has increased, respect for Western institutions has plummeted, and the poverty and disease rates have surged. These social and political effects have made many Russians hostile to the United States, and the effects feed back into economic policies that can cause further damage." William K. Black, *The Best Way to Rob a Bank is to Own One*, (Austin: University of Texas Press, 2005), pp. x-iv, 40, 248-49.

54 Adam Nagourney, "Worries in G.O.P. about Disarray in McCain Camp," *The New York Times*, May 25, 2008, p. 1. With offices in New York, Moscow and 23 other locations, Traxys management team, headed by CEO Mark S. Kristoff, acquired a majority stake in Traxys in 2006 in a buyout sponsored by Pegasus and Kelso & Company. See www.traxys.com. If Sogem and Considar, the predecessor firms to Traxys, were involved with trading metals during the oligarchization of Russia, this buyout helped launder those proceeds.

55 Michael Cooper, "Savior or Machiavelli, McCain Aide Carries On," *The New York Times*, October 23, 2007.

56 Matthew Mosk, "Top McCain Adviser Has Found Success Mixing Money, Politics," *The Washington Post*, June 26, 2008, p. 1. The *Post* article describes how relationships become "lucrative commodities" citing instances where Davis, as campaign

manager, hired a vendor of campaign services in which he was also an investor.

57 Adam Nagourney, "McCain Orders Shake-Up of His Campaign," *The New York Times*, July 3, 2008.

58 A Harvard University professor and 'shock therapy' advocate, Jeffrey Sachs downplays the key role he played in the deprivations forced on the Russian people. He has since transferred to Columbia University where in September 2006 George Soros pledged $50 million to a Sachs-led Millennium Promise to help eradicate extreme poverty in Africa. The recurring behavior patterns associated with Mr. Soros and his Open Society operations suggest this effort may be a means to survey natural resources in Africa for acquisition by Chinese firms reinvesting U.S. purchasing power.

59 BBC News "Profile of Anatoly Chubais," March 17, 2005 (available online).

60 Ibid.

61 Rather than include professionals skilled in law and finance to advise on the employee ownership component of the Russian privatization program, the Harvard advisory team retained Joseph Blasi, a sociologist at Rutgers University who was previously part of the Harvard Project on Kibbutz Studies.

62 In July 2008, Thomas Mirow, newly appointed president of the European Bank for Reconstruction and Development (founded at the end of the Cold War to bring markets to former communist countries), said that he saw "encouraging signs" in Russia, in particular that Chubais could play an influential role in negotiating a new accord between Russia and the European Union. Katrin Bennhold and Alison Smale, "New Head of Development Bank Puts Focus on Russia," *The New York Times*, July 5, 2008, p. B2.

63 In 1993, in the lead-up to the loans-for-shares fraud, Potanin's bank (Oneximbank) became the paying agent for Finance Ministry bonds. In 1994, Oneximbank became the depository and paying agent for treasury obligations and in 1995 became the Russian Federation's authorized bank for dealing with bankrupt enterprises, a key component in the loans for shares fraud.

64 "How to Make a Billion Dollars," *Frontline*, October 2003, http://www.pbs.org/frontlineworld/stories/moscow/billionaires.html Friedman's 1962 book, *Capitalism and Freedom*,

provided Russian reformers with guidelines for minimizing the influence of government. Friedman's prescription provided the intellectual authority that privatization architects could cite for their belief (or the pretense of belief) that this massive fraud was a means to maximize personal and social freedom.

65 In his previous job as secretary of state in the German Finance Ministry, Mr. Mirow traveled widely in Russia. Katrin Bennhold and Alison Smale, "New Head of Development Bank Puts Focus on Russia," *The New York Times*, July 5, 2008, p. B2.

66 See David McClintick, "How Harvard Lost Russia," *Institutional Investor*, January 2006.

67 This Hungarian-born Ashkenazi multi-billionaire co-founded in 1973 the Quantum Fund, one of the first hedge funds. The fund reportedly generated a 3,365% return over the next 10 years. His speculation on the British pound earned him a reputation for "bankrupting" the Bank of England. As part of Europe's exchange rate mechanism, the bank maintained an artificial exchange rate with the Deutschmark as the U.K. economy weakened (along with the pound sterling) while the German economy improved. In September 1992 Soros led other investors in exerting pressure on the pound by short-selling more than $10 billion of pounds sterling, igniting "Black Wednesday" (September 16, 1992) when the bank was forced to borrow £15 billion to defend a rapidly devaluing currency, reportedly earning Soros $1.1 billion.

68 An assessment of the power-of-association political dynamics in Ukraine was provided to the Russian embassy in Washington during the widely heralded "Orange Revolution" of November 2004.

69 McCain is the only sitting member of Congress ever to head one of the democracy groups. After taking over in January 1993, he shifted much the institute's focus from Latin America to the former Soviet bloc. Under his leadership, the institute has grown to 400 employees working in 70 countries with a budget of about $78 million as he solicited funds from some 560 defense contractors, lobbying firms, oil companies and other donors, many with interests before Senate committes on which he served. John Dowd, his personal attorney in the Keating Five scandal, served as the institute's general counsel. Critics have long charged the institute with improper meddling in pursuit of a neoconservative

agenda. In 2002, the institute was criticized after George Folsom, its president at the time, praised a coup attempt against Venezuelan president Hugo Chavez. A former U.S. ambassador to Haiti has asserted that institute operatives undermined reconciliation efforts among Haitian political rivals, contributing to a coup in 2004. Mike McIntire, "McCain's Lobbyist Laden Group," *The New York Times*, July 28, 2008, p. 1.

70 Billy House, "'Democracy builders drawing ire,'" *Arizona Republic*, July 16, 2006.

71 Seldom did media reports include a reference to the more recent attempt by Mossad agents to poison Hamas leader Khaled Meshal in Jordan in 1998. When the attempted murder was discovered and two Mossad agents were apprehended by Jordanian authorities, Tel Aviv reluctantly agreed to provide an antidote. Since 1991, Meshal has lived in Damascus where he currently resides.

72 Andrew Osborn, "Orange revolution grinds to a halt as Yushchenko sacks entire government," Independent.co.uk, September 9, 2005.

73 Landon Thomas, Jr., "The Man Who May Become the Richest Rothschild," *The New York Times*, March 9, 2007, p. C1. Adolph Hitler sought to conquer Russia knowing that its vast resources could sustain his quest for global dominance. Ukraine, the center of agricultural and manufacturing for the Soviet Union, also served as the center of much of its nuclear weaponry, including its nuclear-armed submarine fleet.

74 In March 2008, Russian security officials reported the arrest of two brothers with links to British interests who were gathering classified data for foreign firms. Ilya Zaslavsky is a TNK-BP manager while his brother Alexander is head of the British Council's Moscow Alumni Club. BBC News, March 20, 2008.

75 "Beyond Transition," an excerpt from the 1998 report of Donald N. Jensen, Associate Director of REF/RL, The World Bank Group. See http://www.worldbank.org/html/prddr/trans/feb98/bigseven.htm

76 Charitable giving by Russia's Ashkenazi elite appears to remain in the broader Jewish community. For example, Vladimir Potanin donates to New York's Guggenheim Museum while Mikhail Fridman donates to the Jewish Museum of New York. With Sibneft acquired by Gazprom, only two large independent

oil companies remain: TNK-BP controlled by Fridman and Lukoil controlled by Vagit Alekperov.

77 Landon Thomas Jr., "Can the New Rich Buy Respect? One Ukrainian Oligarch Is Trying," *The New York Times*, August 8, 2008, p. C1.

78 Catrina Stewart and Matt Siegel, "Nevzlin Goes on Trial in Absentia for Murder," *The Moscow Times*, March 20, 2008, p. 5.

79 "Variety: Johnny Depp to make movie of spy poisoning," CNN.com, January 13, 2007.

80 Congressman Tom Lantos also participated in the July 13, 2005 Helsinki Commission briefing titled "The Yukos Affair and Its Implications for Politics and Business in Russia." The commission is also known as the U.S. Commission on Security and Cooperation in Europe. Its mandate is to ensure that the rule of law protects human rights and basic freedoms in countries under its jurisdiction. Nevzlin's testimony showed how the rule of law has routinely been displaced by belief in the (corrupted) authority of law: "…it is my opinion that the rule of Russia law is the cornerstone of civil society because it serves to protect the rights and freedoms of all citizens… The lives of many hundreds of thousands of people have been harmed forever as a result of the abuses of the Russian government, which has violated basic human rights and its own laws again and again." Similar to Greenspan vouching for the financial soundness of Lincoln S&L in the early stages of that control fraud, we now know that systemic corruption of the authority of law was key to the control fraud inflicted on Russia. Similarly, corruption of the lawful authority of Israel's sovereignty is all that stands between Leonid Nevzlin and his prosecution for murder under Russian law. Nevzlin's full statement is posted online at a Khodorkovsky-related website: http/www.khodorkovsky.infor/docs/nevzlin briefing2. See also "The U.S. to play the Yukos card again?," *Pravda,* July 7, 2005.

81 In April 2007 Moscow sought a reversal of his asylum status after Berezovsky called for the use of force to remove Putin from office. Terry Macalister, Ian Cobain and Simon Tisdall, "Diplomatic rift as Russia says: give us Berezovsky," *Guardian.co.uk*, April 19, 2007.

82 For the past four years, Ashkenazi reporter Arkady Ostrovsky

has been the Moscow correspondent for the London-based *Financial Times* where his portrayal of Khodorkovsky proved unfailingly sympathetic. Even as late as March 2007, Ostrovsky described (in an autobiographical sketch about his own childhood in Moscow) how Khodorkovsky "was arrested in 2003 and watched from a prison cell as his company was destroyed by the state." Arkady Ostrovsky, "A difference in class," *Financial Times*, March 3-4, 2007, p. 3.

83 Catherine Belton, "Kremlin's public enemy number two fights back," *Financial Times*, February 25-25, 2007.

84 Paul Klebnikov, *Godfather of the Kremlin* (New York: Harcourt, Inc., 2000).

85 Ibid., p. 92.

86 Ibid., p. 181.

87 Ibid., pp. 257-268.

88 Ibid., p. 320.

89 Avi Issacharoff and Barak Ravid, "Olmert: No chance for deal with Palestinians on Jerusalem this year," *Haaretz*, July 28, 2008.

Chapter 6: Money, Democracy and the Great Divide

1 Sasha Issenberg, "McCain: It's about the economy," *Boston Globe*, December 18, 2007.

2 Reporting on findings by the Congressional Budget Office in David Cay Johnson, "Report Says the Rich are Getting Richer Faster, Much Faster," *The New York Times*, December 15, 2007, p. 3.

3 Internal Revenue Service data reported in David Cay Johnson, "'05 Incomes, On Average, Still Below 2000 Peak," *The New York Times*, August 21, 2007, p. C1.

4 Justin Lahart and Kelly Evans, "Trapped in the Middle," *The Wall Street Journal*, April 19-20, 2008, p. 1.

5 The "supply side" term was coined by Jude Wanniski in 1975 and popularized in *The Wall Street Journal* by Wanniski, economist Arthur Laffer and *Journal* editorial page editor Robert Bartley. Columbia University economist Robert Mundell was often associated with supply-side theory. Mundell received the 1999 Nobel prize in economic science for his analysis of monetary and fiscal policy under different exchange rate regimes.

6 Dow Jones & Company, the parent company of *The Wall Street*

Journal, was acquired by Rupert Murdoch's News Corp. in August 2007.

7 See General Explanation of the Economic Recovery Tax Act of 1981 (H.R.4242), 97th Congress; Public Law 97-4), Joint Committee on Taxation, JCS 71-81, December 29, 1981.

8 William K. Black, *The Best Way to Rob a Bank Is to Own One* (Austin: University of Texas Press, 2005), p. 37. Black served in numerous senior positions in the area of thrift oversight, including Director of Litigation for the Federal Home Loan Bank Board in Washington, D.C.

9 Interest payments received by individuals on U.S. government securities ("treasuries") are reported by approximately 4% of U.S. taxpayers. Those taxpayers are dominantly upper-income households. To extend the mortgage metaphor: supply-side subsidies ensured that those few who used our mortgage (deficits) to purchase the house also received the bulk of the interest payments on that mortgage.

10 Investment banks and other financial firms pay agencies to rate assets they intend to sell as securities. Oftentimes the firms will seek a preliminary assessment before agreeing to pay the rating agency for the assessment. If the risk rating is lower than anticipated for the securities, the firm will shop elsewhere. Michael Grynbaum, "Study Finds Flawed Practices at Rating Firms," *The New York Times*, July 9, 2008, p. C1. Standard & Poor's Rating Services, the largest bond-rating firm by revenue, is a unit of McGraw-Hill Companies. A July 8, 2008 report by the Securities and Exchange Commission included revealing emails among S&P staffers, including one that read "it could be structured by cows and we would rate it." Another read: "Let's hope we are all wealthy and retired by the time this house of cards falters" while another proposed adjusting rating criteria "because of the ongoing threat of losing deals." Aaron Lucchetti, "S&P Email: 'We Should Not Be Rating It,'" *Wall Street Journal*, August 2-3, 2008, p. B1.

11 As under secretary of defense for policy, Paul Wolfowitz supervised the drafting of a 1992 "Defense Planning Guide" providing military leaders a coherent strategic framework to evaluate force and training options. Under the direction of Secretary of Defense Cheney, the "defense strategy objectives" sought "to

prevent the re-emergence of a new rival" with a "new order that holds the promise of convincing potential competitors that they need not aspire to a greater role or pursue a more aggressive posture to protect their legitimate interests" and "new mechanisms for deterring potential competitors from even aspiring to a large regional or global role." Patrick E. Tyler, "U.S. Strategy Plan Calls for Insuring No Rivals Develop a One-Superpower World." *The New York Times*, March 8, 1992.

12 LTCM included two Nobel laureate economists on its board. Harvard Professor Robert C. Merton and Stanford Professor Myron S. Scholes shared the 1997 prize for a method to determine the value of derivatives.

13 Stanford Kurland, former president of Countrywide Financial Corporation, one of the largest originators of subprime mortgages, founded a firm to buy discounted mortgages. Louis Story, "Pouncing on The Wounded of Wall Street," *The New York Times*, April 4, 2008, p. 1.

14 Jenny Anderson and Louise Story, "Fortunes Reverse for a Bank and Its Lender," *The New York Times*, June 10, 2008, p. C1.

15 Jenny Anderson, "Burdened by Mortgages, Lehman's Options Narrow," *The New York Times*, August 22, 2008, p. C1.

16 A tax deduction is allowed for the cost of pension plan contributions. In addition, the earnings accumulate tax-free and tax preferences are allowed on distribution. The tax expenditure estimates by budget function for fiscal years 2007-2011 indicate a total cost of $760.3 billion for employer-sponsored plans, individual retirement plans and plans covering partners and sole proprietors (Keogh plans). Joint Committee on Taxation, *Estimates of Federal Tax Expenditures for Fiscal years 2007-2011* (Washington, D.C.: U.S. Government Printing Office, September 24, 2007), pp. 34-35. The fiscal cost of the home mortgage interest deduction for the five-year period (2007-2011) is estimated to total $430.2 billion.

17 During his first year as President, Reagan appointed Greenspan to his Economic Policy Advisory Board and named him chair of the National Commission on Social Security Reform. Richard Nixon resigned soon after selecting Greenspan to chair his Council of Economic Advisers. Gerald Ford retained him as chairman until Carter' s election.

18 For instance New York developer Harry Macklowe bought seven Midtown Manhattan office towers for nearly $7 billion, using only $50 million of his own money (seven-tenths of one percent).

19 In 1986, the U.S. General Accounting Office (GAO) described this phenomenon as a "closed system of finance." In 2004, the GAO was renamed the General Accountability Office.

20 An oligarchy implies governance or control by a small group of people for their own interests.

21 The *Criminal State* series will chronicle how organized crime pre-positioned Ronald Reagan for the presidency.

22 For instance, in the largest initial public offering in U.S. history, Visa went public with an $18 billion public offering in March 2008. Wall Street firms stand to collect upward of $500 million in underwriting fees from the sale. Eric Dash, "Big Payday for Wall St. In Visa's Public Offering," *The New York Times*, March 19, 2008, p. C3.

23 The *Criminal State* series will describe how debt-based monetization methods worsen the systemic dysfunctions created by the closed system of finance. Human dignity and informed choice suggest that the solution lies in the direction of monetization secured by the physical capital essential for healthy communities.

24 In May 2008, Fed Chief Ben Bernanke, Greenspan's successor, opened a lending facility for banks and even brokers to swap up to $350 billion of their unsellable securities for cash or treasuries. This "trash for cash" agenda (again backed by our full faith and credit) led critics to describe the Federal Reserve as "a monetary bordello." Gretchen Morgenson, "What a Deal: Trash for Treasuries," *The New York Times*, May 18, 2008, p. BU1.

25 Average pay was $14.2 million in 2007 based on reported compensation for CEOs of Standard & Poor's 500 companies. That figure is based on preliminary data from The Corporate Library drawing on 211 proxy statements filed through April 9, 2008. The median pay was $8.8 million.

26 Jeanne Sahadi, "CEO pay: 364 times more than workers," CNNMoney.com, August 29, 2007.

27 As of May 2008, Kohlberg, Kravis Roberts & Co. had completed 160 transactions with an enterprise value of more than $410 billion. Marc Gunther, "Private Equity Goes Green," *Fortune*, May 1, 2008.

28 Mehlman focuses on "strategic public affairs" as he communicates the public benefits of private equity to governments, third parties and non-governmental organizations. Mehlman also serves as a trustee of the U.S. Holocaust Memorial Museum. Press Release of April 16, Kohlberg Kravis Roberts & Co.

29 Bank shares are cheap and likely to rebound as the economy improves. In a replay of the pre-staging of the S&L fraud, the private equity firms seek managerial control without the regulations intended to protect bank depositors as well as taxpayers who provide the full faith and credit that stands behind the various guarantees and subsidies provided to banks. "The Banks and Private Equity," (op-ed), *The New York Times*, August 3, 2008.

30 Jenny Anderson, "Willing To Lease Your Bridge," *The New York Times*, August 27, 2008, p. C1.

31 "Where's the Prosperity," *The New York Times*, August 27, 2008, p A 22.

32 David E. Sanger, "Beyond the Trade Pact Collapse," *The New York Times*, August 3, 2008.

33 Peter S. Goodman, "U.S. and Global Economies Slipping in Unison," *The New York Times*, August 24, 2008, p. 1.

34 David Barboza, "Little-Known Entrepreneurs Putting China Near Top of Billionaires' List," *The New York Times*, November 7, 2007. *Forbes* identified 66 billionaires in China.

35 "China has 146 billionaires," *China Daily*, January 1, 2008.

36 Stijn Claessens, Simeon Djankov and Larry H.P. Lang, "Who Controls East Asian Corporations?" (Washington, D.C.: The World Bank, 1999).

37 "Where's the Prosperity," *The New York Times*, August 27, 2008, p A 22.

38 David Cay Johnston, "Average US Income in 2006 Showed First Rise Over 2000," *The New York Times*, August 26,2008, p. C3.

39 While counsel to the Senate Committee on Finance, the author shared responsibility for crafting federal laws that increased funds in the hands of pension fund managers from approximately $800 billon in 1980 ($1,770 billion in 2007 dollars) to $16,600 billion by March 30, 2007.

40 Javier Santiso, "Sovereign wealth funds boost development," *The Globalist*, March 21, 2008.

41 Sovereign wealth funds are among the biggest speculators in the

trading of oil and other commodities like corn and cotton in the U.S. David Cho, "Sovereign Funds Become Big Speculators," *The Washington Post*, August 12 2008, p. D1.

42 Steven Weisman, "2 Foreign Funds Agree to Shun 'Political' Deals," *The New York Times*, March 21, 2008.

43 David Gross, "SWF Seeks Loving American Man," Slate.com, January 24, 2008.

44 In July 2008, Defense Secretary Robert M. Gates acknowledged that America's long-term national security now depends on eliminating the conditions that foster extremism by understanding and addressing "the grievances that lie at the heart of insurgencies." Josh White, "Gates Sees Terrorism Remaining Enemy No. 1," *The Washington Post*, July 31, 2008, p. 1.

45 As a governing council under fundamentalist Judaism, the Sanhedrin was all-powerful because it was accountable only to itself. Akin to a Sanhedrin, a global capital market likewise answers only to itself based on consensus-derived commercial principles enforced by the World Trade Organization with technical and financial assistance provided by the World Bank Group. The *Criminal State* series will describe how complementary monetization methods can create locale-attuned purchasing power able to match unmet needs to underutilized local capacities as a means to counter the impact on communities of this finance-fixated governing system.

46 See Donella Meadows, "Places to Intervene in a System," *Whole Earth Review*, Winter 1997.

47 Israel Shahak, *Jewish History, Jewish Religion* (London: Pluto Press, 1994), p. 51.

48 Ibid., p. 58.

49 Ibid., p. 89.

Chapter 7: The New Anti-Semitism

1 The entire quote reads: "The new anti-Semitism appears in the guise of 'political criticism of Israel,' consisting of a discriminatory approach and double standard towards the state of Jews, while questioning its right to exist." Natan Sharansky, "Anti-Semitism Is Our Problem," *Haaretz,* August 10, 2003. A dedicated Zionist, Sharansky immigrated to Israel in 1986 as part of a prisoner exchange after ten years confinement in the Soviet Union. Named minister of industry and trade in 1996 and

minister of the interior in 1999, in February 2003 he was appointed minister without portfolio responsible for Jerusalem, social and Diaspora affairs. He resigned from the government in May 2005 to protest Ariel Sharon's disengagement plan for Gaza. President G.W. Bush lauded his 2004 book, *The Case For Democracy*. Sharansky was awarded the Presidential Medal of Freedom in December 2006, the first Israeli to receive that award. He received the Congressional Gold Medal in 1986. Only three others have received both awards: Pope John Paul II, Mother Teresa and Nelson Mandela. When Sharansky moved to Israel, he formed the Zionist Forum, an umbrella organization dedicated to helping new Israeli immigrants from the former Soviet Union. A $20,000 relocation allowance was provided to Russian Jews. Guilford Glazer of Knoxville, Tennessee-based Glazer Steel, Inc., was reportedly a key financier for this relocation process. Former first lady Nancy Reagan presented Sharansky with the 2008 Ronald Reagan Freedom Award in a June 4, 2008 ceremony in Washington, D.C. "Nancy Reagan Will Present Natan Sharansky 2008 Ronald Reagan Freedom Award," *Jewish Russian Telegraph*, February 28, 2008.

2 Remarks to Jewish leaders in Cleveland, February 25, 2008.

3 See "Global Anti-Semitism Review Act," October 8, 2004 (S. 2292) posted online at http://www.state.gov/g/drl/ris/79640.htm

4 The May 23, 2006 press release announced the appointment of Gregg Rickman as the "first special envoy for monitoring and combating anti-Semitism." Rickman helped investigate the United Nations Oil-for-Food Program and the retention by Swiss banks of assets belonging to Holocaust victims and their heirs. http://useu.usmision.gov

5 Email to author of December 4, 2004 from Massachusetts Institute of Technology Professor Noam Chomsky, available online at www.criminalstate.org.

6 David McCullough, *Truman* (New York: Simon & Schuster, 1992), p. 614.

7 Michael T. Benson, *Harry S. Truman and the Founding of Israel* (Westport: Praeger, 1997), pp. 9, 47-49, 53-58, 67, 181. Christian dispensationalism offers a Biblical interpretation of the role played by the return of Jews to Israel as a prerequisite to the resurrection of Jesus Christ and the final assumption of believers into heaven ("rapture") during the "end-times."

8 Memorandum of Conversation by Secretary of State [Recognition of Israel], Top Secret, Washington, D.C., May 12, 1948, reproduced in Donald Neff, *Fallen Pillars* (Washington, D.C.: Institute for Palestine Studies, 1995), pp. 221-223.

9 Feinberg received from Truman a personal 17-page letter of thanks and an offer that he declined to serve as U.S. Ambassador to Israel. Grant T. Smith, *America's Defense Line* (Washington, DC: Institute for Research: Middle Eastern Policy, 2008), pp. 40-41, 290.

10 See Norman G. Finkelstein, *Beyond Chutzpah—On the Misuse of Anti-Semitism and the Abuse of History* (Berkeley: University of California Press, 2005).

11 Quoted in James Besser, "Jewish Criticism of Carter Intensifies," *Jewish Week*, December 15, 2006.

12 Martin Peretz, "Carter's Legacy," *The Spine* (weblog of *The New Republic*), November 26, 2006.

13 Norman G. Finkelstein, *The Holocaust Industry* (New York: Verso, 2000).

14 Jennifer Howard, "Calif. Press Will Publish Controversial Book on Israel," *The Chronicle of Higher Education*, July 22, 2006, p. 1

15 Yossi Melman, "Israel denies entry to high-profile critic Norman Finkelstein," *Haaretz*, May 25, 2008.

16 Paul Findley, *They Dare to Speak Out* (Chicago: Lawrence Hill Books, 1985), Chapter Six.

17 Ibid, p. 192.

18 For example, if an AWACS had been in operation in 1967, the preemptive component of the Six-Day War would not be in dispute. Nor would the details of the Israeli attack on the *USS Liberty*, including the eight hours of aerial surveillance by Israeli aircraft prior to commencing a two-hour air and naval attack

19 The *Criminal State* series will document how such psy-ops are routinely deployed against individuals who have firsthand evidence that incriminates this network of operatives in transgenerational criminality. In the interim, see analyses and postings on www.criminalstate.org.

20 A.M. Rosenthal, "On My Mind: The Deadly Cargo," *The New York Times*, October 22, 1999.

21 Stephen Miller, "A.M. Rosenthal, Influential *The New York Times* Editor, Dies at 84," *The New York Times*, May 11, 2006.

22 Rosenthal also exposed Loral's sale of missile guidance systems

to China and protested Clinton's approval of the sale. A.M. Rosenthal, "On My Mind; The Missile Business," *The New York Times*, April 10, 1998. Bernard Schwartz, Loral's CEO, was Bill Clinton's top fundraiser in 1996, the same year Loral stock sold for $72 a share. Loral was fined $20 million. In effect, the 2002 fine punished the shareholders (largely tax-subsidized pension plans). In 2003, Loral declared bankruptcy. The government insider on that theft, Stephen Bryen, was then the deputy under secretary of defense for technology security policy (1981-1988). Bryen now serves on the Advisory Board of JINSA, the Jewish Institute for National Security Affairs.

23 In 1963, Fulbright convened hearings before the Committee on Foreign Relations concerning the funding sources for foreign agents influencing public opinion and policy through media campaigns and other propaganda. The hearings confirmed that at least $5 million ($27.5 million in 2007 dollars) were funds directly from the quasi-governmental Jewish Agency. An international thought leader, Fulbright won election to the Senate in 1944 and served five terms, including serving the longest of any chairman of the Foreign Relations Committee (1959-1974). Fulbright's lengthy absences from the state became a political vulnerability that Governor Dale Bumpers seized to defeat Fulbright in November 1974. Though Bumpers largely refused out-of-state funding for his modest $300,000 campaign, it is also clear that Fulbright considered himself a target of the Israel lobby whose operatives he considered should comply with the Foreign Agents Registration Act. With his removal, Tel Aviv could avoid potentially embarrassing disclosures by a high-profile Senator about foreign funding sources for pro-Israeli political operations in the U.S.

24 The *Criminal State* series will describe the interstate node-and-network imbedding of this corruption dating from the Prohibition era. Evidence abounds of the federal/state/local imbedding of this *modus operandi* across generations.

25 John J. Fialka, "Jewish Groups Increase Campaign Donations, Target Them Precisely," *Wall Street Journal*, August 3, 1983, p. 1.

26 Quoted in Paul Findley, "Blow to Pro-Israel Lobby in the U.S.," *Washington Report on Middle East Affairs*, March 1997, p. 16.

27 From October 1984 to April 1992, Diller served as chairman and

CEO of Fox, Inc., parent company of Fox Broadcasting Company and Twentieth Century Fox. In 1978, control of Twentieth Century Fox passed to investors Marvin Davis and Marc Rich. In 1983, Rich was indicted in federal court for evading $48 million in taxes and charged with 51 counts of tax fraud and orchestrating illegal oil sales with Iran during the hostage crisis (1979-1981). In 1985, Rich's half interest was sold to News Corp. controlled by Rupert Murdoch. Six months later, Davis sold his interest to Fox. Murdoch recruited Diller from Paramount to run the studio and Murdoch implemented Diller's plan for a television network. After becoming an American citizen in 1985, the Australian Murdoch gained Federal Communications Commission approval to acquire Metromedia's television properties, creating Fox Broadcasting Company. Though never convicted, Rich was pardoned by President Bill Clinton in January 2001 citing clemency pleas from Israeli officials including the head of the Mossad and Prime Minister Ehud Barak.

28 John Pilger, "From triumph to torture," *The Guardian*, July 2, 2008.

29 Mohammed Omer, "A Voice for the Voiceless: On Winning the 2008 Martha Gellhorn Prize for Journalism," *Washington Report on Middle East Affairs*, August 2008, p. 15.

30 "Anti-Semitism and the *USS Liberty* Inquiry," http://www.usslibertyinquiry.com/misc/antisemitism/ html.

31 Helen Nugent, "Chief Rabbi Flays Church over Vote on Israel Assets," *Times* (London), February 17, 2006.

32 "ADL rips new UN human rights body as tool of Arabs, Muslims," *Haaretz,* November 29, 2006.

33 According to Foxman, "The appointment of Desmond Tutu as head of the fact-finding mission to Beit Hanun is an extension of the anti-Israel kangaroo court tactics used by the UN Human Rights Council." Quoted in Herb Keinon, "Israel won't bar Desmond Tutu's entry," *Jerusalem Post*, December 3, 2006.

34 Associated Press, "Israel to deny UN official entry for comparing Israel to Nazis," *Haaretz*, April 9, 2008. In an article that irked his pro-Israeli critics titled, "Slouching Towards a Palestinian Holocaust," Falk wrote that "it is especially painful for me, as an American Jew, to feel compelled to portray the ongoing and intensifying abuse of the Palestinian people by Israel through a reliance on such an inflammatory metaphor as a 'holocaust.'" He

then asked: "Is it an irresponsible overstatement to associate the treatment of Palestinians with this criminalized Nazi record of collective atrocity? I think not. The recent developments in Gaza are especially disturbing because they express so vividly a deliberate intention on the part of Israel and its allies to subject an entire human community to life-endangering conditions of utmost cruelty." Marc Perlman, "U.N. Taps America Jewish Critic of Israel as Rights Expert," Forward.com, March 27, 2008.

35 Mahoud al-Zahar, "No Peace Without Hamas," *The Washington Post*, April 17, 2008, p. A23.

36 Isabel Kershner, "Palestinians Fight Israelis In Gaza; Toll Exceeds 21," *The New York Times*, April 17, 2008, p. A6. The day before the attack, Avigdor Lieberman, chairman of the far-right Yisrael Beiteinu (Our Home) party urged that Carter cancel his plans, saying such talks would only heighten terror. Reuters, "Lieberman to Carter: Meeting Meshal will only heighten terror," *Haaretz*, April 16, 2008.

37 Reuters, "Report: Netanyahu says 9/11 terror attacks good for Israel," *Haaretz*, April 16, 2008

38 Patricia Cohen, "Essay Linking Liberal Jews and Anti-Semitism Sparks a Furor," *The New York Times*, January 31, 2007, p. B1.

39 Fernanda Santos, "New York Rabbi Finds Friends in Iran and Enemies at Home," *The New York Times*, January 15, 2007.

40 Bradley Burston, "Jews who make Satan look good," *Haaretz*, December 15, 2006.

41 DPA, "UN Secretary General calls Holocaust deniers 'misguided individuals,'" *Haaretz*, January 20, 2008.

42 "ADL unleashes ads condemning Swiss energy deal with Iran," *Haaretz*, April 9, 2008.

43 Yossi Melman, "Polish PM: There is no Polish culture without Jewish culture," *Haaretz*, April 9, 2008; Barak Ravid, "Polish PM: Iran's comment on Israel annuls right to place in int'l community," *Haaretz*, April 9, 2008.

44 Max Deveson, "US Jewish lobby gains new voice," BBC News, Washington, April 16, 2008.

45 Klein quoted in Paul Katz, "Breaking ranks with U.S. Jewish 'establishment' on the occupation," *Haaretz*, April 16, 2008.

46 Born in Moscow in 1973 to a Jewish couple, Brin and his family left Russia in 1977. "Google co-founder: My family left Russia because of anti-Semitism," *Haaretz*, May 18, 2005.

47 Associated Press, "Peres urges world youth to fight anti-Semitism using Facebook," *Haaretz,* January 29, 2008.

48 See "IT Security" in Appendix A and posted online at www.criminalstate.org

49 The circumstances whereby this chart was obtained from an Israeli source will be described in the *Criminal State.* series.

50 The full text of this email exchange is posted online at www.criminalstate.org.

51 Visible displays of support for Israel are a means to signal potential pro-Israeli fundraisers, particularly for anyone considering a presidential race. Delaware Senator Joe Biden, a potential 2008 presidential candidate, announced in December 2006 that he would press for greater access to Nazi-era files, claiming "further delay in release of this archive material would be unjust to Holocaust survivors." Associated Press, "U.S. Senator presses for greater access to Nazi-era files," *Haaretz,* December 29, 2006.

52 Elliott Abrams, *Faith or Fear—How Jews Can Survive in a Christian America* (New York: The Free Press, 1997).

53 Israel Shahak, *Jewish History, Jewish Religion* (New York: Pluto Press, 1994), p. 8.

54 Ibid., p. 9.

55 Responses ranged from a low of 34% in the United Kingdom to a high of 72% in Spain. EU-wide, 42% agreed with the statement: Jews still talk too much about the Holocaust." "Manifestations of Anti-Semitism in the European Union—Belgium," posted at http://www.jewishvirtuallibrary.org/jsource/anti-semitism/report_belgium.html

56 The John Hagee Ministries operate largely in the U.S. and the U.K.

57 Kurtzer also served as U.S. ambassador to Egypt. As a member of the State Department Policy Planning staff during the Reagan Administration, he was a speechwriter for Secretary of State George Schultz who now serves as co-chair of the Committee on the Present Danger. During his 29 years of public service, he also served as Deputy Assistant Secretary of State for Near Eastern Affairs and Principal Deputy Assistant Secretary of State for Intelligence and Research. From 1977-1979, he served as Dean of Yeshiva College. He presently serves as the S. Daniel Abraham Professor of Middle East Policy Studies at Princeton University's Woodrow Wilson School of Public and International Affairs.

58. Anschel Pfeffer, "Dennis Ross, Daniel Kurtzer slam Bush's Mideast policy," *Haaretz*, May 14, 2008. Kurtzer may have been the advisor who inserted in Obama's June 2008 AIPAC speech a promise that "Jerusalem will remain the capital of Israel, and it must remain undivided." Obama had to quickly explain himself when the statement outraged Palestinians, alarmed Muslims and raised concerns among moderates worldwide.

59 Neela Banerjee and Michael Luo, "McCain Chides Pastor Over Sermon on Holocaust," *The New York Times*, May 23, 2008, p. A15.

60 Associated Press, "U.S. evangelist pledges $6 million in contributions to Israel," *Haaretz*, April 6, 2008; Associated Press, "Hagee: Israel Must Control All Jerusalem," *Haaretz*, April 7, 2008.

61 On May 22, 2008, McCain announced his rejection of Hagee's endorsement after an audio recording surfaced in which the preacher said that God sent Adolf Hitler to help Jews reach the promised land. Libby Quaid, "McCain Rejects Pastor's Endorsement," ABC News (online) May 22, 2008.

62 "Lieberman Address to Christians United for Israel," July 16, 2007, posted on Lieberman's Senate website: http://lieberman.senate.gov/newsroom/release.dfm?id=279110

63 Andrew Miga, "Lieberman to speak at conference hosted by Hagee," May 28, 2008, Associated Press online.

64 Reuters, "Pre-WW2 Churchill article says Jews partly to blame for anti-Semitism," *Haaretz*, November 3, 2007.

65 Elliott Abrams, *Faith or Fear* (New York: Free Press, 1997), p. 196.

66 Ibid., p. 193. (emphasis in original)

67 Israel Shahak, *Jewish History, Jewish Religion* (New York: Pluto Press, 1994).

68 Ibid., p. 71.

69 Prinz migrated to the U.S. in 1937 with the sponsorship of Rabbi Stephen Wise, an adviser to Franklin Roosevelt and Harry Truman. Prinz lectured widely for the United Jewish Appeal established in the 1920s by Golda Meir and others intent on funding the Zionist movement. Settling in Newark, New Jersey, Rabbi Prinz helped organize the Conference of Presidents of Major American Jewish Organizations. In the fall of 1963, the conference reportedly offered the funding to help Senator John F. Kennedy finish his presidential campaign provided he would

turn over to them control of U.S. policy in the Middle East, an account that will be chronicled in the *Criminal State* series. Prinz served as conference president, 1965-67. The Conference membership is made up of 51 Jewish organizations dedicated to mobilizing support for Israel.

70 David Rose, "The Gaza Bombshell," *Vanity Fair*, April 2008.

71 The text reads: "We gather to mark a momentous occasion. Sixty years ago in Tel Aviv, David Ben-Gurion proclaimed Israel's independence, founded on the 'natural right of the Jewish people to be masters of their own fate.' What followed was more than the establishment of a new country. It was the redemption of an ancient promise given to Abraham and Moses and David—a homeland for the chosen people of Eretz Yisrael." Associated Press, "Text of President Bush's speech to the Knesset, the Israeli parliament, as provided by the White House," May 15, 2008.

72 "Israeli think tank: Muslim anti-Semitism is strategic danger for Israel," *Haaretz*, April 22, 2008.

73 Ora Koren, "Kissinger: Timetable required to combat global nuclear threat," *Haaretz*, May 14, 2008.

Chapter 8: Would Obama Be Better?

1 The support of James Crown and Penny Pritzker, Chicago Jewish scions, helped establish Obama in the Jewish community. Pritzker, Obama's national finance chair, previously donated funds to George W. Bush. Early support from Jewish mega-donor Alan Solomont gave Obama credibility early on in the community of heavyweight fundraisers. "Barack Obama: The Kosher Connection," *The Jewish Daily Forward*, August 21, 2008.

2 Reuters, "Hedge fund managers set new payout records in 2007," April 16, 2008. Soros was not the top-paid hedge fund operator. According to Institutional Investor's *Alpha Magazine*, John Paulson took home \$3.7 billion in 2007 when he profited from money borrowed to bet on the collapse of the U.S. subprime mortgage market. James Simons at Renaissance Technologies took home \$2.8 billion. The top 50 hedge fund managers pocketed an estimated \$29 billion in 2007.

3 Associated Press, "U.S. Presidential hopeful Obama launches Hebrew blog in Israel," *Haaretz*, April 11, 2008.

4 In his March 2, 2007 speech, Senator Obama pledged his "strong commitment to the security of Israel: our strongest ally in the

region and its only established democracy. That will always be my starting point."

5 "Obama: Israel's security sacrosanct," *Jerusalem Post* online edition, February 27, 2008.

6 Associated Press, "U.S. Presidential hopeful Obama launches Hebrew blog in Israel," *Haaretz*, April 11, 2008.

7 Ewen Macskill, Daniel Nasaw and Suzanne Goldenburg, "Clinton makes threat against Iran as voters go to polls," Guardian.co.uk, April 22, 2008.

8 In the indirect way that *the people in between* wage unconventional warfare, that political promise often emerges as a commitment to move the U.S. embassy from Tel Aviv to Jerusalem in order to suggest that Jerusalem and not Tel Aviv is the capital. Akiva Eldar, "Jewish functionaries are stirring up the Clinton-Obama race," *Haaretz*, February 15, 2008. To create consensus around Jerusalem as the capital, *Haaretz* routinely reports the Israeli government as based not in Tel Aviv but Jerusalem. Thus, for example, the May 11, 2008 issue of *Haaretz* reported, "Jerusalem has decided not to issue any official comment." From Yoav Stern and Barak Ravid, "Ex-IDF Chief: Hezbollah control of Lebanon may benefit Israel."

9 In addition to wire fencing and concrete walling, sections will include electrified fencing, trenches, roads for patrol vehicles, electronic ground and fence sensors, thermal imaging and video cameras, unmanned aerial vehicles, sniper towers and razor wire. Construction began in 2002. As of July 2008, the barrier was 57% complete, much of it constructed inside the West Bank, leading opponents to characterize it as a land grab. In July 2004, the International Court of Justice in The Hague issued an advisory opinion describing the routing of the barrier inside the West Bank as a violation of Israeli obligations under international law.

10 Appealing to pro-Israeli interests has become a rite of passage for potential presidential candidates. Senator Joe Biden of Delaware promised, as chairman of the Senate Committee on Foreign Relations, to hasten the release of Nazi-era files on the Holocaust. Campaign finance records could quantify the impact of that announcement on Biden's early fundraising. Tom Lantos served as an aide to Senator Biden (1978-79).

11 "Palestinians say opposition tour of holy site could cause bloodshed." CNN.com, September 27, 2000.

12 From the Commission findings: "From the Defense Minister himself we know that this consideration did not concern him in the least, and that it was necessary to forestall this possibility as a humanitarian obligation and also to prevent the political damage it would entail. In our view, the Minister of Defense made a grave mistake when he ignored the danger of acts of revenge and bloodshed by the Phalangists against the population in the refugee camps." The Commission further reported: "We shall remark here that it is ostensibly puzzling that the Defense Minister did not in any way make the Prime Minister privy to the decision on having the Phalangists enter the camps." The full text of the commission report can be found at http://www.jewishvirtuallibrary.org/jsource/History/kahan.html.

13 Ibid.

14 This ongoing phenomenon will be detailed in the *Criminal State* series

15 Dr. Steve Sauerberg ran for the Republican nomination after a young wealthy political newcomer (Steve Greenberg, age 35) opted out of mounting a challenge to Durbin. Sam Youngman, "One Durbin challenger in, another out," *The Hill*, May 14, 2007.

16 In June 2008, the Office of Thrift Supervision (OTS) accused Schumer, a member of the Senate Banking Committee, of sparking a bank run when he released a June 28 letter expressing concerns about the viability of IndyMac, a California-based lender with assets of $32 billion and deposits of $19 billion. The OTS announced July 12 that it was transferring control of IndyMac to the Federal Deposit Insurance Corporation. "Schumer: Don't blame me for IndyMac failure," CNN.com, July 13, 2008.

17 Quoted in John J. Mearsheimer and Stephen M. Walt, *The Israel Lobby and U.S. Foreign Policy* (New York: Farrar, Strauss and Giroux, 2007), p. 153. The authors explain that the Reid quote was accessed from AIPAC's website on January 14, 2005 but had been removed by May 2007.

18 Quoted in Shmuel Rosner, "U.S. Jewish leader worried by thrust of White House campaign," *Haaretz*, February 12, 2008.

19 "Obama: Israel's security sacrosanct," *Jerusalem Post* online edition, February 27, 2008.

20 In June 2008, Libyan leader Moamer al Qadhafi offered his theory for Barack Obama's support of Israel: "We suspect he may

fear being killed by Israeli agents and meet the same fate as Kennedy when he promised to look into Israel's nuclear program." *Reuters*, "Gadaffi: We fear Israel may kill Barack Obama just as it did JFK," *Haaretz*, June 6, 2008.

21 Israeli envoy Dan Gillerman said that Carter "went to the region with soiled hands and came back with bloody hands after shaking the hand of Khaled Meshal, the leader of Hamas." Gillerman said it was "a shame" to see Carter, who had done "good things" as a former president, "turn into what I believe to be a bigot." Associated Press, "Israeli envoy to UN calls Carter 'a bigot' for meeting Meshal," *Haaretz*, April 25, 2008. That comment elicited a rare rebuke when the U.S. Embassy in Tel Aviv expressed its dissatisfaction with the disrespectful comments about the former president.

22 Associated Press, "Obama slams Carter for meeting Hamas, tries to reassure Jewish voters," *Haaretz*, April 16, 2008.

23 A video excerpt from a Wright sermon was posted on Youtube.com http://www/youtube.com/ watch?v=Fnl431s1r6s

24 David Nitkin and Harry Merritt, "A new twist on an intriguing family history," *Baltimore Sun*, March 2, 2007.

25 Adi Schwartz, "'Israeli Miracle' is developing strong ties with Communist China," *Haaretz*, August 8, 2008.

26 Associated Press, "McCain blasts Obama for saying Iran poses lesser threat than Soviets," *Haaretz*, May 20, 2008.

27 Stephen J. Solarz, a New York Congressman (1975-93), boasted to columnist Robert Novak about his many meetings with Saddam Hussein. While pro-Israeli policy makers were meeting with the Iraqi dictator, U.S. policy makers were being urged to isolate the former ally because he posed a threat to Israel and, with his weapons of mass destruction, to U.S. national security. Solarz is a member of the Committee on the Present Danger.

28 When the CIA, the State Department and the Pentagon determined in 1974 that Israel had produced and stockpiled nuclear weapons, Tel Aviv was also suspected of providing nuclear materials, equipment and technology to Iran, South Africa and other countries. Amir Oren, "CIA: We said back in 1974 that Israel had nuclear weapons," *Haaretz*, January 13, 2008.

29 Patrick Healy, "Clinton and Obama Court Jewish Vote," *The New York Times*, March 14, 2007. Not to be outdone at the March

2007 AIPAC conference, Hillary Clinton featured Israeli music on the sound system at her reception along with a sign featuring her name in Hebrew.

30 In 1991, Jeremiah Wright, Obama's black liberation preacher at Trinity United Church of Christ, gave a sermon titled "Audacity to Hope" based on Bible passage 1 Samuel 1:1-18. Bill Clinton's hometown is Hope, Arkansas, the reason Clinton titled his autobiography, *Between Hope and History*.

31 *Time*, October 23, 2006. *See also* Joe Klein, "The Fresh Face," October 15, 2006. See www.time.com/magazine.

32 Jeff Zeleny, "Book Sales Lifted Obamas' Income in 2007 to a Total of $4.2 Million," *The New York Times*, April 17, 2008.

33 *Time* described Stein's Chicago business practices as "The Octopus" in an April 1945 article chronicling how he intimidated the top talent of that era by monopolizing bookings at hotels and ballrooms for whom he and his organized crime colleagues also provided floor shows, liquor and table favors. As advertisers began to sponsor radio programs, he purchased "great hunks of choice network time" where he allowed only MCA bands and performers. With his monopoly profits, he acquired the Rolls Royce and Buick agencies in Chicago and could also supply real estate, insurance and bonds. With his bands and radio stars signed to MCA, he bought up the contracts of Hollywood stars, including Errol Flynn, Bette Davis and Betty Grable. At the time, Stein was reported to have offices in Chicago, New York, Hollywood, Cleveland, Dallas, San Francisco and London. "The Octopus," *Time*, April 23, 1945. The MCA-Reagan connection will be chronicled in the *Criminal State* series.

34 Nicholas D. Kristof, "Obama: Man of the World," *The New York Times*, March 6, 2007, p. A23.

35 Ben White and Edward Luce, "Obama takes on Clinton for Wall Street cash," *Financial Times*, March 8, 2007, p. 6.

36 Mike McIntire, "Clintons Made $109 Million In Last 8 Years," *The New York Times*, April 5, 2008, p. 1.

37 www.ted.com/index.php/talks/view/id/53.

38 Kelefa Sanneh, "Project Trinity," *The New Yorker*, April 7, 2008.

39 The Black population is taken from U.S. Census Bureau figures for 2004 that report 36,121,000 Blacks or African Americans in an overall population of approximately 300 million (281.4

million in 2000). This number includes those who reported only Black in addition to 1.8 million people who reported Black as well as one or more other races.

40 Howard M. Sachar, *A History of the Jews in America* (New York: Alfred A Knopf, 1992), p. 803.

41 "Jews Going to Paris with Bill of Rights," *The New York Times*, December 18, 1918.

42 Anti-Zionist Orthodox Jews of Neturei Karta refer to him as "Stephen Wise: The Chief Saboteur" for his alleged delay of legislation leading to formation of the War Refugee Board. Moshe Shonfeld, *The Holocaust Victims Accuse - Documents and Testimony on Jewish War Criminals* (Brooklyn: Neturei Karta of USA, 1977), pp. 43-57.

43 David McCullough, *Truman* (New York: Simon & Schuster, 1992), p. 369; Robert J. Donovan, *Conflict & Crisis* (Columbia: University of Missouri Press, 1977), pp. 312-20.

44 Israel Shahak, *Jewish History, Jewish Religion* (London: Pluto Press, 1994), p. 103.

45 Ibid., pp. 10, 51, 103

46 Ibid., p. 103.

47 Barack Obama, "My Plan For Iraq," *The New York Times*, July 14, 2008.

48 See Jon Cohen and Jennifer Agiesta, "3 in 10 Americans Admit to Race Bias," *The Washington Post*, June 22, 2008, p. 1.

49 http://www.youtube.com/watch?v=yAZm080dLfe.

50 Jake Tapper, "Writing Raising Questions About Obama's Electability," ABC News, April 29, 2008.

51 Mary Mitchell (columnist), "Why Obama 'denounced' Farrakhan," *Chicago Sun-Times*, March 2, 2008.

52 See Israel Shahak, *Jewish History, Jewish Religion* (London: Pluto Press, 1994), p. 97.

53 Darryl Fears, "House Issues An Apology For Slavery," *The Washington Post*, July 30, 2008, p. A3.

54 Reuters, "Obama slams Bush, former pres. Clinton's mideast diplomacy, *Haaretz,* April 21 2008

55 Serge Schmemann, "Netanyahu Defiantly Defending Botched Assassination Attempt," *The New York Times*, October 7, 1997.

56 This theme was reinforced by House Majority Leader Tom DeLay in a speech he delivered to the Israeli Knesset on July 30, 2003, four months after the U.S. was induced to invade Iraq. In

his speech, DeLay cited President Bush and his reaffirmation of "America's support for Israel's security and our commitment to fight 'terrorism wherever it is found.'"

57 Matthew Kalman, *The San Francisco Chronicle* (SFGate.com), July 21, 2006.

58 Yoav Stern and Barak Ravid, "Ex-IDF Chief: Hezbollah control of Lebanon may benefit Israel," *Haaretz,* May 5, 2008.

59 "Hezbollah Wins Major Concessions in Lebanon," CBS News (online), May 15, 2008. See also "Lebanon forms unity gov't which gives Hezbollah veto power," *Haaretz*, July 11, 2008.

60 *Profiles in Courage* (1956) was a book authored by John F. Kennedy that helped him gain a national reputation. The book won the 1957 Pulitzer Prize for biography. Kennedy assistant and historian Theodore Sorensen is widely credited with writing much of the book.

61 For example, the report of the 9/11 Commission cites the motivation of Khalid Sheikh Mohammed, the "mastermind" of the attacks: "KSM's animus toward the United States stemmed not from his experiences there as a student, but rather from his violent disagreement with U.S. foreign policy favoring Israel." *9/11 Commission Report* (Washington, D.C.: National Commission on Terrorist Attacks Upon the United States, 2004), p. 147.

62 The founding of Israel is forever linked by extremist Jews with terrorism. That war was rationalized by appeals to the victimized status of the broader community of displaced Jews in need of a place to reside in the post-WWII era. For example, the April 1948 massacre at Deir Yassin killed 254 Palestinians, about half of them women, children and the elderly. Many of the bodies were thrown into wells. At the direction of two future Israeli Prime Ministers, Menachem Begin and Yitzhak Shamir, 25 male villagers were forced into trucks and paraded through Jerusalem before being driven to a nearby stone quarry and executed Nazi-style. The remaining villagers were taken to East Jerusalem before their village was bulldozed for an airfield. The massacre was assisted by Haganah militia under the control of David Ben-Gurion. Irgun leader Menachem Begin later conceded that terrorism served its intended effect: "Arabs throughout the country, induced to believe wild tales of 'Irgun butchery,' were seized with limitless panic and started to flee for their lives. The mass flight soon developed into a maddened, uncontrollable stampede. The political

and economic significance of this development can hardly be overestimated." After displaying heaps of Palestinian corpses, speaker trucks drove through Arab communities threatening their residents with another Deir Yassin. Walid Khalid (ed.), *From Haven to Conquest: Readings in Zionism and the Palestine Problem until 1948* (Washington, D.C.: Institute for Palestine Studies, 1987), pp. 761-768. Moshe Dayan led a similar massacre in the Hebron Hills where 80 to 100 residents were slaughtered and the village razed. Begin also planned the bombing of the King David Hotel in Jerusalem in July 1946, a terrorist attack that injured 45 and killed 91, including 41 Arabs, 28 Brits, 17 Jews, and five others. Begin quoted in Robert Fisk, "Arabs and Jews unite to commemorate massacre," Independent.co.uk, March 15, 2001. The value of lost Palestinian immovable property (homes, shops, warehouses and such) was at least $480 million in 1947 dollars ($3.7 billion in 2007 dollars). Zionist/Israeli forces committed 33 massacres altogether. See http://www.ifamericansknew.org. Jewish terrorists groups also sought to assassinate British Foreign Secretary Ernest Bevin who viewed the creation of Israel as "so manifestly unjust to the Arabs that it is difficult to see how we could reconcile it with conscience." British Cabinet Minutes CP47/259, September 18, 1947, p. 4; "Jewish groups plotted to kill Bevin," *The Telegraph*, May 22, 2003.

63 Quoted in John J. Mearsheimer and Stephen M. Walt, *The Israel Lobby* (New York: Farrar, Strauss and Giroux, 2007), p. 89 citing Begin's comment from Amnon Kapeliuk, "Begin and the 'Beasts,'" *New Statesman*, June 25, 1982, p. 12. Eitan's comment is from David K. Shipler, "Most West Bank Arabs Blaming U.S. for Impasse," *The New York Times*, April 14, 1983.

64 Israel Shahak, *Jewish History, Jewish Religion* (London: Pluto Press, 1994), p. x.

65 "Obama promises 'unshakable commitment' to Israel if elected," *Haaretz*, May 23, 2008; "Barack Obama: The Kosher Connection," *The Jewish Daily Forward*, August 21, 2008.

66 Jeff Zeleny, "Obama Asks Jewish Voters to Judge Him on His Policies," *The New York Times*, May 23, 2008.

67 Jodi Kantor, "As Obama Heads to Florida, Jews There Have Their Doubts," *The New York Times*, May 22, 2008, p. 1.

68 Ibid.

69 Akiva Eldar, "U.S. fumes after Israeli envoy to UN brands Carter 'a bigot,'" *Haaretz*, April 27, 2008.

70 Reuters, "Obama says Bush policies strengthened Iran, Hamas," *Haaretz*, May 17, 2008.

71 David Brooks, "Obama Admires Bush," *The New York Times*, May 16, 2008.

72 See David Frum and Richard Perle, *An End to Evil: How to Win the War on Terror* (New York: Random House, 2003).

73 Ethan Bronner, "Israel Holds Peace Talks With Syria," *The New York Times*, May 22, 2008.

74 The day after Hillary Clinton dropped out of the 2008 Democratic primary, Obama appointed 37-year old Jason Furman to head his economic policy team. A fan of former Treasury Secretary Robert Rubin whose "Wall Street realism" granted deference to bond markets, Furman heads the Brookings Institution's Hamilton Project that proposes reforming rather than rejecting the free-trade agenda launched by Friedman, embraced by Reagan and imbedded in law by the Rubin-advised Bill Clinton.

75 Carter had also criticized Obama by questioning his substance and experience to be president. "Jimmy Carter shunted to sidelines in Democratic Convention," *Haaretz*, August 26, 2008.

76 Brett Lieberman and Nathan Guttman, "Jimmy Carter Conspicuously Absent From Podium," *Forward*, August 28, 2008.

Chapter 9: The Way Forward

1 Though characterized as his Farewell Address, Washington's comments were not a speech but an open letter to the public published in the form of a speech on September 19, 1796. In addition to cautioning against permanent foreign alliances, he warned against the perils to the fledgling republic of political polarization and factionalism. One of the U.S. Senate's most enduring traditions is the annual reading of President Washington's Farewell Address.

2 Former Secretary of State Madeleine Albright welcomed a delegation of Georgians to the Democratic Party convention in Denver. Peter Baker, "Guns Silent, Moscow and Tbilisi Open New Front in Denver," *The New York Times*, August 26, 2008, p. A16.

3 *The New York Times* and *The Washington Post* fueled U.S.-Russia

tensions with bellicose editorials. See "Who Needs Russia," *The Washington Post*, August 23, 2008, p. A14; "Stuck in Georgia," *The New York Times*, August 27, 2008, p. A22.

4 Clifford J. Levy, "Putin Suggests U.S. Provocation in Georgia Clash," *The New York Times*, August 29, 2008, p. 1. McCain foreign policy adviser Randy Scheunemann lobbied for the Georgian government until March 2008. Michael Cooper, "In Split Role, McCain Adviser Is Sometimes a Lobbyist," *The New York Times*, August 14, 2008, p. A20.

5 Michael Luo and Sarah Wheaton, "List of McCain Fund-Raisers Includes Prominent Lobbyists," *The New York Times*, April 21, 2008, p. A 17.

6 In mid-May 2008, McCain's campaign announced new restrictions on the lobbying activities of staff members and others connected to the campaign. "Lobbying Policies," *The Washington Post*, May 20, 2008, p. A4.

7 Sally Quinn, "The Man Who Would Succeed Saddam," *The Washington Post*, November 24, 2003, p. C1.

8 Aram Roston, *The Man Who Pushed America To War* (New York: Nation Books, 2008), p. 174.

9 As will be chronicled in the *Criminal State* series, those identified in this account routinely target family members of the wealthy and the politically influential in order to influence decision-making, often by drawing the 'mark' into discrediting circumstances with which they can be portrayed as guilty by association. For example, Jimmy Carter's brother "Billy" was drawn into a scandal involving Libyan oil contracts for Charter Oil, a firm in which Carl Lindner and Armand Hammer had a stake. When Neil Bush was given a cameo directorship on the board of a corrupt Colorado S&L, that position associated his father, G.H.W. Bush, with that nationwide fraud. Similarly, it was a clumsy cash contribution to Richard Nixon's reelection campaign by political sophisticate Armand Hammer that helped trigger the Watergate hearings that led to impeachment proceedings and Nixon's resignation that brought Gerald Ford to the White House.

10 Matthew Mosk, "McCain Pushed Land Swap That Benefits Backer," *The New York Times*, May 9, 2008, p. 1.

11 William K. Black, *The Best Way to Rob a Bank is to Own One* (Austin: University of Texas Press, 2005), pp. 63-65.

12 David D. Kirkpatrick and Jim Rutenberg, "McCain, a Benefactor Poses a Challenge," *The New York Times*, April 22, 2008, p. 1.

13 After a career in New York in the commodities business, Diamond began a land development career in Arizona where he attended elementary school, high school and college. As Chairman of Diamond Ventures, Inc., he spearheaded the building of the Jewish Community Center in Tucson along with Diamond Ventures' top three executives: David Goldstein, Kenneth Abrahams and Mark Weinberg.

14 From 1995 to January 2002, McCain fundraiser Lewis Eisenberg served as Chairman of the Port Authority of New York and New Jersey that owned the World Trade Center at the time of the 9/11 attacks. A long-time Republican Party activist and member of the Republican Jewish Coalition, Eisenberg previously served as Finance Chairman of the Republican National Committee. In March 2008, he was appointed the RNC's "Victory Finance Chairman" to lead nationwide fundraising for McCain. On July 24, 2001, Leonard Silverstein signed a 99-year, $3.2 billion lease taking control of the World Trade Center seven weeks before the attacks that killed 2,749 people and toppled ten million square feet of commercial space in the twin towers and five other buildings. In December 2004, a jury determined that the impact of two Boeing 767 passenger jets crashing 16 minutes apart was two separate incidents leaving insurers responsible for up to $1.1 billion per occurrence. Phil Hirschkorn, CNN.com, December 6, 2004. In additional actions, Mr. Silverstein won a total of nearly $4.6 billion in insurance payments to cover his losses. In March 2008, he sought damages of $12.3 billion from airlines and airport security companies for the 9/11 attack claiming $8.4 billion for replacement value and $3.9 billion in other costs, including $100 million a year in rent to the Port Authority, $300 million a year in lost rental income, the costs of marketing and leasing the new buildings and prejudgment interest. If he prevails, Silverstein said he would repay the insurance companies. Anemona Hartocollis, "Developer Sues to Win $12.3 Billion in 9/11 Attack," *The New York Times*, March 27, 2008. For his 99-year lease, "Silverstein put up only $14 million of his own money." Alison Frankel, "Double Indemnity," Law.com, September 3, 2002.

15 Paul Klebnikov, *Godfather of the Kremlin* (New York: Harcourt,

2000), pp. 158; Marshall Goldman, *The Piratization of Russia* (New York: Routledge, 2003), p. 183; David Hoffman, *The Oligarchs* (New York: Public Affairs, 2002), p. 527, note 26.

16 Richard N. Haass, "The Age of Nonpolarity," *Foreign Affairs*, May/June 2008, pp. 44-56. Born in Brooklyn, Haass is president of the Council on Foreign Relations. He served as director of policy planning for the U.S. Department of State from January 2001 to June 2003 during the war-planning period. He was previously director of foreign policy studies at the Brookings Institution specializing in Near East affairs, a position incorporated into the Saban Center for Middle East Policy directed by Martin Indyk, co-founder of the Washington Institute for Near East Policies with Barbi Weinberg, wife of AIPAC Chairman Emeritus Lawrence Weinberg of Los Angeles.

17 David Hoffman, *The Oligarchs* (New York: Public Affairs, 2002), p. 360.

18 The shift of mainstream media into pro-Israeli hands will be chronicled in the *Criminal State* series.

19 The role of popular culture in "preparing the minds" and displacing facts with beliefs will be chronicled in the *Criminal State* series.

20 Associated Press, "More controversy for Oprah's book club?," MSNBC.com January 17, 2006.

21 Rachael Donadio, "The Story of 'Night'," *The New York Times*, January 20, 2008.

22 "2008 Pulitzer Prizes for Letters, Drama and Music," *The New York Times*, April 7, 2008.

23 "Barack Obama: We will keep Israel's security a priority," Haaretz.com TV, May 11, 2008.

24 Anshel Pfeffer, "Jews bend over backward to stay neutral in U.S. vote," *Haaretz*, May 9, 2008.

25 Israel Shahak warns of the "myth of the Aryan" race as well as the "myth of the Jewish race" in cautioning against the perils of "Jewish segregationism and chauvinism." He cautions: "those Jews who refuse to come to terms with the Jewish past… have become its slaves and are repeating it in zionist and Israeli policies. The State of Israel now fulfills towards the oppressed peasants of many countries—not only in the Middle East but also far beyond it—a role not unlike a bailiff to the imperial

oppressor. It is characteristic and instructive that Israel's major role in arming the forces of the Somoza regime in Nicaragua, and those of Guatemala, El Salvador, Chile and the rest has not given rise to any wide public debate in Israel or among *organized* Jewish communities in the diaspora." Israel Shahak, *Jewish History, Jewish Religion* (London: Pluto Press, 1994), p. 72.

26 Michael T. Benson, *Harry S. Truman and the Founding of Israel* (Westport: Praeger, 1997), p. 120.

27 Defense Secretary Donald Rumsfeld sought "information dominance" by recruiting more than 75 retired military officers to portray Iraq as an urgent threat. By associating their analysis with their military service, their comments became what Rumsfeld called "message-force multipliers." Cooperative broadcast networks and print media spread Pentagon-shaped information portrayed as independent military analysis by authoritative military sources. David Barstow, "Behind TV Analysis, Pentagon's Hidden Hand," *The New York Times*, April 20, 2008.

28 Based on evidence confirming the trans-generational and imbedded nature of this treason, Committee members should also consider whether to reconstitute the Office of the Alien Property Custodian along with the accompanying authority to seize assets.

29 Rowan Scarborough, "U.S. troops would enforce peace under Army study," *The Washington Times*, September 10, 2001

30 The Board "provides advice to the President concerning the quality and adequacy of the intelligence collection, of analysis and estimates, or counterintelligence, and of other intelligence activities."

31 Though such coordination has periodically been confirmed, election law violations continue with impunity, including AIPAC's creation and coordination of political action committees to favor Israeli interests. See Grant F. Smith, *Foreign Agents* (Washington, D.C.: Institute for Research: Middle East Affairs, 2007), pp. 75-99.

32 Originally enacted in October 1917, the Act generally provides the president with broad discretion to order restrictions on trade with nations known to be hostile to the United States.

33 The debacle in Iraq included the airlifting of $12 billion in shrink-wrapped $100 bills into Iraq in 2003. Transported on pallets in C-130s, the nearly 281 million notes, weighing 363

tons, were sent from New York to Baghdad for disbursement to Iraqi ministries as part of a Development Fund for Iraq. David Pallister, "How the US sent $12bn in cash to Iraq. And watched it vanish," *The Guardian*, February 8, 2007. A key goal of complementary exchanges systems is to remove *the people in between* by identifying how best to imbed currencies in communities so that local liquidity is no longer solely dependent on a foreign currency, a unitary currency or a central monetization agency wed to a globalizing economy. In addition to reducing interest payments to the carriage trade, the goal should be to encourage demonstration models showing how locally attuned exchange systems can relieve the fiscal pressure for services such as education, health care, clean energy and environmental restoration.

34 At what point does public money that passes through private hands lose its public character? Similarly, at what point does public property that passes into private hands (as in Russia) lose its public character? The law generally imposes no statute of limitations on fraud where indices of conspiracy are present. Should a lien be placed on such properties to secure proceeds required to pay for public services that would otherwise be affordable but for this systemic corruption?

35 For example, the GAO should attempt to quantify the financial costs to the U.S. when Loral, under the leadership of Clinton campaign contributor Bernard L. Schwartz, transferred information helpful to improving the reliability and accuracy of China's missiles. See Christopher Marques, "Satellite Maker Fined $20 Million in China Trade Secrets Case," *The New York Times*, January 10, 2002.

36 Shmuel Rosner, "Pelosi: I trust all presidential candidates when it comes to Israel," *Haaretz*, May 18, 2008. That announcement came ten days after Hollywood producer Harvey Weinstein, a supporter of Hillary Clinton, promised to cut campaign contributions to Democrats unless Pelosi supported his plans to fund a revote in primaries in Michigan and Florida. "Harvey Weinstein Pushing for Florida, Michigan and Hillary," Ground Report, May 8, 2008. http://www.groundreport.com/article.php?articleID=2860715&action=print_article. Weinstein was joined in that quest by Governor Ed Rendell of Pennsylvania and Governor Jon Corzine of New Jersey. See Jon S. Corzine and Edward G.

Rendell, "Delegates We Need," *The Washington Post*, March 11, 2008, p. A19. Corzine, a former co-chairman of Goldman Sachs, was elected governor in November 2006 following the resignation of Governor James E. McGreevey who resigned effective November 15, 2004 after he was threatened with a sexual harassment lawsuit by Israeli citizen Golan Cipel with whom McGreevey conceded a gay relationship. Cipel allegedly requested $5 million to quash the suit. McGreevey had appointed Cipel as a $110,000 per year adviser to the state's department of homeland security. McGreevey had also been criticized for his attempt to elevate Charles Kushner, his top contributor, to run the multi-billion-dollar Port Authority of New York and New Jersey. Laura Mansnerus, "A Governor Resigns: Overview; McGreevey Steps Down After Disclosing a Gay Affair, *The New York Times*, August 13, 2004. A former U.S. Senator (2001 to 2006), Corzine resigned to take his seat as Governor. In August 2005, news outlets reported that Corzine had forgiven in 2004 a $470,000 mortgage loan granted in 2002 to girlfriend Carla Katz, president of New Jersey's largest union, the Communication Workers of America. Eric Pfeiffer, "State of Corruption," *National Review Online*, August 12, 2005. David Kocieniewski, "Corzine Gave $470,000 Loan to Head of Union," *The New York Times*, August 4, 2005. Corzine spent more than $62 million on his Senate campaign, the most expensive Senate campaign in U.S. history. His combined expenditures for public office exceed $100 million to date, one-quarter of a reported $400 million-plus in personal wealth accumulated during his tenure at Goldman Sachs.

37 Barak Ravid, "FM Livni to Pelosi: No peace agreement with PA likely in 2008," *Haaretz*, May 20, 2008.

38 Barak Ravid and Amos Harel, "Olmert to Pelosi: Impose naval blockade on Iran," *Haaretz*, May 21, 2008.

39 "Israel-Syria confirm peace talks," BBC News (online), May 21, 2008.

40 Uzi Mahnaimi, "Tzipi Livni: terrorist-hunter secret of woman tipped to lead Israel," *Sunday Times* (London), June 1, 2008.

41 In January 2008, Paul Wolfowitz was appointed chairman of the State Department International Security Advisory Board.

42 Reuters, "U.S. Homeland Security seeks to adopt Israeli airport standards," *Haaretz*, May 29, 2008.

43 Mark Mazzetti, "Military Death Toll Rises in Afghanistan as Taliban Regain Strength," *The New York Times*, July 2, 2008, p. A5.

44 James Zogby, "Bush Visits the Messy World He Created," *Washington Watch*, May 19, 2008.

INDEX

A

B

C

S

T

U

V

W

Y

Z